Flying Through HOLLYWOOD By the Seat of My Pants

From the Man
Who Brought You
I Was a Teenage Werewolf
and
Muscle Beach Party

Sam Arkoff

With Richard Trubo

A Birch Lane Press Book
Published by Carol Publishing Group

Copyright © 1992 by Sam Arkoff

All rights reserved. No part of this book may be reproduced in any form, except by a newspaper or magazine reviewer who wishes to quote brief passages in connection with a review.

A Birch Lane Press Book
Published by Carol Publishing Group
Birch Lane Press is a registered trademark of Carol
 Communications, Inc.

Editorial Offices: 600 Madison Avenue, New York, N.Y. 10022
Sales & Distribution Offices: 120 Enterprise Avenue, Secaucus, N.J. 07094

In Canada: Canadian Manda Group, P.O. Box 920, Station U,
 Toronto, Ontario M8Z 5P9

Queries regarding rights and permissions should be addressed to Carol Publishing Group, 600 Madison Avenue, New York, N.Y. 10022

Carol Publishing Group books are available at special discounts for bulk purchases, for sales promotions, fund raising, or educational purposes. Special editions can be created to specifications. For details, contact: Special Sales Department, Carol Publishing Group, 120 Enterprise Avenue, Secaucus, N.J. 07094

Manufactured in the United States of America
10 9 8 7 6 5 4 3 2 1

Library of Congress-in-Publication Data

Arkoff, Sam.
 Flying through Hollywood by the seat of my pants : from the man who brought you I was a teenage werewolf and Muscle beach party / by Sam Arkoff with Richard Trubo.
  p. cm.
 "A Birch Lane Press book."
 ISBN 1-55972-107-3
  1. Arkoff, Sam. 2. Motion picture producers and directors—United States—Biography. I. Trubo, Richard. II. Title.
 PN1998.3.A75A3 1992
 791.43′0232′092—dc20
  [B]   92-6069
                                                                       CIP

To my wife, Hilda,
who has flown with me all the way.

Acknowledgments

Dozens of people played an important role in making American International Pictures a challenge and a pleasure throughout the book; others, however, who somehow didn't otherwise get into these pages, deserve mention and thanks as well. They include Barbara Boyle, Dennis Brown, Harold "Hal" Brown, Marge Carr, Murray Cohen, Stanley Dudelson, Fred Feitshans, Karin Garrity, Michael Gerety, Richard Graff, Norman Herman, Louis "Deke" Heyward, William Immerman, Lucy Keister, Ann Lander, Ruth Pologe Levinson, David Melamed, Julian Myers, Steve Previn, Elliot Schick, Judy Schwam, Jerry Schwartz, Mort Siegel, Al Simms, Jules Stein, Larry Steinfeld, Robert Steuer, Jerry Sussman, Mickey Zide, and Richard Zimbert. My apologies to those people who I may have unwittingly left out of this list or the book itself.

Flying Through
HOLLYWOOD
By the Seat
of My Pants

1

They laughed when I turned the projectors on to show *I Was a Teenage Werewolf* back in 1957. But when the cash registers started ringing, all of Hollywood took notice. Upon the picture's release, word of mouth among teenage audiences caused lines at theaters and traffic jams at drive-ins from Los Angeles to Hackensack.

Now they call me a "living legend," which worries me. When I hear the word "legend," I think of someone who is horizontal. And while I'm not a tall man, I am still vertical. And still making movies. Let me tell you how.

Whenever you do something right, there's usually a guiding principle behind it. Mine is not too fancy. My number one commandment—beginning in 1954 when Jim Nicholson and I founded American International Pictures—has always been "Thou shalt not put too much money into any one picture. And with the money you do spend, put it on the screen; don't waste it on the egos of actors or on nonsense that might appeal to some highbrow critics."

The payoffs can be substantial. *I Was a Teenage Werewolf* was shot in six days for $100,000. In its first year, it earned over $2 million in U.S. theatrical receipts alone, which was big money in those days.

With that picture, and with every one that preceded and followed it, we did everything possible—and impossible—to cut costs. And we were merciless. We cut down production schedules by using the same sets for different pictures. We combined locations to save physical moves during production. We even tore pages out of scripts if the director didn't pick up the pace of shooting. When we filmed *Girls in Prison* in 1956, and violent winds created chaos on the set, we instantly wrote a storm into the script rather than lose a day of shooting. Or scenes were cannibalized from one AIP picture and edited into another, like the burning house footage that appeared in more than one of our Edgar Allan Poe movies. Some critics objected. The purpose, however, was to film the meat without the fat. And it worked. We often used ingenuity and imagination instead of money, without tarnishing the quality. We wanted to make the best pictures we possibly could, and discovered ways to do so without spending a fortune.

AIP simply approached moviemaking differently than anyone else. In fact, the content of the films themselves sometimes almost seemed to take a backseat to the titles and the advertising campaigns that were carefully crafted before the first roll of film was ever shot.

Consider the near disaster surrounding *The Beast With 1,000,000 Eyes!*, a 1955 picture that grew out of a wonderful ad campaign that depicted a tentacled, multiple-orbed monster menacing a young, bathing suit-clad woman on the beach. The movie, the ad heralded, was shot in "TerrorScope."

At the time, Joe Levine (who later produced movies like *The Carpetbaggers* and *Two Women*) was our distributor in Boston. Joe loved the title and the ad campaign, and called with a proposal. "When the picture is finished, I want to bring one of New England's biggest exhibitors out to L.A. to see it," he said. "If he likes it, he'll put it in his best theaters with special promotion behind it. Sam, this movie could really be big."

I gulped. This was a Roger Corman picture (although because it was shot nonunion, Roger gave the director's credit to David Kramarsky). And when the editor delivered the work print to us, it didn't even have a beast in it, much less one with a million eyes!

I called Roger, who was already shooting our next picture on location. "Where the hell is the monster footage?!" I asked.

"Sam, I didn't have much money to work with," he explained. "We couldn't shoot *everything*! I gave you as much as I could on a $29,000 budget. *You* put in the beast!"

Roger had gone over budget on his previous movie for us—part of a four-picture deal with AIP—and all he had left was $29,000 for this one. According to Roger, that forced him to cut corners—including deleting the beast from a picture titled *The Beast With 1,000,000 Eyes!*

Jim and I pondered several solutions, from retitling the picture to reediting it. In a panic, we arranged to shoot some extra footage of the only "beast" we could quickly find—a teakettle that we subjected to a hasty face-lift! We poked forty holes in it—not a million, but who was really counting?—and as the camera rolled, we ran steam from the vaporizer through it. The mist was designed to give the "beast" an ominous appearance, but more importantly, it obscured the kettle just enough so viewers couldn't get too clear a look at it. It wouldn't have been a state-of-the-art special effect in the 1990s, but it worked just fine in 1955.

I tried to discourage Levine from making the trip to Los Angeles to preview the film, but he wouldn't listen. "Don't worry," Joe told me. "I can sell the picture to this exhibitor."

A week later, when we finally screened the picture for them, it was a disaster. As the projector rolled, Jim and I kept slumping lower in our seats, and when the beast itself finally appeared on the screen, we almost hit the floor. Before the movie had ended, the exhibitor had seen enough; he stormed out of the screening room, with Levine chasing him up the aisle.

A few hours later, Levine called from his hotel room. "You were right; it was a mistake to bring him out." Then he added, "I've got an idea. I love the title and the advertising for the picture, and I want to buy them from you. I'll give you a check for $100,000 today. But I also want you to burn your film and I'll make a new version of it myself!"

Even the toughest movie critic had never suggested torching our movies. I politely told Levine that we were "flattered" by his offer, but we still thought the picture might find an audience. It was released two weeks later, with the teakettle still in the starring role. Fortunately for us, the ad campaign alone brought young people into the theater.

Okay, neither *I Was a Teenage Werewolf* nor *The Beast With 1,000,000 Eyes!* was *Casablanca* or *From Here to Eternity*. But they were never intended to be. Neither were any of AIP's other five-hundred-plus feature films. From AIP's first movie, *The Fast and the Furious*, to the features I'm making today, one of my overriding philosophies has remained the same: to produce pictures that audiences find entertaining, and that bring in enough money to finance the next movie. Period.

By the late 1970s, we had moved beyond movies like *I Was a Teenage Werewolf, The Astounding She-Monster,* and *High School Hellcats*, and were prosperous enough where we could make bigger features—*The Amityville Horror, Love at First Bite,* and *Dressed to Kill*. In fact, *The Amityville Horror* returned $65 million in U.S. theatrical box office receipts in 1979, earning it a place as the most successful independent feature film up to that time. Even so, the earliest AIP pictures—movies like *Day the World Ended, I Was a Teenage Frankenstein,* and *The Amazing Colossal Man*—still attract a great deal of interest today. They are movies that found their way onto the nation's projectors with bargain-basement budgets and hardly a star or a big-name director. Instead, we parlayed bikinis, bikes, a bit of blood, and a lot of ingenuity and inventiveness into a lengthy string of money-making films.

So, you might ask, why did AIP succeed and remain prosperous when so many other independents failed? The answer was sitting restlessly in homes across America, neglected by movie studios for years: the teenager... the gum-chewing, hamburger-munching adolescent dying to get out of the house on a Friday or Saturday night and yearning for a place to go. The youth whose parents were just as eager to have him or her out of the house for the evening. AIP didn't invent the American teenager, but the big studios lagged so far behind that they must have thought our company did. We offered fast cars (*Hot Rod Gang, Dragstrip Girl*) in the fifties, beach parties (*How to Stuff a Wild Bikini, Beach Blanket Bingo*) in the early sixties, and anger and alienation (*The Wild Angels, The Trip, Wild in the Streets*) in the late sixties. We attracted millions of young people to the movie theaters, and even more often, to drive-ins.

The Hollywood establishment would say, "Oh, AIP, the people who make exploitation movies." Before long, however, those same executives started reading the profit-and-loss reports of picture grosses in the trade newspapers, and discovered that AIP and Disney were the only film companies in town—the *only* ones—that consistently made a profit, year after year. While the major companies struggled to stay in the black, we never had a money-losing year. We weren't doing things big, but we were doing them right.

I've always felt that AIP was simply more honest than its competitors by never soft-pedaling the profit motive. (Not that the majors had any other motive, but they cloaked it under other pretenses.) Of course, what the big studios didn't realize was that our movies literally *had* to make money. A couple of losers back to back, and our entire company would have been in jeopardy. We had to make a profit or close our doors. Failure was a luxury we could not afford.

So while the studios were making their multimillion dollar productions, we financed Francis Ford Coppola's first feature, *Dementia 13*, for less than $50,000 in 1963. While the big studios were paying stars astronomical salaries, AIP was serving as a wonderful training ground for two generations of young actors, writers, and directors who couldn't break into the studios, but could get an opportunity with us; we helped create a lot of future stars, and our list of alumni reads like a Who's Who of Hollywood. Woody Allen directed his first picture (*What's Up, Tiger Lily?*) for us. John Milius (*Dillinger*) got his first directoral chance with AIP, too, as did Ivan Reitman (*Cannibal Girls*) and David Cronenberg (*It Came From Within*). Martin Scorsese directed his first feature (*Boxcar Bertha*) for us, and Brian De Palma made his first horror picture (*Sisters*) at AIP. Producer Paul Maslansky not only made some pictures for us in Europe, but the only movie he ever directed (*Sugar Hill*) was for AIP. After we took over distribution of Ralph Bakshi's *Fritz the Cat*, he directed his next picture (*Heavy Traffic*) for us. Peter Bogdanovich did a variety of odd jobs for us, largely in our editing room, before breaking through as a director.

We gave first starring roles to Charles Bronson (*Machine Gun Kelly*), Mel Gibson (*Mad Max*), and Nick Nolte and Don Johnson (*Return to Macon County*). Jack Nicholson appeared in our horror movies (*The Raven*) and later in our "drug" pictures (*Psych-Out*), and Robert De Niro got the opportunity for an important costarring role (*Bloody Mama*). Peter Fonda played a variety of roles in our protest pictures—a change of pace from the romantic leads he was accustomed to. In picture after picture, AIP gave aspiring actors their first leading roles—Michael Landon, Melanie Griffith, Bruce Dern, Robert Vaughn, Richard Pryor, Cher, Chuck Norris, Dennis Hopper— or an important part boosting their careers that the majors were unwilling to give them—Tom Laughlin, Ed Begley, Jr., Michael "Touch" Connors, Susan Sarandon, Linda Evans, Richard Dreyfuss,

Diane Ladd, Sally Kellerman, Ben Vereen, and Margot Kidder. The entire list could fill up a whole chapter.

In fiscal year 1979-1980, AIP produced three pictures—*Love at First Bite*, *The Amityville Horror*, and *Dressed to Kill*—that achieved such impressive theatrical box office receipts that we grossed more domestically than the Disney Studios. That same year, I merged AIP with Filmways to give my company access to even greater amounts of capital that I'd need to make the bigger (but still not bloated) budget movies that audiences were coming to expect. I continued as president and chief executive of AIP when it became a Filmways subsidiary, but almost immediately, I realized that the marriage wasn't going to work.

The real problem was that Richard Bloch, the chairman of Filmways, wanted to turn the company into a major studio, which wasn't realistic. Within about a year, I had sold my stock in the company and was back to being an independent producing and otherwise involved in pictures under a new AIP logo, Arkoff International Pictures.

Now I've got a deal with several major companies to make the old type of AIP pictures—the kind designed primarily to entertain. Too many people in Hollywood are still part of what I call the "arty-farty" crowd—the highbrow, high-budget filmmakers who seem much more interested in being "auteurs" than making movies for the masses. Five hundred years from now, nobody is going to look back on most of today's movies and call them art in the same sense as the works of Michelangelo or Da Vinci. AIP's pictures have always just taken audiences out of their everyday world and transported them somewhere else for eighty to ninety-five minutes. Half of today's movies use their big budgets, big stars, big directors, and big writers as big drawing cards, but they still don't reach their audiences half as effectively, dollar for dollar, as our pictures always have.

Perhaps much of my success (said modestly) can be attributed to the fact that I was never torn between art and commerce. At AIP, we were always too busy making entertainment pictures for a reasonable price to worry about what the "auteurs" might be thinking. That's why no one was more surprised than me when, in the summer of 1979, the Museum of Modern Art in New York announced plans for a five-week-long retrospective and tribute to American International Pictures. It was the twenty-fifth anniversary of AIP, and the museum had decided to honor our films, which, according to MOMA's program, were "a uniquely American art form." Some of our pictures, said MOMA, had "come to be regarded as classics."

Classics? An American art form? Not too many years earlier, some Hollywood observers had used words like "exploitation" to describe some of our movies. These were pictures intended to be watched on forty-foot-high, drive-in screens through steamed-up windshields, and heard through tinny car speakers over the sound of crunching, buttered popcorn. Now they were being screened in a museum auditorium, in a forum usually reserved for the likes of Matisse, Monet, and Grandma Moses. They had certainly come a long way.

As I told the audience at the opening night of the MOMA retrospective, "I guess if you hang around long enough, anyone can become respectable."

2

The 1950s were just about the worst time to launch a new film company. But Jim Nicholson and I found rolling the dice an irresistible temptation.

It was a time in which the television industry was threatening to do to motion pictures what motion pictures had once done to vaudeville. The studios were in a panic, fearing that they were about to be transformed into ghost towns. Some people thought Jim and I had lost our senses when we started talking seriously about going into the movie business. Nevertheless, we believed, perhaps naively, that we had a real shot at success.

Ever since I first laid eyes on a copy of *Variety* as a teenager, I was determined to be a part of the motion picture industry. Beginning in 1933, I read every page of *Variety* compulsively and began to envision the road from my hometown of Fort Dodge, Iowa, to Hollywood. Logically, there was a much greater likelihood that I'd spend my life in Iowa where they raised corn and hogs rather than cultivated teenage werewolves. But as my career attests, logic often has very little to do with it.

For years, I've told people, "At heart, I'm just an Iowa farm boy." I was born in 1918 and grew up in Fort Dodge, a Norman Rockwell–vintage, county-seat town of less than twenty-thousand people surrounded by farms. My father, Louis Arkoff, was born in Russia, and as a young man was drafted into the army at the time of the Russo-Japanese War of 1905. On the troop train to the Siberian front, he decided he had no interest in fighting for anti-Semitic Russia, so he and a group of Jews and non-Jews deserted and made their way to New York, the gateway to the Promised Land.

Ultimately, my father arrived in Fort Dodge, where he met my mother, Helen Lurie. She was a very attractive young lady who had immigrated to the United States from Latvia in 1914 to join her three brothers, who were already in this country and were owners of two clothing stores in Fort Dodge. She and my father married in 1916.

My father was a very intelligent man and loved books. Given another birthplace and other circumstances, he probably would have entered a profession. But as an immigrant having to earn a living, he opened his own clothing store in Fort Dodge, working long hours, including on Sunday mornings. He preferred sitting on his wooden chair in the back of the store, reading his books. The regular customers knew to shout, "Louie," which would prompt my father to set down his books and come forward to sell a pair of overalls or shoes. By the age of eight, I worked each Saturday in my father's store, dusting the stacks of clothing and returning unsold shoes to their boxes.

There were never more than fifteen Jewish families in Fort Dodge, including ours and those of my three uncles. We had no synagogue, but on the High Holidays—Rosh Hashanah and Yom Kippur—we'd meet in the Knights of Columbus dance hall, joined by another ten or fifteen families from adjoining towns. My mother kept a kosher home, and our meat was delivered on the interurban train from Des Moines. When I was thirteen, I became a bar mitzvah, having learned the necessary prayers from Old Man Rabiner, who was then in his eighties.

We led a pleasant life in Fort Dodge, although I'm certain my father worried about the Depression and what would happen tomorrow. I suppose my siblings and I knew we'd ultimately wind up elsewhere. There was really no future for us in Fort Dodge. I ultimately led the way West, coming to Los Angeles. My sister, Edith, who writes, and my brother Bob, a doctor, now live in the San Francisco area; my brother Harold is a publisher of several trade magazines and also lives in Los Angeles; another brother, Abe, has been a professor at the University of Hawaii for thirty-five years.

Even so, as a youngster I had plenty of movies in Fort Dodge to keep me entertained and to stir my imagination. Marx Brothers films like *The Cocoanuts* and Johnny Weissmuller's *Tarzan, the Ape Man*—along with a regular array of Saturday afternoon Westerns—played at Fort Dodge's theaters. Before starting work at my father's store, I divided my weekend afternoons between the Rialto, the Iowa, and the Strand, where for a dime each, my friends and I could spend five or six hours, watching the same movies to the point of exhaustion, rushing home only when it was time for dinner or when our fatigued eyes started seeing double.

In those days, the movie houses had no concession stands, since their owners were convinced that food items like candy and popcorn were nothing but a nuisance that stuck to the seats and dirtied up the place. Nevertheless, the Skouras brothers, Greek-American producers and exhibitors (one of whom, Spyros, was president of Twentieth Century-Fox for two decades), helped bring Greek immigrants into the country and set them up in small candy stores as close as possible to the Skouras's theaters, often next door. Yet even in communities where these candy shops didn't exist, it was always easy to sneak in a Snickers bar or some peanut brittle to crunch on while watching Tom Mix, Buck Jones, or Ken Maynard gallop across the screen. Today, of course, theaters seem to be, first and foremost, dispensers of confections; the movies often almost seem like an afterthought.

During the Depression, theater owners by necessity became the supreme showmen in their towns, forced to use gimmicks to get people through their doors. I remember them sponsoring "dish night," where they'd offer a dish to every female patron; regular customers eventually could complete an entire set. Or they'd have "bank night," where they would have a drawing for a cash prize.

During junior high and high school, I gradually became an even bigger movie buff. In most of Fort Dodge's theaters, movies would change two or three times a week, so to see everything, I often cut classes and snuck into the theaters through a back door, making sure to leave in enough time to get to my dad's store on schedule on the days when I was expected there. "I can always catch up on my math homework," I'd tell my friends, "but these movies are going to be gone in a few days."

In the late 1920s, "talkies" were revolutionizing the motion picture business, and although stars like Charlie Chaplin lamented the trend—"Movies need dialogue as much as Beethoven symphonies need lyrics," he complained—I couldn't get enough of what the publicity posters heralded as "pictures that talk like living people." One afternoon in 1929, my friends and I went to see *Weary River*, a film starring Richard Barthelmess, a popular actor whom Lillian Gish once described as having "the most beautiful face of any man who ever went before a camera." In those early days of "talkies," the sound wasn't part of the film, but was actually on a separate disc that revolved on a turntable next to the projector. Unfortunately, the sound would slip out of sync periodically. During this particular screening of *Weary River*, while Barthelmess and his leading lady were canoeing down the river, *his* pronouncements of love began coming out of *her* mouth, and vice versa. It was amusing at first, but the projectionist made no attempt to fix it. Before long, the audience became impatient, stamping their feet on the floor and clapping their hands. That was about as disorderly as people in Fort Dodge ever got.

A turning point for me came in 1933. My Uncle Louie and Aunt Bessie lived on the south side of Chicago, and when the World's Fair opened there, they invited me to spend ten days with them to see the exposition. My parents bought me a special ten-dollar, round-trip excursion ticket on the Illinois Central Railroad, and I was off to Chicago.

The fair was impressive. Sally Rand and her fans were the headliners, and they certainly attracted my attention. But perhaps more important, Chicago was where I discovered my first issue of *Variety*, the show business weekly, in the magazine rack of a candy store on South State Street. Although the newspaper was filled with entertainment lingo, I immediately became addicted. I read that *Variety* from cover to cover, and although I didn't comprehend a lot of it—these publications generally aren't written for small-town boys from Iowa—I absorbed enough to feel that I was suddenly more than a spectator, but rather was becoming a show business insider. I assimilated news about the Hollywood studios, the pictures being made, and the well-known directors and producers. For a fifteen-year-old kid who already loved the movies, *Variety* was exciting reading.

When I returned home, I discovered that no one in town knew about or had ever read this publication. I talked Hogan, the proprietor of

Hogan's Pool Hall, into ordering *Variety* for me on a regular basis. For fifteen cents every week, I became Fort Dodge's closet Hollywoodian, with *Variety* providing my crash course in how show business worked. I never had the chutzpah to ever say to anyone, "I want to be a movie producer someday." But that's where I set my sights.

After high school and a year at Fort Dodge Junior College, I enrolled at the University of Colorado just because I wanted to get out of Iowa for awhile. Growing up in Iowa, I also had never seen a mountain before, and I figured Colorado would be the place to find one. As the Depression worsened, however, my money soon ran out in Colorado and I transferred to the University of Iowa, where I worked my way through school. I majored in speech, and sometimes imagined myself as a criminal lawyer, a dashing, somewhat overweight Clarence Darrow-type. Even so, my heart was still in the movies. Yes, I made some time for chess and some card games, and even a little for studying. But mostly I went to the movies.

One theater in Iowa City showed foreign films about twice a month; I was going through my arty stage, and never missed any of them. Some of my university friends were from New York City, elitists who thought that civilization ended at the Hudson River; they had brought a heavy dose of snobbery and pseudointellectualism with them to Iowa. We would only see movies by certain directors, and if they had English subtitles, all the better. At the end of the movie, unless the camera panned the sky as the lovers sank lusting in the sand, we didn't think it was art.

My friends and I would talk late into the night about every nuance in the latest film we had seen... "Jean Renoir showed such sensitivity in that closing scene"... "Sergei Eisenstein towers over any American director you could name." We'd analyze and reanalyze until we ran out of superlatives. If only those highbrow classmates had known that someday I'd be making movies like *I Was a Teenage Werewolf* and *The Brain Eaters*, they would have run me out of the theater.

I entered the air force in the summer of 1942, still a year short of getting my degree from the University of Iowa. In the aftermath of Pearl Harbor, I was caught up in the patriotic, anti-Hitler, anti-Hirohito fervor of the times. I showed up for my physical at Fort Des Moines with some level of enthusiasm, but tipping the scales at about 230 pounds, I wasn't quite the spitting image of Gary Cooper in *Sergeant York*. Add to that my high blood pressure, and I flunked two army physicals. But after consuming a hefty dose of an antihypertensive medication prescribed by a military doctor—taking enough of it to lower the blood pressure of an entire platoon—my blood pressure measurements were normal, and I was a few rubber stamps away from becoming a private in the air force.

I endured thirty days of basic training at Kearns, Utah, which was such a new camp that it had no obstacle course (thank God!), so we just marched all day in the dust, helping me lose thirty pounds in the process. After that, the air force was assigning new recruits into jobs as radio operators, aircraft mechanics, and weathermen, none of which interested me. The commanding officers looked me over, agreed that I wasn't suited for any of these assignments, and granted my request for training at cryptographic school (codes and ciphers) instead, which at least sounded interesting.

After my training, I was shipped to the Portuguese Azores with a twenty-two-man unit responsible for encoding and decoding messages going to and from the Northern African Theater. Since the Azores were neutral during the war, everyone in my unit changed from his uniform into civilian clothes during our flight to the islands. At times, we lived in Azorean hotels also housing German soldiers, some of whom were in civvies, too. If we had been caught and the Germans had won the war, we probably would have been shot, not a particularly comfortable way to go. I was always one for comfort.

After the Second Front was opened by the Allies, the Germans disappeared from the Azores, and my unit went back into uniform. At that time, Special Services sent over a thin, gregarious fellow with big ears and an engaging sense of humor. His name was Hank McCune. Before the war, Hank had been a radio announcer who aspired to become a comic. I, of course, was interested in show business, and the two of us agreed to create and produce a live variety show, called *A.P.O. Zoot*, for the troops. I talked the captain in charge of Special Services into letting us put on the live show on one of the outdoor stages normally reserved for movies. Hank and one of the radio operators wrote the script, and, for costumes, we surreptitiously got some uniforms and had them tailored to look like zoot suits. The production was not Tony Award caliber, but it gave me a sense of being in the entertainment business.

After the war, I married Hilda Rusoff, a young woman I had met on a blind date near the end of 1942 while stationed at Payne Field in the state of Washington. Maury Wiss, a friend from Fort Dodge, was serving in the Canadian Air Force across the border near Vancouver, and he helped arrange my first date with Hilda, on which she was given the chance of going out with either a Rhodes scholar or a good dancer. She chose the Rhodes scholar, but got me instead. I was neither an academic genius, nor was I particularly light on my feet.

A native of Winnipeg, Hilda was as opinionated as I was. She was bright, insightful, very pretty, and quite thin. I called her "slim," a label she preferred to what most people called her—"skinny." Frankly, at 230 pounds, I would have gladly accepted either one.

I immediately sensed that my relationship with Hilda might last more than just an evening, which it did. We stayed in touch by mail throughout the war, and when I returned from overseas, Hilda and I began seeing each other again. Upon my discharge, our relationship became more serious. When the conversation turned to marriage, my debating skills became extremely useful. At night, when things became romantic, I would say, "Maybe we should get married." By morning, however, my rational side took over, and I'd tell her, "Well, I do want to be a lawyer and get into the film business, so maybe we should wait."

Ultimately, Hilda became tired of my rationalizations. She told me, "Make up your mind, Sam!" I finally did. We got married in Winnepeg on December 16, 1945.

Hilda is the ninth of ten children; the first five were born in Russia, while the remaining ones came along after the family had immigrated to Canada. Although all of her siblings are gone now, we remain great believers in family. (In 1991, there was a meeting of the Rusoff clan that attracted nearly one hundred family members, and in which a double-decker bus was chartered to take everyone on a tour of the many houses in Winnipeg in which the Rusoffs had lived over the years—and had been asked to leave when the boys became a little too rambunctious and rendered things like swinging doors unusable; a year earlier, the Arkoff family had a reunion of its own: by comparison, we were a more orderly group, being far smaller, but no less loving.)

Almost immediately after our wedding, Hilda and I headed for Los Angeles. By then, I knew that I wasn't destined for a career as a motion picture actor or director, but I still wanted somehow to get into the movie business, and I figured L.A. was the place to be. Ostensibly, I had settled in California to go to law school, but I was aiming for something beyond a legal career. Entertainment law, I figured, might eventually open some doors for me into motion picture production.

With the support of the G.I. Bill, I enrolled at Loyola Law School in Los Angeles, which had reopened after the war with a class of eighty students, all veterans. For someone like me, the Loyola program was ideal: It was close to dozens of movie theaters. And when it came to choosing between analyzing the intricacies of *Marbury* v. *Madison* and catching the premiere of *The Best Years of Our Lives* or *Gilda*, the movies prevailed almost every time. Hardly a day passed when I didn't see at least one double feature. Fortunately, I befriended some fellow students who never missed a class, and I benefited immensely from their conscientious notetaking, eventually passing the bar on my first try. Our law school curricula program was compressed into twenty-seven months, with a review course for the bar examination at night; of the eighty students in my class, twenty of us graduated and nineteen passed the bar, the best record ever for any law school in California or elsewhere. Of the nineteen, eight became judges; I was the only one in the group to desert the dignified cloisters of the law for a career in the more lurid industry of motion pictures.

During this same time, Hank McCune had shifted his sights from radio to television. The earliest postwar TV sets were small—eight- or ten-inch screens were common—but many appliance stores could barely keep them in stock. As TV's popularity grew, so did the interest of a lot of radio performers in breaking into this new medium. Hank was one of them.

While I was in law school, Hank gave me a call. "I need a lawyer"—as far as Hank was concerned, even though I was only partway through law school, I was already qualified as an attorney—"and I need someone with good business instincts," he told me. He thought I had done a good job in *A.P.O. Zoot*, and he figured I might work cheap; since he had no money, he planned to offer me a partnership in the new venture he had in mind.

"I see myself as the next Jack Benny," Hank would tell me. He didn't look like Benny, nor was his sense of humor as sharp. But television stations were in the market for new programming. So in

1947, while I was still in law school, Hank and I decided to try to break into the medium together with one of its first situation comedies, *The Hank McCune Show*.

At the time, nearly everything else on the small screen was live and couldn't be shown at any other times of day, except by kinescope, which was very poor quality. But Hank had another idea. "Let's shoot the program on sixteen-millimeter film, and then self-syndicate it to independent stations throughout the country," he said. "A filmed program is good quality, can be shown at different times in different cities, and then can even be rebroadcast as well."

In that era, when Hollywood wasn't giving TV stations any of its feature films to show, nor were the studios permitting their contract actors to work on the new medium, most stations had representatives actively looking for programs. Through some hard-selling and fast-talking, we were able to convince enough of them to give *The Hank McCune Show* a shot. We assembled a cast and crew and went into production. Hank and I were fifty-fifty partners in the enterprise; I handled the legal and business side of the operation, as well as looking over the scripts for problems and occasionally making suggestions for their improvement.

Once the show finally debuted, many of the critics weren't kind. One called the program "stilted and cheaply produced." (We were certainly guilty of the second charge, and perhaps even the first.) Another categorized it as a "screwball" comedy about the "empty-headed adventures" of an inoffensive "bumbler."

We grossed a maximum of about $2,000 a show, which was barely enough to pay for the film, the lab work, and a few props. The actors got anything that was left over, which wasn't much. Nevertheless, there was no shortage of actors—as well as writers and directors—who were radio veterans eager to learn the new TV game, or were novices in the entertainment business looking for their first break. We gave them that chance, they got experience in TV, and the spirit on the set was great.

Neither Hank nor I received a penny from the show. Some weeks, we didn't even have the money to produce a new episode, so I'd send out Western Union telegrams to the stations, explaining, "Play last week's show over again." In those days, when many TV stations were experimental and were on the air for only a few hours daily, you could get away with things like that.

Fortunately, I didn't need to rely on *The Hank McCune Show* for my living expenses. The G.I. Bill was helping out, and Hilda had a good job. I felt like a kept man—not a bad feeling. She managed the office of Dr. Barney Kully, a prominent ear, nose, and throat specialist who cared for a number of celebrities and movie moguls (including Louis B. Mayer and Darryl F. Zanuck). Not only was Hilda making $750 a month, but just as important to me, she arranged with some of her show business patients for me to visit the major studio lots. It sure beat immersing myself in my law school textbooks.

During those visits to the studio lots, I was struck by the large numbers of people on the sets—usually fifty to one hundred people on each crew—and how little they seemed to be doing. To me, it seemed apparent that there was an enormous amount of waste. After all, I was accustomed to making a TV show for about $2,000 a week, and even though the money spent on those studio pictures wasn't mine, I used to practically break out in a sweat watching the way those movies were being made. I resolved that if I ever got the chance to make motion pictures, I would do it with fewer people and less money than what I had witnessed. It made quite an impression on me.

Upon graduating from law school in 1948, I went to work for Abe Gottfried, a lawyer in downtown L.A., for $150 a month, while continuing to work with Hank on the show. Then, in early 1950, I received a phone call that became an important landmark for the program: The Maxin Agency, representing the Peter Paul candy company that manufactured Mounds and Almond Joy, was interested in sponsoring *The Hank McCune Show* on the NBC network. In those days, the advertising agencies created most of the TV shows for their clients and then took them to the networks; the Peter Paul company thought it had a winner in Hank McCune.

Hoping to take advantage of my skills as a lawyer, Hank and I decided that I would fly to New York to meet with NBC's attorneys to work out the details of our debut on the network. The NBC lawyers were extremely friendly, acted delighted to have our show on the network schedule, and then invited me to lunch at a restaurant in Times Square, which apparently consisted mostly of imbibing in three martinis. After those three drinks, however, my negotiating skills disintegrated. We agreed to some basic terms, and as I staggered back to my room at the Hotel Astor, I wondered, "I hope I didn't give the store away!" As I stared up at the Camel cigarette billboard blowing smoke into Times Square, I realized I may have blown it, too.

On the second day of negotiations, I limited myself to drinking

Pepsi-Cola and coffee. I retraced my legal steps, was able to renegotiate some of the more important points I had stumbled over the previous afternoon, and came away with an acceptable deal. "I'm never going to drink again during lunch," I promised myself. I've never faltered in that commitment.

The McCune show became the first NBC comedy program on film. Our deal with NBC called for a weekly budget of $5,500 for each thirty-minute episode. It wasn't a lot of money, but Hank and I were used to making shows for $2,000, and getting a lot for very little. Ironically, the bigger-name network stars weren't getting too much more than us. During the first year of Milton Berle's *Texaco Star Theatre*, his budget was $15,000 for a one-hour program. We weren't that far out of the ballpark, and for the first time, I was able to draw an advance of $150 a show plus expenses. As it turned out, there were never any profits to share, but we didn't care: We had a network show on the bright, shining new medium of television.

The Hank McCune Show debuted on NBC in the 10:30 time slot on Sunday nights, competing for viewers against ABC's *Bowling Headliners*. In its review of the network version of the McCune show, *Variety* seemed most intrigued by the laugh track that had been interspersed through the program, the first time it had ever been utilized on TV:

> Although the show is lensed on film without a studio audience, there are chuckles and yocks dubbed in. Whether this induces a jovial mood in home viewers is still to be determined, but the practice may have unlimited possibilities if it's spread to include canned peals of hilarity, thunderous ovations and gasps of sympathy.

As I frequently pointed out to friends and critics alike, the laugh track was the network's idea, not ours. Hank and I never liked it, and over the years, it had been our dark secret that we were an innocent party to the introduction of this intrusive aspect of TV. But a network executive explained it to us this way: "The viewer sitting in his living room, by himself or perhaps with another family member or two, will feel the 'community spirit' that audience laughter can provide, and he'll be more likely to chuckle himself during the show." I often wondered if that was his polite way of telling me that our program wasn't funny enough to get laughs without some prompting.

From the beginning, NBC had difficulty dealing with Hank. The network wanted to approve every script, and Hank balked at most of their recommended changes. At the last minute, he would sometimes reinsert lines about which both the NBC "continuity" executives and I had raised doubts. One time, the network censors ordered the name "Paramount Studios" yanked from the script; when Hank vehemently objected, they overreacted; they not only deleted "Paramount," but soon thereafter eliminated the show itself from NBC's schedule.

With the McCune show buried, I couldn't exactly retreat to the comfort of my law practice, since there wasn't much comfort to it. But when Hilda became pregnant with our first child, I was forced to become more serious about law. In 1950, when she was a month away from delivering Louis, our first born, she quit her job with Dr. Kully, and we were living solely on the income from my law practice, which by then was about $275 a month.

I had moved into a small office at the Lawyers Building in Hollywood, just a couple of blocks from Sunset and Vine. Many of my clients were "one-lung producers," independent filmmakers who made movies on shoestring budgets. For about $25,000 a picture, these small-time filmmakers would shoot two Westerns simultaneously at Griffith Park or the Iverson Ranch, using the same cast and the same horses for both films. Even the story lines were nearly identical, although they might change the way the villain sneered or the hero rode off into the sunset.

Invariably, however, these producers would run out of money before they finished their movies, and I would be hired to clean up the messes, get the pictures completed, and find a distributor. Most of the filmmakers couldn't pay me with cash, so I accepted a percentage of their pictures in exchange for my legal services. In most cases, that was like taking no payment at all.

One day in 1951, a fellow named Alex Gordon walked into my office with a case for me to handle. Alex was a sweet guy who loved old movie stars, and, in fact, eventually became one of the original partners in the production wing of AIP. He had come to the States from England, and had dreams of making movies himself, although some of the early films he became involved in probably shouldn't have been made at all.

One of those movies was *Outlaw Marshal*, written and produced by Johnny Carpenter, a stuntman turned actor. He had gathered together some investors from Utah to finance the film, but before it was finished, nearly every disaster that could possibly befall a movie had struck this one. Carpenter's original budget of $20,000 was unrealistic, and before long, he had spent nearly triple that amount. Bills weren't paid. The lab placed a lien on the film. Most of the actors were waiting for their paychecks. Even those who were paid didn't have taxes withheld and sent to the government. In short, it was a film that was slipping from one banana peel to the next.

Alex asked me, "Is there some way you can salvage *Outlaw Marshal*?" I was able to get a look at the footage in the lab and tried hard to contain my dismay. The movie didn't have much of a story line, with a lot of aimless horse chases and guns being fired from one edge of the screen to the other. Maybe the plot itself was beyond salvaging, but I set out to extricate the film from its financial and legal woes.

I started by contacting the backers of *Outlaw Marshal*, one of whom had successfully manipulated his wife into a starring role in the film. Already, even before the movie was finished, the investors were wondering why they hadn't seen a return on their money. To my horror, I discovered that in his enthusiasm to raise funds, Carpenter had sold a total of 161 percent interest in the movie. If the picture had ultimately become a hit, he would have been in the same predicament as Zero Mostel in Mel Brooks's *The Producers*, falling further into debt with each dollar of profit the picture made.

After some tough negotiating, however, everyone in the Utah group agreed to accept a reduced interest in *Outlaw Marshal*. Dozens of phone calls later, I settled the labor claims and talked the laboratory into giving Carpenter a little more time to pay his debts. With the help of Richard Gordon, Alex's brother, I also got a commitment from United Artists to release the movie.

Even so, many months passed before enough of the bills were finally paid so the film could finally leave the lab and head for the theaters. By this time, the Utah investors were convinced that they were never going to see a dime on their investment—which by then was not an unreasonable conclusion. One of our investor meetings lasted for more than twelve hours, during which there were a lot of threats, lost tempers, and even tears. One of the backers shouted, "I would have been better off buying the Brooklyn Bridge!" At that moment, the Brooklyn Bridge might have been a better investment.

"Look," I told them, "the only way this film will ever have a chance of making money is if it gets into the theaters. If you hold up its release because of your own personal grievances, you're going to guarantee the sacrifice of the money you've already put in."

Outlaw Marshal finally was released, and while it was never a smash, it did earn some money. Nevertheless, those investors from Utah may still be impatiently waiting for a full return—and so am I. I was awarded a piece of the film as my "payment" for the legal work I did. There were a lot of losers in that project, including me.

By the end of 1951, I had two children, Louis and Donna, and a happy home life. But I was still looking for a way to get beyond the legal work for those "one-lung producers" and become involved with filmmaking myself. Months had gone by since the demise of *The Hank McCune Show*, and I was itching to get back into production. It took a near disaster in my personal life, however, to finally set the wheels in motion.

3

In 1952, on a Saturday evening in February, my life dramatically changed. For a while, it seemed as though it might end.

I had spent most of the day with my wife and two small children at the bar mitzvah of my nephew, Ted Rusoff. I had developed a headache that became more severe as the day wore on, and I finally excused myself to go home. That night, as the headache grew even worse, I lapsed into a coma.

At age thirty-three, I had suffered a cerebral hemorrhage, a type of stroke that kills many of its victims. In the hospital, I remained unconscious, with the doctors unable to predict whether I would ever awaken. After seven long days, with my wife and other family members holding vigil, I finally did emerge from the coma.

The doctor's prognosis, however, was chilling. "We can't say with any certainty what's going to happen," he said. "Some people who survive cerebral hemorrhages live very long lives. Others continue to have problems, and some of them don't pull through. The next five years will be critical; if you make it that far, you have a good chance of leading a normal life."

In the hospital, and then during a three-month-long recovery at home, I had a lot of time to think. My son, Louis, was two, and my daughter, Donna, was barely six months old. If I died, I had images of my children never getting to know their father, only learning about me years later through what they were told by their mother. And God knows the terrible financial position I'd leave her in. I realized that there were no assurances about my future, and that I might not be around forever. So I decided I needed to make a lot of money quickly. Not only had my illness run up thousands of dollars in medical bills, but I felt the need to leave behind some financial security for my family—a lot more money than I was making.

I also made another decision: It was finally time to pursue those dreams that, for the most part, I had put on hold. I had not gone to law school to practice law. My legal practice was paying most of the bills, but it wasn't fulfilling my dreams or making me a rich man. I needed an ownership interest in something with which I could quickly build some financial assets. I resolved that it was time to make movies.

Despite my newfound determination, I didn't know quite how to get started. Fortunately, only a few weeks after my return to my law practice, Alex Gordon reentered my life, beginning a series of events that eventually led to the creation of American International Pictures.

Alex and I would occasionally get together and talk about our options for making pictures. Bela Lugosi was an old family friend of the Gordons, and his career was floundering at the time. Lugosi was seventy years old, and more than two decades had passed since he achieved fame as Dracula and in other horror roles. He was looking for new films, but at this stage in his career, not much was being offered to him.

At the same time, Alex teamed up with Edward Wood Jr. to write a new screenplay for the Hungarian actor and called it *The Atomic Monster*. Alex took the script to Realart, a small film company making most of its money by reissuing movies from the Universal library under new titles. In those days—before the proliferation of television and long before home video—movies didn't have much value after their theatrical release had run its course, moving from the big downtown theaters to the outlying communities and finally to the smaller neighborhoods. But with fresh titles, Realart was pumping new life—and for Realart, new profits—into films that had sat on the shelves for years.

Alex presented his script for *The Atomic Monster* to Jack Broder, Realart's president. They discussed the project, and Broder agreed to read the screenplay. A week later, however, Broder called Gordon, expressing a lack of interest in producing the film. But that was only the beginning of the saga.

A few months later, when Realart reissued an early 1940s Lon Chaney Jr. movie, *Man Made Monster*, it carried the new title, *The Atomic Monster*. When Alex found out about it, he was outraged.

"They stole my title!" he told me. "I left the script with Broder, and before you know it, my title is on one of his movies! Aren't there any ethics in this town?"

I tried to calm Alex down. "There's really no way you can protect that title," I said. "The stories in the two scripts are different, and titles can't be copyrighted. There's something called 'unfair competition,' but it doesn't apply here. You may feel violated, but I don't see any basis for damages."

Alex looked devastated.

"If you want me to," I finally added, "I'll talk to Broder."

The next day, I showed up at Realart's office. Before meeting Broder, I introduced myself to a thin fellow in a dark suit and tie who occupied a desk near the office entrance. He was about five-foot-ten and couldn't have weighed more than 130 pounds. His name was James Nicholson. Nicholson, I learned, was Realart's sales manager. One of his responsibilities was retitling the company's reissued films. During our meeting, Broder called Nicholson into the office, and Jim pleaded innocent to the charges.

"Did you ever see a script that came across my desk called *The Atomic Monster*?" asked Broder.

"No, I never did," Jim said. "I'm thinking up new titles all the time, and when I came up with *The Atomic Monster*, it was an original."

After Jim left the room, I lit up a cigar as Broder and I continued to talk. I knew Alex had no legal basis to stand on, and that he could never prove damages in a court of law. But I continued to argue my case as though he could.

"Look, Jack, this is a serious matter," I said. "The use of Alex's title may have been inadvertent, but his script was sitting here in your office, and the title moved from the script to your movie. It seems to me like a clear case of title infringement. My client is entitled to compensation, and if we have to take it to court, it's going to cost everyone a lot in legal fees."

I was bluffing, of course. It was one of a handful of things I had learned in law school.

"What will it take to settle this?" Broder asked.

"I think my client would be content with $500," I said. "Content" wasn't a strong enough word; Alex would be ecstatic!

Broder thought for a second. "OK, I can have my secretary draw up a letter to that effect, and we'll get you a check right away."

No one was more surprised than me—unless it was Jim Nicholson. Jim, in fact, was astonished that I had gotten *any* money out of Broder, who had a reputation for being, well, frugal. Jim called me two days after that meeting at Realart.

"I never saw Broder give anyone anything, particularly when something has no merit," he chuckled. "There are a lot of people in this town who could use someone like you. Why don't we have lunch?"

Over the next few months, Jim and I stayed in contact. He knew about my background in production with the McCune television show and would call me occasionally to see if I had any suggestions for salvaging various troubled film projects that were brought into Realart. Usually, they were beyond rescue. But it gave Jim and me an opportunity to talk.

Jim was born in Florida in 1916 and had moved to San Francisco as a teenager. In high school, he worked as an usher and then a projectionist at the El Rey Theater. By age twenty-one, he had been promoted to manager.

Soon thereafter, Jim moved to Omaha to manage two theaters for the Goldberg chain. He met and married his wife, Sylvia, there, where she worked as a theater usherette. She was a blonde with brown eyes, and they decided to move to Los Angeles, where Jim began working in radio as a writer and announcer before returning to the theater business. He leased and operated a chain of four movie houses that he named the Academy of Proven Hits, which ran old movies, many of them classics like *Casablanca* and *The Grapes of Wrath*. On New Year's Day in 1949, one of his theaters showed the Rose Bowl Game on its oversized screen, opening the gates for what eventually became the lucrative field of closed-circuit viewing of sporting events.

Business boomed at the Academy of Proven Hits, but before long other theater chains copied Jim's concept, which gradually thinned out his audiences. When times got particularly tough, the stress may have finally taken a toll upon Jim's health. Unexpectedly, his lung collapsed, he was hospitalized and was forced to stop working. As his medical bills soared, he had to sell his theaters. When he recovered, he went to work for Jack Broder, not only retitling old Universal films, but pairing them into double bills of a similar genre—two crime pictures, two horror pictures, etc.—for distribution.

During our lunches Jim and I would talk continuously about the current state of the film business, which was dreadful and only becoming worse. At times, our discussions must have sounded like we were making persuasive arguments to stay as far away from the movie industry as possible. After all, the picture business was in a genuine panic in the early 1950s, with changes—most of them negative—occurring with the speed of a zoom shot.

Jim and I talked about the television revolution which was in high gear, tempting millions of people who had once regularly attended movies to stay home, watching live dramas on the *Kraft Television Theater*, the comedic antics of Lucy and Desi, and Ed Murrow's relentless cross-examination on *Person to Person*. Many Americans reasoned, "Why spend money going out to the movies when we can be entertained at home for free?" According to one survey, the average household in the U.S. spent $47.12 a year going to the movies in 1946; by 1952, that figure had decreased to $27.82, a 42 percent decline.

For a time, the major film studios thought they could play hardball with television and win. Most of the old movie moguls—from Mayer to Zanuck to Cohn—had misjudged just how powerful TV was becoming, maintaining an unwavering loyalty to the concept of motion pictures. In league with the exhibitor organizations, they turned their backs on television, refusing to allow their film libraries on the small screen, and prohibiting their big movie stars from appearing on the tube. They also launched an expensive advertising campaign, heralding the slogan "Movies Are Better Than Ever."

Nevertheless, the public remained glued to its TV sets, and a few film stars eventually began to defect to the new medium. Before long, the TV steamroller couldn't be stopped.

Jim and I would discuss whether there were any opportunities left in the theatrical film business, any way to get our foot in the door. At least on the surface, however, the picture looked grim. During the fifties, 7,000 of the nation's 21,000 single-standing theaters folded. Even the majestic Fox downtown theaters—the 5,000-seaters in cities like Los Angeles, San Francisco, Detroit, and St. Louis that had done quite well during World War II—were becoming modern dinosaurs as millions of Americans made an exodus to the suburbs, enticed there by thousands of new tract homes.

"A lot of those new suburban homeowners are returning veterans who recently got married," Jim said. "They're raising families and are content to just stay home on Saturday nights in front of the TV."

I agreed. "Even the people who are still in the cities aren't spending much time anymore in the downtown movie palaces," I said. "There's less and less parking available downtown, and a lot of those old theaters aren't being kept up very well." In fact, theaters like the Roxy in New York, which had 6,000 seats and a lobby the size of Yankee Stadium, went from opulence to obsolescence almost overnight.

The remaining movie houses continued to suffer with the changing times. "The studios just aren't making as many movies as they used to," Jim said. "A lot of theater owners are getting desperate for new pictures to exhibit. Television has scared the studios into decreasing their production of feature films."

Coinciding with the proliferation of TV, a major Supreme Court antitrust ruling threw the majors into even more turmoil. And as a lawyer, that court decision particularly interested me. It had a dramatic impact upon the studios and their longstanding operation of their own chains of theaters, particularly the important first-run houses in the nation's largest cities. Warner Bros. had its Warner Theatres. Twentieth Century-Fox had its Fox Theaters. Paramount, MGM, and RKO had their own movie houses, too. Each studio played its own movies in its own theaters—and in each other's theaters, too—so nearly all the exhibition money ended up in their own pockets. In essence, the studios owned and controlled the box office.

But the court decision changed all that. And it created new opportunities for movie producers outside of the studio system.

What happened transformed the movie business. The so-called "consent decree" forced a division between film production and distribution. The net effect was that the studios had to divest themselves of their theater operations. In the process, it might have provided Jim and me with an opening we were looking for.

"This decree has changed everything," I explained to Jim during one of our meetings. "In the past, each of the studios knew it could make forty to sixty pictures a year, and sell or license them in advance in a single package to its own theaters, as well as exchange them with the theaters of the other major companies. That left the independent theater owners dangling far down the ladder of priorities. The studios had a vested interest in keeping things just as they were, since it assured them that their movies would immediately start earning back their production expenses."

Under that old system, the majors could confidently plan ahead. They'd schedule a certain number of "A" or relatively expensive pictures a year, and a particular number of "B" or low-budget second features,* plus program Westerns, serials, and short subjects. At the same time, they could keep actors, producers, directors, and screenwriters under contract, assigning the Bogarts, Cagneys, Gables, and Grables to three or four movies a year and their featured actors to even more.

But with the consent decree, the studios felt that nothing was assured any longer. "Overnight, these theaters have become independent entities," I reasoned. "The studios have to sell each of their movies separately to the exhibitors making the highest bid or offering longer runs or bigger theaters. The majors don't necessarily have the inside track anymore."

Of course, a good old boy network persisted for a while, and the studios still maintained backdoor connections on the bidding with friendly distributors and exhibitors whom they had worked with for decades. In fact, some of the theater chain executives would congregate every Monday for their so-called "Boys Club" meetings, and illegally divide the available pictures among themselves; these circuits felt obligated to book most of the pictures from the majors, including the weaker ones. With the independents, however, their negotiations were much tougher.

Still, there was more uncertainty than ever before, and studio executives felt they could no longer keep production at an accelerated level, and thus could not afford to keep their expensive contract lists. Jim and I would look through *Variety*, and we could see the impact in

---

*In general, the "B" pictures were the studios' "action" movies. The early Warner action films—starring Cagney, Bogart, and Robinson—were considered "B's," and were some of the most popular motion pictures of the times. By contrast, the "A" movies were the prestige pictures like *The Story of Louis Pasteur*, which Warner Bros. promoted as "starring *Mr.* Paul Muni," and Fox's *Wilson*, an overly long, deadly dull film about the twenty-eighth President, which Darryl Zanuck and Fox produced to impress the critics.

article after article. "All types of films are feeling the brunt of the cutbacks," I said, "especially the inexpensive action, Western, and crime subjects starring second-tier contract actors. They're just gone from the production schedules. The theory must be that people can see similar kinds of 'cheapies' on TV."

For someone like me who loved movies—and wanted to make them—the deterioration of the studios was quite noticeable. Hilda and I lived in Burbank, just a block from the Warner studios, and by the early to mid-1950s, half of their sound stages were idle or in disrepair. The major filmmakers tried to fight back, digging into their foxholes and trying to create their own D-Day offensive against the intrusions of TV. The studios produced film "spectaculars" that might lure people out of their homes—musicals like *Singin' in the Rain* and *Show Boat* topped the list, along with Biblical epics like *The Robe*. Some films dealt with controversial themes; others featured 3-D images, stereophonic sound, improved color film, CinemaScope, and Cinerama.

Nevertheless, there were still no real signs of resuscitation. So when Jim and I would tell friends that we were thinking of launching a new motion picture enterprise, they figured we had gone crazy. Nevertheless, amid the panic that was running through Hollywood, we began making plans for our own independent film distribution company. Jim actually had been thinking in that direction for some time. My own interests were more toward production, thanks to my experience with *The Hank McCune Show* and my knowledge of how to produce inexpensively. Even so, I recognized that we just didn't have the money to make movies. Distribution, then, seemed like a good place to start, particularly since Jim already knew a lot about it.

"I don't know where in the hell we're going to get films to distribute," I once said. But when you're excited about starting a new business, you don't concern yourself with the minor details, or even some of the major ones. We just assumed the movies would turn up somewhere.

Jim and I had a vision of how we could find our niche in the motion picture industry. During our planning sessions, that vision took form, with our reasoning going something like this:

> The TV revolution has reduced the number of bigger pictures being made and is driving the smaller pictures into hiding.

Nevertheless, a lot of theaters desperately need product and some of it doesn't have to be blockbuster material.

With the consent decree fully implemented, independently made films have a better chance of being shown in theaters that were once studio-owned.

Later, we began to recognize the potential of tapping the teenage market, too. TV might have been keeping parents at home, but teenagers needed to get out of the house and be with kids their own age—and the parents couldn't wait for them to leave. There's some primeval, tribal thing, where boys want to be with boys, girls want to be with girls, and eventually they want to be with each other. They need a place to go with their friends and their dates. They also had a lot more spending money than kids did in the Depression era, thanks to allowances from their parents or their own jobs in fast-food restaurants. We eventually realized that if we concentrated on movies aimed at the youth market, we might be able to create a lucrative niche for ourselves.

After months of discussion, Jim and I decided to start living out some of our dreams. Almost everything in Tinseltown had changed, but we were convinced that if we approached our new venture conservatively, we could avoid drowning in red ink and becoming another Hollywood statistic.

We actually became one of only a handful of independents still operating in Hollywood. Samuel Goldwyn was well into his seventies and, along with Disney, the only big independent, but after *Hans Christian Andersen* was released in 1952, he went three years before making his next movie. David O. Selznick, who had made *Gone With the Wind* and other big films, talked of making more pictures, but he had lost his patron, Jock Whitney, and his production schedule skidded to a halt. Smaller independents like Monogram and Republic were trying to hang on by making inexpensive Westerns, but before the decade was out, Monogram became Allied Artists and Republic had folded its movie operations. Lippert Pictures was the only small independent of any real consequence when Jim and I launched our company, but even Lippert faded away in the latter part of the fifties, unable to see any future for theatrical films.

From the start, Jim and I wanted to name our new enterprise American International Pictures, but another California company had called itself American Pictures. So for the time being, we settled for American Releasing Corporation—and immediately gave new meaning to the term "shoestring budget." ARC was launched with a total investment of $3,000, made up of $1,000 each from Jim and me, and another $1,000 from Joseph Moritz, an exhibitor for whom Jim had once worked.

Jim and I became joint executive officers, although he assumed the title of president to my more modest vice presidency. While we gave Moritz the title of treasurer, he really played no role in the day-to-day functioning of ARC.

Jim needed a salary to live on, so he drew a weekly paycheck of $150. I relied on my law practice for income, never drawing any money out of ARC for the first two years. Because I was more interested in production than distribution, I envisioned ARC as a sideline business for me, particularly in those early days when we really weren't certain in what direction the company would head.

Our first office was in the Lawyers Building, across the hall from my own law office. We were just blocks from the heart of town—the Palladium, the Brown Derby, Hollywood Boulevard. Jim occupied one of ARC's small cubicles, and his wife, Sylvia, who worked as our secretary, occupied the other. One afternoon, with our name on the door and the telephones connected, Jim and I looked at each other and almost at the same time, said, "All we need now is a movie to distribute!"

4

About the same time that Jim Nicholson and I were looking for our first property, a young filmmaker named Roger Corman was seeking a distributor for the new action film he was producing. Called *The Fast and the Furious*, it was one of several pictures whose rushes we looked at, and it was the one that most piqued our interest.

Starring John Ireland, *The Fast and the Furious* was the story of a fugitive who commandeers both Dorothy Malone and her automobile and joins a car race heading for the Mexican border. Naturally, in true Hollywood fashion, Ireland and Malone fall in love at the fade-out.

Corman himself had an engineering degree from Stanford University, but his real love was movies. At age twenty-seven, he had produced his first picture, a horror film called *The Monster From the Ocean Floor*, which he made on a shoestring budget. After making a distribution deal for that movie, he used that money to produce *The Fast and the Furious*.

When we screened the still unfinished movie, Jim and I liked a lot of what we saw. The racing scenes weren't bad, particularly considering that John Ireland—and Corman himself—did some of the driving.

Later, we found out that Roger didn't have the money to hire race-car drivers, so he ended up behind the wheel in one of the climactic scenes, in which Ireland was supposed to shoot past him to victory. Roger, however, couldn't bear to lose, even in his own movie, and as the camera rolled, he got caught up in the excitement of the moment, pressed the accelerator to the floor, and left Ireland in the dust, ruining the shot. The scene had to be redone. It was one of the few instances in Roger's career in which he let something interfere with keeping costs to the bare minimum.

Of course, Jim and I realized that *The Fast and the Furious* was no *Gone With the Wind*. But not too many pictures are. Both Ireland and Malone had some name value, and we concluded that the movie had enough positive elements that we might be able to make some money with it. We needed a picture, and we had finally found one.

We decided between ourselves that if we could work out a deal with Roger, we would make *The Fast and the Furious* our first release. Roger said that both Republic and Columbia were interested in releasing the picture, too, but he was looking at all his options.

"I already have these other distribution offers from established companies," Roger told us. "But I can see myself falling into the pattern of most independent producers, which is putting out your money, making the film, sending it into distribution, and getting your money back a year later, hopefully along with a profit. I'm looking for a quicker return than that so I can have some cash to start my next movie. What can you offer me?"

Jim and I began calculating the deal we would put on the table. We knew we would soon need some additional pictures, and Roger seemed like a likely source. So we came up with the following plan:

"Roger, we'd like to distribute *The Fast and the Furious* as part of a four-picture deal. We'll raise the money for your next three pictures by going out on the road with you, meeting with the franchise holders, showing them *The Fast and the Furious*, and asking them to advance us the money for your next pictures."

None of us knew whether this strategy would work. It would mean talking the territorial distributors—called "states righters" or "franchise holders"—into booking the movie and financing others sight unseen.

The states righters dated back to the era of the nickelodeons, the first motion picture theaters. The nickelodeons were nothing more than converted stores in which chairs were set up in front of a movie screen. The states righters supplied short, silent pictures (and later feature-length movies) to the exhibitors in their particular territories, since there weren't any national distributors. The studios steadily bought up the states righters, however, thus creating their own network for national distribution, with Columbia (after its first big hit, *It Happened One Night*) being the last of the current studios to buy out its territorial distributors. When we entered the business, we realized that the states righters—who needed pictures for their territories—were a key to getting our pictures into the theaters. If we could get advances from them, too, they would also be critical to getting our pictures made.

"It sounds like it has possibilities," Roger said in response to my offer. "Let's see how much money we can raise over the next thirty days."

From his years with Realart, Jim knew many of these regional distributors, so with his guidance, we arranged a cross-country trip with Roger to four key metropolitan centers—New York, Chicago, Atlanta, and New Orleans—where we could meet with franchise holders from other nearby areas as well. We used the company's $3,000 start-up nest egg to finance the mission. We knew that if the strategy failed, ARC itself might not survive.

Here was our proposal to the twenty-eight franchise holders that covered the country: "We have *The Fast and the Furious* in the can, and we'd like to lease you the rights to release it in your territory. Also, we're going to deliver three additional movies from Roger Corman. We'll relinquish an extra five percent fee to you if you agree to put up money when each picture is delivered to you. But if you come up with the money at the *start* of principal photography, we'll give you an extra ten percent."

Money talks. Once we had mentioned increasing their percentage, the franchise holders were eager to sign on the dotted line. They agreed to put up advance guarantees not only for *The Fast and the Furious*, but ultimately for Roger's next three movies. By the time we returned home, we had commitments to cover Roger's future film-making costs.

As cooperative as the franchise holders were in the early days, however, they and the exhibitors they supplied treated us like a "comfort station"—someone to call and support when nothing else was available to play in their theaters. We eventually realized that we'd need to assume more aggressive control over our own distribution, and thus over a period of about four years, we took over most of these franchise contracts ourselves, waiting for them to expire so we could have our own national distribution organization.

Meanwhile, Roger went to work on his next picture as we prepared for the release of *The Fast and the Furious*. The reviews for that first movie were mixed, but Jack Moffitt of *The Hollywood Reporter* had just the reaction we wanted:

"This action-jammed film about sports car racing gives the exhibitor something that will appeal to young audiences on the second half of a double bill."

The movie, which cost $50,000 to produce, plus prints and ads, grossed a quarter of a million.

We promised Roger about $60,000 to produce his next picture—a deal that was made with a handshake. Over the years, we'd regularly discuss future projects with him, come to an agreement on scripts and budgets, but usually did not go through the formality of signing a written contract until much later. I was the only lawyer at the company and there were many other demands on my time since I was handling all the day-to-day crises, from business transactions to production problems. So I'd wait until there were several pictures that needed contracts before I'd draw up any of them. Even without something in writing, however, we trusted Roger to deliver his pictures on time. He also sensed that Jim and I were the type of businessmen who would always pay him promptly, and we did.

At that time, I was also the "company pessimist." I would tell Jim, "Let's keep our expectations from becoming too inflated." I knew that in Hollywood, everyone associated with every picture always seems convinced that they're working on the next Academy Award winner or box office bonanza, or both. However, from the inception of ARC, I always believed that to get an accurate sense of a picture's potential, you have to charge admission to it. "I never get overly excited about any picture until I see how paying customers react to it," I would say.

Even so, I was hopeful about the contribution Roger might make to the company. In fact, when he was making movies for us, it seemed as though he had been born with natural instincts for cutting corners. First and foremost, he was a creative, no-frills producer who, in my opinion, directed some of his own movies only because he couldn't find another director who was as good at saving money as he was. Someone once said that Roger could make a film in a phone booth for the cost of a call to New York and finish it before the three minutes were up. And that wasn't even much of an exaggeration.

Roger's next film for us was *Five Guns West*, a Civil War-era Western that was also his first attempt at directing. Today, kids go to film school for four years to learn how to direct. Roger, always resourceful, tried to teach himself in a single day by shooting an eight-minute short at the beach with a few actor friends. He filmed *Five Guns West* in nine days.

On it, Roger was prepared for everything—except for the torrential rainstorm during the first day of shooting. He was so annoyed by the rain that on his way to the set, he stopped his car by the side of the road and threw up. Who said filmmaking wasn't glamorous?

In *Five Guns West*, as with so many other Corman pictures, Roger was skimpy with extras. When I saw the rushes, I'd complain, "For God's sakes, Roger, extras are cheap! Give them a beer and a lunch, and they'll do almost anything for you! Flesh out your scenes with a few more bodies!"

But Roger had other ideas. He purchased some stock footage of a legion of Indians on the warpath, and in the editing room he spliced them around close-ups of the few actors actually hired for the movie. As for the few extras he did get to ride into and out of the sunset, most were Easterners who had never been on horseback in their lives, except perhaps on a merry-go-round. Many would have had trouble on Shetland ponies, much less something more challenging, and they spent as much time falling from their horses as riding them. It was an equestrian's nightmare.

As prolific as Roger would become, I realized that for ARC to have a steady stream of pictures to release, we'd still have to develop other sources of movies—or produce some of our own.

"We need more than Roger," I told Jim one morning. "He can give us about four pictures a year, but we can't run a company on that. There aren't that many independent movies around for us to distribute. Maybe it's time to think about making movies ourselves."

Jim was hesitant. "How are we going to get the money to produce the movies?" he asked. "It takes a lot of capital and constant cash flow, Sam. I don't think it's in the cards."

I pleaded my case. I told Jim that we could either find the money or the credit. "I know how to produce inexpensively," I said. "I did it for a long time on Hank McCune's TV show. Hank and I put together a thirty-minute network program for $5,500, nonunion in sixteen-millimeter black and white. Our pictures don't have to cost a lot of money."

At the time, banks just weren't funding independent filmmakers, largely because they were as skeptical about the survival of theatrical pictures as most of the people in Hollywood. There were also limited tax breaks for film producers, with the exception of the ability to virtually write off the total cost of a picture in six months; that tax law eventually became valuable for us in our planning, for we knew that we could take the tax savings from those write-offs and invest them in our next pictures.

I went to Pathe Laboratories, sat down with its owners, and laid out a plan. "Jim and I are going to make pictures, but we need your help. Give us credit on our front-end lab work—the dailies and the negatives—and we'll bring you our release-print business."

Then I proposed the second part of my idea.

"We also need a loan at the beginning of each production schedule. If you loan us $25,000 for each black-and-white picture—and $35,000 for each color picture—we'll buy all our prints from you—on credit, of course. At the time, I was also representing a group of creditors who were trying to settle their legal dispute with a Los Angeles housing development called Glen-Aire that had sunk into financial difficulties. "Once that case is settled," I told Pathe executives, "I will have a big fee coming, which I'll pledge as collateral for the advance you'd be putting up." Much to my surprise, they accepted my offer. Actually, it took another ten years before that fee was paid to me, but Pathe never had to rely on it for its own payment.

There were other people to contact, too. We went back to the franchise holders for advances on the movies that we would eventually deliver to them. Foreign distributors, mostly in the United Kingdom, also fronted us some money. We made a deal with Nat Cohen and Stuart Levy at Anglo-Amalgamated in England, receiving an advance of about $12,000 a picture. We relied on a foreign agent in New York to handle the rest of our overseas licensing for about a $5,000 advance per movie. Actors and directors agreed to defer their salaries for a time. It may have seemed like a patchwork way of financing movies, but we had no other choice. And once everything was pieced together, we had just enough money to produce the next picture. For many of our movies, we were able to put together $50,000 in cash and deferments per film. Of course, a single big mistake could have undermined the entire company. But we put every penny back into the business to try to keep the product flowing. And it did.

To keep the wheels turning, Jim and I worked closely, in the early years spending at least half of every day together, and later at least a third of each day. Jim was the best title man I ever knew; he had a talent for coming up with titles that could create excitement on marquees from coast to coast. And in those early days, that was just what we needed. Exhibitors were not going to hold onto our movies and wait for word of mouth to build an audience: We needed to get people to buy tickets immediately, on that very first weekend. "Since we have no big-name stars, no bestselling books, no hit plays, or well-known directors, the title and the ads are going to have to get young people into the theaters," I told Jim. And that's just what they did.

While Jim was relaxing at home in the evening, he would create a title or two that he then brought with him into the office the next morning. "What do you think of this one?" he would ask. A few of them were duds, but most were "grabbers"... *I Was a Teenage Werewolf, The Amazing Colossal Man, It Conquered the World, Reform School Girl, Diary of a High School Bride*, to name a few. Jim was also terrific at creating the basic concept of an ad, the copy lines, and the type of artwork that would be necessary to make it into one cohesive package. He had to work differently than the studios, who would simply use the portraits of the stars of their pictures in their ads; we had no stars, so Jim had to rely on strong titles and catch lines.

Jim would pass on his ideas to Al Kallis, a talented artist whom we had hired to create the artwork for our posters and advertising—a job he held for more than fifteen years. Milt Moritz, our head of advertising and publicity, would take Jim's titles and concepts and Al's artwork and develop ad campaigns that seized potential moviegoers by the lapels and dragged them into the theaters. For instance:

Beach Blanket Bingo: "When 10,000 Bodies Hit 5,000 Blankets!"

Bloody Mama: "When It Comes to Killing...Mama Knows Best!"

High School Hellcats: "The *Facts* About the Taboo Sororities That Give Them What They Want!"

Diary of a High School Bride: "It's Not True What They Say... We Married for Love...!"

Once the artwork was done, and before investing any more time and money, we took steps to reduce our risks in a very risky business. For the pictures aimed at young audiences, we would test Milt's ad campaigns with some high school and college kids, as well as a few advertising executives. We also showed it to some handpicked exhibitors whose judgment we trusted—the ones who were more than just real estate men and concession operators. If the reaction was positive, we moved ahead, creating the story line, commissioning the script, and preparing for the actual shooting. At times, our writers and producers pulled ideas right from Kallis's artwork, like the time they added a scene to *Flesh and the Spur*, a 1957 Western, which copied Al's drawing of actress Marla English, nearly naked and about to be burned at the stake. The majors thought we were crazy, working "back assward" because we had the title, the artwork, and the catch lines finished before we ever gave approval to have a screenplay written. But we reasoned, "Why make the picture if the public isn't likely to buy it?" Some theater owners were convinced that some of our ad campaigns were better than the movies themselves. As one of them said, "Can I make a suggestion? I'm in love with the advertising that you boys create with your pictures. Why don't you put sprocket holes in the posters and throw the movies away?!"

From the beginning, our most prolific screenwriter was Lou Rusoff, my brother-in-law. He had written for Canadian radio and television before coming to California in 1950, where he wrote for a number of TV programs, among them, *Terry and the Pirates*. For AIP, he wrote about thirty pictures, including several early films produced or directed by Roger Corman (*Apache Woman, Oklahoma Woman, Day the World Ended, It Conquered the World*). Often, he was working on five or six scripts simultaneously—not only his own, but rewriting other people's screenplays when emergencies occurred and the original writers were unavailable. He also eventually produced some of the AIP movies he wrote (*Panic in Year Zero, Suicide Battalion, Hot Rod Gang, Beach Party*). More than any other writer, Lou had a real appreciation for what we were trying to do. He understood how to keep costs down by limiting the number of sets and locations. He framed his scripts beautifully into our titles and artwork. And he always kept a sense of humor, which was a real virtue under hectic circumstances.

The Beast With 1,000,000 Eyes! was one of Jim's million-dollar titles that he brought into the office one morning. It became the fourth film in Roger's four-picture deal.

As I've written earlier, since Roger had gone over budget on *Five Guns West*, he had to make *The Beast With 1,000,000 Eyes!* with only $29,000 remaining in his four-movie contract. Consequently, he made the picture with a nonunion crew and actors, which is not the way to make friends in Hollywood. Most of the movie was filmed in Palm Springs and other nearby desert towns near Los Angeles, and watchdogs from the Screen Actors Guild and IATSE (International Alliance of Theatrical Stage Employees) were chasing the cast and crew from one location to another, trying to shut down work on the film. Desperate to avoid union harassment, the crew shot the last two days at a soundstage on La Cienega Boulevard. Roger never officially took credit for the picture, and although he contends that he kept hands off during the production, he was reported lurking behind the sand dunes throughout.

The Beast With 1,000,000 Eyes! was the story of a strange interplanetary craft that lands in the desert, inhabited by a being that feeds off the minds of living things. In its attempt to take over the world, it forces blackbirds to attack a rancher, and a cow to trample a man to death. The beast emits ominous warnings ("Hate and malice are the keys to power in my world!"), but eventually emerges from the spacecraft and is killed after it slips into the body of a rat.

Even with a great title, however, a picture still has to deliver what's promised, and Corman had neglected to put a beast in the film. He just didn't have the money for it, Roger explained. So Jim and I had to scramble to turn an eight-dollar teakettle into the monster with a million eyes. That was what filmmaking was like in the fifties.

Although we eventually had four features under our belt, all of them had been released as second features, and that began to create some problems. It meant receiving only a flat amount of money from exhibitors, no matter how many people bought tickets. While the fee for a second feature sometimes went as high as five hundred dollars a week in a big theater, it could be as low as fifteen dollars in a small one! And that just wasn't enough to get us by. The movie at the top of the bill provided by the majors got a piece of the action—that is, a percentage of the gross revenue. We were on the outside looking in, even though our picture was often the one that audiences wanted to see most.

One day, I saw the writing on the wall—and it wasn't encouraging. "I don't think we can stay in business indefinitely by making second features," I told Jim. "If we're always at the bottom of the bill, we're never going to grow, and maybe not even make our investment back."

We mulled over our options for a few days, and almost simultaneously, we both came up with the same solution. "What do you think about creating our own combinations?" Jim asked me. "We'll combine two pictures of the same genre—two science-fiction films or two horror features—and sell them to theater owners for what they're paying the major studios for just one feature. It's the same concept that I was using at Realart."

The studios had been approaching double bills differently. They'd play a big picture at the top of the bill—perhaps a musical—and then book it with a second, less-expensive feature from a completely different genre—maybe a Western or action movie. They thought they'd draw a more diversified audience that way. But at about this time, I was becoming convinced of the potential of the teenage market. And I felt that to get the youth audiences into the theaters, we'd have to grab them with two features on the same subject, selling them "a night of science fiction" or "a night of fast cars."

There were other factors at play, too. With people moving out to the suburbs, a lot of drive-ins were opening on the outskirts of town, where the population was mushrooming. Teenagers were the drive-ins' biggest audience, and if we were going to be making films to appeal to kids who have wheels, we could find a ready group of exhibitors in the drive-in owners, and turn those outdoor theaters from "last-run" into "first-run" venues. I felt we should be targeting ourselves on the "passion pits."

Also, the studios were overlooking the summers as a time to target audiences with new pictures. Because many theaters weren't air-conditioned, the studios believed that people just wouldn't go to the movies in the summer. But teenagers would.

Before Jim ever recognized the power of youthful moviegoers, I began to see the value of aiming pictures at this teenage market—which also included the dating crowd into their mid-twenties. I often marveled at how the studios were ignoring them. The studio chiefs apparently didn't understand that their primary audience had changed, that movies were no longer the major form of entertainment for adult Americans. To the big studios, the youth culture was an unknown entity. But I could see who was going to the movies, and it was young people.

Over the years, the studios had almost always missed the mark whenever they did make a "youth" or "teenage" picture. As entertaining as *Black Beauty, Tom Sawyer,* or *The Wizard of Oz* were, they were family pictures that might appeal to younger children or adults, but not to teenage moviegoers. In fact, movies never had been made primarily for teenagers with characters to whom they could really relate. Filmmakers like Walt Disney thought that all youngsters in the eight-to-eighteen age group were the same, as though a high school student enjoyed the same movies as his elementary school brother or sister. We knew better. Maybe parents still think of their sixteen- and seventeen-year-olds as "innocent," but we realized that they had other strong interests—including the opposite sex—that Disney and the studios were largely ignoring.

When the majors did make movies with adolescent characters, they were often played by actresses like Joan Crawford, who might portray a nineteen-year-old shopgirl even though she herself was fast approaching middle age at the time. The Crawford character typically had an elegant apartment—the kind no shopgirl could afford unless she had a sugar daddy or was an heiress to the Rockefeller fortune. When teenagers watched Crawford playing adolescent parts, they would talk back to the theater screen, yelling things like, "She's older than my mother!"

I also recognized that the studios were off target when they released movies like Mickey Rooney's Andy Hardy series, which were really lectures. Andy's father was a judge—a tall, stern, but loving man—who would overhear his son's mischievous plans and warn him, "Be careful; you'll get into trouble." In picture after picture, Andy would ignore his father's advice, get into messes and try futilely to get out of them. In the final reel, he had to confess his transgressions in a heart-to-heart. "You told me not to, but now I'm in trouble," Andy would admit. His father would scold him but then help Andy get out of trouble. Just before the end titles, Andy would exclaim, "Gee, Dad, I'll never do anything you tell me not to again." The adults in the audience would heave a collective sigh of relief. It was a morality play that parents loved—and that made kids nauseous! The last thing teenagers wanted was a lecture during an evening of entertainment.

I convinced Jim that we should give adolescent audiences what they almost never had. When American International Pictures eventually made its teen movies—films like *Hot Rod Girls* and *Beach Party*—the actors were young and they played characters just like the kids sitting in the theater seats. The story lines revolved around teenagers who thought about the opposite sex twenty-four hours a day—sometimes more—just like real adolescents do (although the sex in the pictures was generally treated lightly and amusingly). The plots dealt with both the agonies and the ecstasies of growing up. I remembered my own youth well enough to realize that if kids wanted a lecture, they wouldn't go to the movies—they'd stay home with their parents or cuddle up with a copy of the Bible. Our feelings were, "If you want to send a message, call Western Union."

Over the years, AIP sometimes led the way in motion picture trends; other times, we followed closely behind. When it came to the youth market—and to combinations—we led the pack.

In 1956, we agreed to give the idea of combinations a try, even though our first one wasn't aimed exclusively at teenagers. We combined two science fiction films—*Day the World Ended* and *The Phantom From 10,000 Leagues*—and sent them out together. Each picture was approximately eighty minutes long, shorter than many features, but that was by design. Early on, we became convinced that pictures had to move fast; you could lose your audience if there was a lag in the story line. Even today, I'm still a believer that many movies would be 50 percent better if they were 20 percent shorter.

Of course, not all directors agree. Most, in fact, treasure every foot of film they have shot. To them, cutting a scene that doesn't play well is like cutting off one of their children's hands. For that reason, I never believed in giving directors the final cut. Harry Cohn, who built Columbia Pictures, once said, "When my ass gets tired, the picture's too long!" I suppose some asses have greater endurance than others, but even with the studios today, most directors have contracts that limit their movies to no more than one hundred or one hundred and twenty minutes. Nevertheless, many directors exceed that length, and the studios are often reluctant to hold them to their contractual agreements. Several directors have admitted to me, "Once my picture was screened for a preview audience, I finally realized it was too long, so I went ahead and cut it." But too many directors remain stubborn, refusing to cut their movies until they've already been seen by the critics and the early audiences, and thus it's virtually too late to go back into the editing room.

Day the World Ended, which starred Richard Denning, ran for eighty-one minutes, and was shot in ten days (in living Superscope!) at a cost of $96,000. Roger directed it, and it capitalized on America's heightened anxiety over nuclear war, and coincided with a growing epidemic of Americans building bomb shelters in their backyards. The movie tells the story of the daughter of a retired navy captain and her boyfriend who survive a nuclear war ("Total Destruction Day") because they are hiding behind a mountain, making love when the bomb falls. (Of course, the story was based on the best scientific evidence available at the time—along with a lot of poetic license.) Unfortunately, the captain's isolated ranch house is invaded by the only other survivors of the holocaust, including the daughter's brother, who has been transformed into a three-eyed mutant. She faints when she sees the mutant, not recognizing it as her sibling.

We needed a monster outfit for the movie and turned to Paul Blaisdell, a local actor, to create it. Paul was short in stature (five-foot-two, 120 pounds), but seemed to rise to just about any challenge we gave him. We asked for a monster suit made of rubber to fit the three-eyed, seven-foot-tall mutant, and with the promise of five hundred dollars, he immediately went to work in his garage in Topanga Canyon.

Paul, however, fell behind schedule in completing the costume, and I had to start pestering him for it. Finally, several days later, he told me it was finished, and he propped it up in the passenger seat of his car and drove to the set. Others may have swerved off the Hollywood Freeway at the sight of Paul's three-eyed driving companion.

As the cameras were nearly ready to start rolling, we discovered that Paul had intentionally made the monster suit so *he* could fit into it. The seven-foot-tall Schwarzenegger type we had hired for the part just laughed when he looked at the Billy Barty-sized outfit. There was no time to redo the costume, and it was difficult to find a five-foot-two actor on such "short" notice—so, as he had planned, Paul volunteered. He slipped into the suit, and we began filming.

Roger was shooting at the Sportsman's Lodge, a restaurant in the San Fernando Valley. I had arranged to use the lodge's pond, from which diners could catch fish and have them cooked for dinner. The pond and its waterfall would be used for a scene in which the heroine (played by Lori Nelson) is bathing in the falls, and faints when she sees the monster (her brother), who then carries her off to safety.

Lori was taller than Paul, and probably weighed twenty-five pounds more than him, too. So when Paul picked her up, he was straining like an Olympic weight lifter. To make matters worse, it was over one hundred degrees outside that day, and inside the monster suit, Paul must have thought he had stumbled into Dante's Inferno. As he valiantly tried to carry Lori, he stepped in a gopher hole and collapsed, with Lori landing on top of him. We eventually had to shoot the scene with Paul holding Lori's upper body, while members of the crew supported her lower torso and legs, and tried to stay out of the view of the camera.

Meanwhile, the script also called for Paul to intentionally fall to the ground near the end of the movie, this time during the monster's death scene. So as the camera rolled, Paul toppled over on cue, ending up in water up to his nose.

"Cut," shouted Roger. "That's a take."

As everyone began moving equipment to prepare for the next shot, Paul laid there in the pond, unable to move. He tried getting up, first by rolling to his right, then to his left, but he couldn't budge in his waterlogged suit. He could probably see his life flashing in front of him, including the ridiculous obituary that would describe how he drowned in a three-eyed monster suit.

Two members of the crew, however, finally realized something was wrong. "Hey," one of them shouted, "I think our monster has gone down for the count!" They jumped into the pond, dragged Paul to safety and tore off his monster suit to help him breathe.

In its review of *Day the World Ended*, *Picturegoer* magazine commented: "Hearty congratulations to the players, for they manage to keep their faces straight throughout the film."

Day the World Ended, of course, was just one-half of our first combination. But unfortunately, we didn't have the money to make the second feature ourselves. We had a script ready—*The Phantom From 10,000 Leagues*, written by the prolific Lou Rusoff—and the ad campaign was finished, too ("Sheer Horror as a Living Nightmare Stalks the Ocean Floor!"). All we needed were some investors to put up the money.

We began talking to Jack and Dan Milner, film editors who wanted to produce and direct their own feature. They got excited about *The Phantom From 10,000 Leagues*, and they went looking for some financial backing.

Before long, a group of Japanese-Americans agreed to back the Milners and invest in the movie. They called their group "Nacirema" and anted up $75,000, the entire cost of the picture.

With that kind of money, these were people I wanted to get to know better. I arranged a meeting with them, and they were a cordial—and obviously well-to-do—group of gentlemen. "What does 'Nacirema' mean in Japanese?" I politely asked one of them.

"Nothing," he answered. "It's 'American' spelled backward!"

It sure sounded Japanese to me.

Since *Day the World Ended* cost more than their movie, the investors agreed that AIP would get 60 percent of the incoming share of box office receipts, compared to their 40 percent.

The combination was ready for release in December 1955, billed in our advertising campaign as "The Top Shock Show of All Time!" (We were never ones to understate the clout of our pictures!) But from the beginning, we had to battle for bookings in a lot of cities. Exhibitors everywhere told us, "We want to split up the movies and turn them both into second features."

"That's ridiculous," I told them. "Either show them as a combination or don't show them at all! And we want to be paid on a percentage basis, just like the majors."

"But, Sam, we've never paid you on a percentage basis before."

"Well, things are different now," I said. "We're not making second features anymore. These are two-picture programs."

The exhibitors were stubborn. The pictures were released in September, but by December we had no theater dates. Finally, a quirk of fate got us off the launching pad. A newspaper strike hit Detroit, and as a result, the major studios didn't want to release their movies without newspaper advertising to support them. (This was before the era of TV advertising of movies.) With exhibitors desperate for features, we jumped at the opportunity. We were booked into the Fox Detroit, a magnificent five-thousand-seat movie palace decorated with dozens of colonnades and a gigantic chandelier made up of 1,240 pieces of jeweled glass. The theater was so immense that the owners routinely closed off the balcony, knowing that in the TV era, they could never fill up the entire house. The off-limits balcony was so huge in its own right that people used to joke, "You can shoot deer in the balcony and not bother the folks watching the movie down below."

The combination played in the middle of the Christmas shopping season, when most people were more interested in gift-buying than moviegoing. But we took our limited publicity budget and made the most of every bit of attention we could get in Detroit. We organized miniparades through the streets—our so-called "horror caravans"—with scenes from the movies re-created on flatbed trucks, complete with monsters menacing scantily clad girls, and lightly clad men trying to protect the women by fending off the beasts. It was cold and snowing, and you could have sold the goosebumps and frostbite by the bushel that day. Amid the storm, we dropped our own blizzard of leaflets promoting the pictures.

It wasn't exactly the Rose Parade. But our stunts got great news coverage on local TV and radio, which was the kind of publicity we liked most—free! When we were done, there may not have been a person in Detroit who didn't know that *Day the World Ended* and *The Phantom From 10,000 Leagues* were in town.

The hard work paid off. The combination was a surprise hit in Detroit, and overnight, that encouraged exhibitors in other cities to book us, too. Dates materialized in Los Angeles and New York. Then in Chicago, Boston, and Dallas. We were off and running.

The combination opened on the first Wednesday in January in Los Angeles in six theaters and eight drive-ins, and on the following Tuesday, *Daily Variety* printed the box office receipts for the first half-week. In L.A. alone, our double bill had grossed $140,000. Jim and I were ecstatic—but not nearly as happy as the Japanese-American investors. The Milner brothers, producers of *Phantom*, and some of the Nacirema group showed up in my office the next morning, *Daily Variety* in hand.

"We're here to collect our money," one of them said.

"What are you talking about?" I asked.

"We want our 40 percent of the $140,000."

They were serious.

"Look," I explained, "this isn't the way it works." I turned to the Milners and continued, "You guys have been in the motion picture business for twenty-five years; you should know that you're not going to get your money this quickly. First of all, we'll never see all of that $140,000. The theaters are only going to pay us our cut of the gate, which is 35 percent. Also, the films opened only a week ago; we haven't even sent out a billing yet, much less gotten any money. And before we divide the receipts sixty-forty, we have to deduct our distribution fee, and pay for the advertising and the cost of the prints."

They left my office downcast. For most of them, this was their first experience in filmmaking, and it showed.

Eventually, however, the investors did get their cut of the $140,000—and a lot more. In Los Angeles alone, the double bill ran for four weeks at the Hollywood Theater. During the weekend shows, there were lines blocking the sidewalks—which is probably the best publicity any film can get.

5

At AIP, we were always looking for young actors who we could cast in our teenage pictures, using them again and again as their audience appeal grew. Alex Gordon, on the other hand, was always lobbying for ways to showcase some of his favorite old-time movie stars. While we hired youthful actors who were content eating box lunches and using the bathroom at gas stations near our shooting locations, Alex wanted to treat some of his aging stars to chauffeur-driven limousines and linen tablecloths during meals. While we were robbing the cradles, Alex was robbing the graves.

By 1955, Alex had stepped in to handle publicity for us. When we formed our first production company, Golden State, he became a partner—along with Jim Nicholson, Lou Rusoff, and me—in it. He also took producer credit and handled other tasks on some of our pictures. In that latter capacity, he helped cast some of our movies, often sneaking in stars from the thirties and forties, and pampering them as much as possible. I used to joke with Jim Nicholson, "Alex must visit cemetaries to find some of these old-time actors whom he drags onto the set." On a more serious note, Alex's coddling of these veteran actors ran counter to everything AIP was doing.

The beauty of dealing with young actors is that they are generally easy to handle and fast to learn. With shooting schedules of two weeks or less, we didn't have time for temperamental stars. We didn't have time to deal with unreasonable demands from agents, who generally wouldn't devote much energy to these young actors anyway, since they weren't making enough money to warrant the attention. More than anything, these kids wanted to work in pictures, and they enjoyed being in front of the cameras and spending time with one another. We had wonderful esprit de corps on our sets.

But Alex Gordon had a different vision. The movie that best personified his love for seasoned actors was *Runaway Daughters*. In the film, Alex cast Anna Sten, a Russian-born actress who was well past her prime... by more than twenty years. Sten was an attractive blonde originally discovered by Samuel Goldwyn, who believed that she could become the next Greta Garbo or Marlene Dietrich. But many of her films were flops, and some of her reviews were embarrassing. Finally, Goldwyn gave up on her.

That didn't deter Alex, however. In *Runaway Daughters*, he cast Sten as the mother of a high school girl who flees to Los Angeles to escape her overbearing parents. As our ad campaign put it, the film showed "teenage girls in revolt against today's delinquent parents."

Alex wanted to give Sten top billing—an idea I immediately vetoed.

"Sam, it's a real *coup* to get Anna Sten," Alex insisted.

"I think it could be more like a *coup de grace!*" I complained. "Anna Sten means nothing to our teenage audiences. I see no point in playing to empty seats. Sam Goldwyn couldn't get people into the theaters to see Anna Sten, and I don't think we will either. Alex, we're trying to get *young* people to come to our movies, not senior citizens!"

None of us knew quite what to expect when the shooting of *Runaway Daughters* started at a sound stage we had rented on Sunset Boulevard at Western Avenue. Alex had explained to her, "Miss Sten, this movie has an entire budget of only $90,000. I'm afraid we just can't afford the frills you're used to and certainly deserve."

Sten seemed to be understanding, but also apparently decided that she wasn't going to be deprived. She arrived on the set in her own limousine. She brought her own champagne. And caviar. At AIP, we were much more accustomed to Pepsi-Cola and tuna sandwiches on rye. As Sten surveyed the scene around her, she was probably cursing Samuel Goldwyn's departure from her life.

Runaway Daughters was part of a double bill with *Shake, Rattle and Rock*, our first entry into rock 'n' roll movies. But whether the films focused on music, fast cars, juvenile delinquency, or teenage horror, they were designed to tap into the interests and tastes of America's adolescents. With no lack of modesty, our own trade newsletter, *American News*, credited us with "the rebirth of the movie habit among young Americans." For the most part, however, we never took ourselves too seriously; after all, how could you when you were making pictures with titles like *Girls in Prison, Dragstrip Girl, The She Creature,* and *Hot Rod Girl*?

In 1956, when Roger Corman made *It Conquered the World* for us, we encountered our first problem with censors. Peter Graves starred as a young scientist who successfully thwarts the sinister efforts of an odd-looking, bug-eyed space creature from Venus (one critic called it a "megalomaniac vegetable"), which lands on Earth and attempts to take control. The creature—with a mouth resembling a chain saw and arms that belonged on a crab—enslaves people by piercing their necks with small rubber bats, which forces them into submission. Eventually, good wins out and the monster's eyes are blowtorched as it dies.

Sparing no expense, we used chocolate syrup to simulate the "blood" oozing out of the creature in its death scene; if the movie had been shot in color, the chocolate never would have worked, but in black-and-white, it was perfect. And how could anyone get upset with a monster that bled Hershey's chocolate?

In *Daily Variety*, the reviewer noted that the movie "may call down the wrath of groups concerned with kiddie pix fare. But it must be admitted that the packed house of moppets at the show caught appeared to relish the gore."

However, when AIP shipped *It Conquered the World* to the United Kingdom for a routine screening by its film review board, we never got a response. During repeated phone calls, they never gave me an answer on whether or not the movie would be approved for distribution in the U.K. And I was infuriated since we already had a date for release with ABC, the English circuit.

I flew to London to meet personally with John Travelian, the chief of England's review board. I couldn't figure out what the problem was; after all, there was only minimal violence in the movie. However, it wasn't only the violence that was causing the problems in the U.K.

"First of all, it's the blowtorch, Sam," said Travelian. "You've got the monster being destroyed by a blowtorch."

"Come on," I said, "you approve movies with a lot more violence than an attack upon a monster who looks like a vegetable!"

"Well, here's our real concern, Sam. Is this creature an animal or a human?"

"How do I know? What difference does it make?"

"Well, it doesn't look like a human to me. It looks like an animal. And we don't want to offend people who have animals. The animal protection groups complain to us whenever they see cruelty to animals on film. And I don't want to deal with that kind of aggravation."

I was somewhat amused by his logic. After all, I've often heard it said that the English frequently have more compassion for animals than for children. "Look," I said, "this being is from another planet. In fact, that's what humans from Venus look like! Our scientific research department can back it up! If you get any complaints, refer them to me."

Eventually, Travelian was persuaded, and the movie got a passing seal. Fortunately, no one ever requested the scientific research.

It Conquered the World was released in combination with *The She Creature*, a picture directed by Edward Cahn. During those early years, we had a mixture of new, hungry directors along with some veterans. The old-time directors were happy to get the assignments. Later, once the television networks started making ninety- and one hundred and twenty-minute features on their own, they began hiring some of these veteran directors. Until then, the directors were just pleased to get work, and we gave them a lot of it.

Edward Cahn's directorial credits dated back to the early thirties. Probably his best-known film was *Law and Order*, a 1932 Western in which Walter Huston portrayed Wyatt Earp. For us, he made movies like *Girls in Prison, Suicide Battalion, Voodoo Woman, Invasion of the Saucer-Men,* and *The She Creature*. And he always did high-quality, high-efficiency work.

Like many AIP pictures, the concept for *The She Creature* came off the front pages of the newspapers. It grew out of news stories about Bridey Murphy and the claims by a woman of reliving her past lives while hypnotized. Lou Rusoff wrote the provocative script, which tells of an evil hypnotist whose amazing powers allow him to lure an amphibious female creature out of the ocean to murder at his command. Eventually, the creature turns on the hypnotist and kills him, dragging him into the ocean for a chilly, high-salt demise that would send chills through any hypertensive watching his sodium intake.

Alex filled the cast with his usual array of old-time actors, some who dated back to the silent movies—Jack Mulhall, El Brendel, and Franklyn Farnum. But the vivacious Marla English, one of the unhappy teenagers in *Runaway Daughters*, got most of the attention in *The She Creature*, playing the young woman who regresses into a prehistoric, homicidal creature while in various stages of dress and undress.

Using foam rubber and latex, Paul Blaisdell crafted the monster outfit for the movie—complete with tentacles, pointed ears, tail, and bulging breasts. It weighed ninety-two pounds, and as Paul climbed into the unsightly garb, he insisted that it was bulletproof.

"Go ahead," he exclaimed. "Try shooting twenty-two-caliber blank ammunition at it at close range. It's not going to penetrate the material." Because replacement actors were hard to find on short notice, we decided to take Paul's word for it.

Paul was exhausted by the time everyone was ready to photograph the scene where the monster meets its alter ego, the lovely Marla English, AIP's answer to Elizabeth Taylor. Paul was told to hold his standing position while the crew moved the lights into place. Marla lay comfortably on a couch.

"How come you always have it so easy?" Paul grumbled inside the costume.

"What do you mean?" Marla asked.

"Why is it that I always have to stand while you get to lie on your back?"

Marla chuckled. "You sound like some of my boyfriends."

Fast and Furious
by Mark Thomas McGee

The *Los Angeles Times* critic said that Marla English's "tangible endowments are such that her 'acting' is, we suppose, irrelevant." The censors, however, were apparently not as taken with her—and her monstrous incarnation—even before the picture had been completed. We had submitted the script to the Production Code office, and Jim got a call from one of its officials.

"From the looks of the script, this she creature isn't wearing any clothes," he said. "Is that true?"

"Yes," Jim told him. "But the monster is covered with scales and seaweed."

"Even on the top?"

"Yes," Jim said, annoyed with the call. "There's plenty of seaweed covering her. She's ugly, too!"

"Good," came the reply. "We're glad to hear she's ugly. Let me just advise you to watch the cleavage. Not too much cleavage, please."

Jim slammed down the phone, and scrawled a memo to Cahn, telling him to watch the cleavage. Undoubtedly, the censors watched it quite a bit, too, not to mention the young audiences who couldn't get enough of Marla English.

In March 1956, we formally changed our company name to American International Pictures. The old American Pictures had finally gone out of business, and we grabbed the AIP name.

By that time, we were growing so fast that we moved out of the Lawyers Building into more expansive offices on Sunset Boulevard. We took over one-third of a floor, and Jim and I each had our own offices. In 1956, I also gave up my law practice—or what there was of it—and devoted all my energies to AIP. I hated to put law behind me...I think any professional becomes anxious about giving up what he was trained to do. But as the company expanded, I realized I couldn't do both, and was faced with choosing between law and motion pictures. The movies won out, and for the first time, I began drawing a salary, nearly two years after Jim and I had launched the company.

Leon Blender, who had been in the sales department at Twentieth Century-Fox, joined us as our sales manager. Leon was a great salesman—so talented that we often didn't even bother to show him the movies he was promoting to exhibitors. Leon could sell the pictures better if he *didn't* see them. He'd look at the artwork and perhaps the trailers. Then he'd take the exhibitors golfing, let them win by a stroke or two, and by the eighteenth hole, the movie had been booked.

The rest of our growing staff—from production assistants to publicity people—occupied the other desks. We worked hard, and everyone felt that they were part of the AIP family. There were no civil wars like at other companies. No one let his or her ego get in the way of making the company successful, and everyone knew they could offer suggestions about our projects.

Time after time, we proved that we could translate starvation film budgets into successful movies. Sure, we still heard lofty pronouncements from narcissistic producers at the studios, who continued to feel that they were too dignified to make "exploitation" movies. But we found that these pictures complemented buttered popcorn quite well. While the majors were still adapting versions of Alexandre Dumas or Rudyard Kipling, kids were standing in line to see our *High School Hellcats* and *Motorcycle Gang*.

When our teen movies opened in theaters in middle America, they raised eyebrows. There still hadn't been many youth-oriented pictures by then, and there certainly hadn't been any like these. But even though our movies—or at least the ads for them—were considered daring for the times, most of the films themselves continued to be pretty innocent, particularly by today's standards. There was no seduction, no rape, rarely any nudity. Just kids doing a lot of flirting, maybe a little fighting, and occasionally something that got them into trouble with the law. They weren't the kinds of movies that turned kids into juvenile delinquents, serial killers, or nymphomaniacs.

We were even careful to insert some traffic safety warnings into the dialogue of *Hot Rod Girl*. For instance, as cars zoomed around the San Fernando Drag Strip, the public address announcer cautioned the fans, "Take it easy going home! Play it safe on the road, the same as you do here on the strip!" Later in the picture, when two cars speed toward each other in a game of chicken, and one swerves away before the collision, the driver's "yellow streak" is depicted as common sense. A teenage girl watching the incident comments about the other hot-rodder who seemed quite content to crash, by saying, "He's crazy. He's completely crazy."

In that movie, we didn't even show the car wrecks that occurred at the dragstrip itself—but that was to save money, not to save youthful eyes from viewing the carnage. Just as a hot-rod accident was about to occur, we'd cut to another shot and then come back to show the damage. It costs money to stage crashes, and when you're making a movie for $80,000, you learn to settle for the *sounds* of crashes, and a lot of heavy promotion to get people into the theaters. As the promotional copy indicated, *Hot Rod Girl* was a "2-*See*" movie (some of our "really good" pictures got 3- or 4-*Sees*!). Our ads shouted: "Youth on the loose! *See* the death-defying, 'chicken race'—teenage Russian roulette! *See* teenage terrorists on a speed crazy rampage—violent—reckless!"

When I look back at those teenage pictures, it is hard to believe that any of them were controversial. *The Cool and the Crazy*, a film we distributed in 1958, had ads promising audiences the story of "seven savage punks on a weekend binge of violence." Shot in Kansas City, it depicts a drug pusher introducing a group of high-school delinquents to marijuana, which causes them to behave like zombies, clutching their throats in agony and experiencing torturous withdrawal that could have frightened Timothy Leary into abstinence. Marijuana was treated as such a taboo in the movie that it was referred to only as "M." No one would dare actually say the word!

At the end of *The Cool and the Crazy*, there was even a disclaimer to pacify the little old ladies in tennis shoes. It took the moral high ground, proclaiming that the producers hoped that the film would "raise the guard of teenagers and their parents against the awful perils of narcotic addiction." We hoped it also would raise a little money for AIP.

When Roger Corman first began working with us, he didn't immediately recognize the potential of the teen market that became so critical to AIP's success. His early movies with us, such as *The Fast and the Furious* and *Apache Woman*, were not youth pictures. But before long, we convinced him that this was a viable audience we were tapping.

In 1957, Roger directed one of our more interesting teen pictures, *Rock All Night*. We wanted the movie made quickly, so Roger suggested an adaptation of a half-hour TV drama he had seen called *The Little Guy*. He bought the rights to it, and Chuck Griffith (who had written *It Conquered the World*) was hired to write the script, expanding it into a feature film, with enough music to justify the title.

We signed the Platters, a popular group at the time, to sing and appear throughout *Rock All Night*. There was a catch to the arrangement, however: Just as the seven-day shooting schedule began, the Platters' manager called and said, "I guess I forgot to tell you. The Platters are on tour; they won't be back in L.A. for two weeks."

Two weeks! We became frantic. Chuck Griffith quickly rewrote parts of the script and Roger shot around the group as best he could. After production was finished, the Platters returned to town. We cornered them for just one day's work on the film. Roger couldn't do too much more than shoot them lip-synching a couple of their hit songs, which he cut into the beginning of the movie.

The ads said that the movie was "starring the Platters." That was stretching the truth a bit. But at least they finally made an appearance in the picture.

The Platters weren't the only rock stars who turned up in our movies. At the end of the film *Shake, Rattle and Rock*, a 1957 AIP picture whose story line put rock 'n' roll "on trial," younger and older generations make peace with their wildly differing tastes in music as Fats Domino sings one of his hits, "I'm in Love Again."

It took us many days of negotiations to obtain the rights to Domino's songs, with his record company insisting upon a much higher fee than we were willing to pay. "If you're going to demand that much money," I told one record company executive, "we'll have him sing all his songs live. We've already gotten the permission of the music publisher to do that. We'll just get along without the records themselves."

"Go ahead and try it," he said. "But you'll end up coming back to me."

I didn't quite understand what he meant—at least not until the picture went into production. But as Domino sang his songs with the cameras rolling, something just didn't sound right. It seemed as though he was singing in slow motion. And none of us could figure it out.

The next day, I called the record company executive, and explained our dilemma. "Here's what's going on," he told me. "Once Fats records his songs, we have to speed them up a bit. Fats himself may not even realize it, but his fans seem to enjoy his singing more at a faster speed, and so we doctor it a little. If you were to put him into your movie the way he really sings, audiences may not even recognize him."

He was right. We ended up having to use Fats's recordings in our soundtrack of *Shake, Rattle and Rock*, with him lip-synching them.

Because we were aiming for youth audiences who were enamored with rock 'n' roll, we put up with the eccentricities of rock stars more than we ever did with actors. We often said that the target audience for our movies was a nineteen-year-old boy who made the decision on where to take his girlfriend on Saturday night. That's why most of our movies were geared to appeal to male ticket-buyers...the teenage boys who might be drawn to theaters playing movies with provocative and titillating titles like *Diary of a High School Bride, Girls in Prison*, and *Hot Rod Girl*.

We knew we didn't have to fill every seat in the house to make money. We had to satisfy our audience, not the entire country. Even today, the studios too often try to please everyone—but everyone doesn't go to the movies, and not every movie appeals to every individual.

From the beginning, I believed that we had to target our audience and advertise our pictures for the young dating crowd. We found our niche and stuck with it, and knew who our ticket-buyers were going to be before the cameras ever rolled. When a filmmaker claims, "A good movie will find its audience," he's taking a chance; often, his movie will play to empty houses the first week, and with little or no word of mouth, the exhibitors will pull the picture before the public realizes that it's even there.

Yet despite AIP's growing success, we still had difficulty getting bookings in many theaters, particularly the large flagship movie houses in downtown areas. In those first few years, they'd schedule our pictures when they didn't have any other movies to play, and during the slower times of the year. Fortunately, we could turn with increasing frequency to drive-ins, which weren't necessarily looking for big-budget, first-run pictures.

Drive-ins had more than a twenty-year history before the first AIP picture ever screened at one of these "ozoners." The first drive-in—the Camden Automobile Theater—opened in 1933 in Camden, New Jersey, showing the three-year-old Adolphe Menjou film, *Wife Beware*, and charging twenty-five cents per person. But prior to World War II, there were still only a few drive-ins, mostly in the South. Farmers would plow over their fields and turn them into outdoor movie houses by putting up a screen, perching a few speaker cones on tall poles, and setting up a concession stand. They were often called park-in theaters, and were open only on Friday and Saturday nights.

In the postwar forties and fifties, as car registrations boomed and people moved from the cities to the suburbs, drive-ins were built on inexpensive land in outlying regions where there were no hardtop theaters. In the colder parts of the country, the drive-ins closed during the winter until some began renting heaters to their customers. Of course, the teenagers who helped drive-ins earn the nickname "passion pits"—crowding into backseats in the back rows of drive-ins—really didn't need heaters to keep warm.

At that time, the running gag about drive-ins was "They play last-run movies, right after drug stores." The major studios never really considered them reputable—in fact, unlike today, they nearly ignored the summer moviegoing market altogether, which was when the drive-ins drew their biggest crowds. While we found the summer a lucrative time for releasing pictures, we sometimes had to open our movies in drive-ins or, in some cities, they wouldn't play at all. As the crowds began to respond, putting down their two or three dollars per car to park their gas guzzlers in front of the latest AIP thrillers, we gradually turned the last-run "ozoners" into first-run venues.

As I told Jim, "We aren't being paid much"—a flat fee of anywhere from $50 to $500 per combination per week—"but by booking ourselves into drive-ins throughout the country, we can make it pay off." By 1958, there were 4,063 outdoors screens (compared to 820 in 1948), and we tapped almost every one of them.

Before long, the drive-ins were attracting more than teenagers. While dating adolescents still made up the majority of the drive-in audiences, the outdoor theaters installed playgrounds to lure young families through their gates. By bringing their small children with them, parents eliminated baby-sitting costs, keeping down their expenses for an evening of entertainment.

Even though AIP's pictures continued to play in as many indoor theaters as drive-ins, the drive-ins remained critical to our success. In good weather, a drive-in could draw a gross of two to three times the average hardtop. The drive-ins had been accustomed to paying a flat fee for their movies, whether from AIP or the majors, and these theaters didn't have to submit their grosses on these flat-price pictures. Consequently, many distributors never realized just how successful the drive-ins were.

As much as any other exhibitor, Bill Foreman of the Pacific theater chain recognized how important AIP was to his theaters, particularly the drive-ins. Many drive-in owners were skeptical about turning their theaters into first-run houses, and downright adamant against wavering from their flat-fee arrangement with distributors. But Foreman was receptive to innovation and change.

"About seventy-five percent of my customers are under age twenty-five and they want action movies, which are the kinds of pictures AIP gives us," Foreman said. "So it seems reasonable to pay you a cut of the gate rather than a flat fee." Our percentage varied, and it was never as good as the majors received, at least in the early years, but Foreman was always fair with us, and helped us convince other theater-owners that our movies could hold their own in first run. Foreman was in the vanguard of bright theater executives who realized that the business was not dead, but instead was evolving and undergoing a transformation. He bought land at cheap prices miles away from the downtowns or business districts, but in the midst of growing suburban communities. And he erected playgrounds in his drive-ins and thus attracted young married couples with children, which expanded his audience beyond teenagers in search of the "passion pits." He was a friend who was very helpful to AIP.

Throughout this early period, we were still keeping the costs of our movies strikingly low. All of them cost between $50,000 and $150,000. Meanwhile, the studios were doing everything but printing money to keep their films in the high-budget stratosphere.

6

"Listen to this one."

Jim Nicholson was tossing around titles one morning in 1957 during our morning meeting.

"Sam, I came up with this title last night: *I Was a Teenage Werewolf*. What do you think?"

I was stunned. "My God, it's terrific," I told him.

At the same time, however, I wasn't sure quite how middle America would react to it over their morning cup of coffee. There had never been a teenage horror picture before; during the twenties and thirties when horror movies were thriving, neither Karloff, Lugosi, nor Chaney ever entered into the world of adolescence, nor were there teenagers in their pictures. Maybe they had a good reason. My wife echoed the advice I received from a lot of people. "It's a great title. But don't you dare use it."

Jim had created the title to put on a story idea brought to AIP by a producer named Herman Cohen. And for the next few days, Jim and I talked about the title again and again. Should we really use it? If we do, how will the public react? We tested the title on a few people who we trusted. Some were theater-owners who had a good sense of their audiences and what the public would buy. One of them said, "It's a great gag, but I don't know if the public will come. There's never been a teenage horror picture before." Yet almost to a person, they loved the name. *I Was a Teenage Werewolf* was a million-dollar title on what would become a $100,000 movie.

To take first things first, the title is a magnificent piece of composition. It has a haunting quality about it, and I ought to caution you that if you let it pierce your consciousness it will echo in your brain in a constant refrain—*I Was a Teenage Werewolf, I Was a Teenage Werewolf.* The title, in other words, is by way of being a little monster itself.

—S. A. Desick, *Los Angeles Examiner*

Herman Cohen was a personable fellow who, like Nicholson, had begun his motion picture career as a theater manager, running Detroit's Fox Theater, a house that he later owned in part. At age twenty-three, Herman came to Hollywood to make movies, and went on to produce *Crime and Passion*, starring Barbara Stanwyck and Sterling Hayden. When we finally reached the decision to go ahead with *I Was a Teenage Werewolf*, we hired Herman, then twenty-nine, to produce it.

While Jim and I began working on the film's promotion and advertising ("The *most* amazing motion picture of our time!... You won't believe your eyes!"), Herman cowrote the script (with Aben Kandel, both sharing the single pen name, Ralph Thornton).

When the script was completed, Herman turned it over to Gene Fowler Jr. *Teenage Werewolf* became Fowler's directorial debut, but he already had an impressive track record as an editor of movies like William Wellman's *Ox-Bow Incident*, as well as director Fritz Lang's films of the 1950s. Fowler was looking for a chance to direct, and salivated at the chance with *Teenage Werewolf*. Even so, he had enough doubts about the commercial potential of the project that when he was offered either a standard fee, or less up-front money and a percentage of the movie, he bit on the flat salary. If his decision had been different, he would have ultimately made much more money.

Once the preproduction schedule was announced in the trades, still weeks before the movie was shot and eventually released, AIP's phone began ringing off the hook. Newspapers and magazines across the country were calling us for stories and interviews with the people behind the movie. Comedians on TV shows were making jokes based on the *Teenage Werewolf* title. Overnight, the picture was getting millions of dollars worth of free publicity, long before it had ever reached the theaters.

Herman, however, was concerned about some of that attention. A couple of his colleagues warned him, "Herman, you're not going to put your name on that picture, are you? Not with a title like that!"

Not long afterward, Herman's secretary rushed into his office and said, "Mr. Cohen, *Time* magazine is on the phone. The reporter wants to know if Herman Cohen is the producer of this forthcoming picture! What shall I tell him?"

It took him only a second to respond. "*Time* magazine! Tell them it's Herman Cohen, all right! And put the call through to me!"

Time did a story on the movie. So did *Look* and *Life*. Bob Hope and Jack Benny joked about it in their acts. At one point, I said to Jim, "I hope the gags—and the title itself—aren't stale by the time we finally release the picture." But that was an unwarranted fear. We continued to get incredible mileage out of the title.

In the process, a lot of people began taking credit for the title. Herman was among them, claiming that he and Jim had come up with it together. But, in fact, it was the creation of Jim alone. As the saying goes, "Success has many fathers; failure's a bastard," and this picture looked like it would be a success.

Meanwhile, as Gene Fowler was scouting locations, Herman was reviewing with us his final list of the actors he was considering for the lead in the movie. A young Jack Nicholson was near the top of the list; so was Scott Marlowe. But neither was ranked as high as an unknown actor named Michael Landon. We eventually hired the twenty-year-old Landon, giving him his first starring role. His salary: $1,000.

At the time, Landon was a hungry actor living with his wife in a sparse, one-room apartment. Before his first paycheck arrived, Herman took him to the grocery store to fill up his empty refrigerator and cupboards. Even a werewolf needs to eat regularly.

Landon portrays a surly high school youth, a chronic troublemaker who fights dirty with his classmates in schoolyard set-tos. His character also has a few other idiosyncrasies—for instance, when he is startled by the sound of a ringing school bell, he grows fangs and a blanket of facial hair, and brutally devours a leotard-clad coed practicing gymnastics in the Rockdale High gymnasium. No wonder he had trouble making friends.

The film was shot in just six days. Landon was a real professional before the cameras and gave a superb performance. Fowler built dramatic intensity well throughout the picture, and cameraman Joseph La Shelle proved why he had won the Academy Award for his work on the 1944 classic, *Laura*.

Teenage Werewolf was a turning point for AIP. Immediately upon its release in June 1957, the movie with the extraordinary title became one of the country's surprise successes. It earned back its production costs in the first two weeks and became one of our biggest grossing movies of the era. As one critic said, "The picture has become a monster in its own right."

Instantly, AIP was no longer the ugly duckling of Hollywood that ached for respectability. Many of the critics who had ignored us since the beginning—even some of the "artier" types—were suddenly taking notice. In *Partisan Review*, critic Robert Brustein dissected *Teenage Werewolf* and some of our sequels to it, treating them like the works of European "auteurs." Burstein wrote, "What these films seem to be saying, in their underground manner, is that... the adolescent feels victimized by society—turned into a monster by society."

Today, *I Was a Teenage Werewolf* is a cult movie, still shown at film festivals around the world each year. Even so, Michael Landon himself was a little slower to come around. Long after he had achieved enormous success in television, he rarely acknowledged that he had starred in *Teenage Werewolf*, probably on the advice of his agents, lawyers, and business advisors, who suggested to him that this picture was beneath his dignity and stature (or more likely, beneath theirs). From time to time, however, we made it somewhat difficult for him to completely escape his past, rereleasing the film and promoting it as "starring Michael Landon, star of *Bonanza*."

But, in fact, most of the public knew about his role in the picture anyway. In the mid-1980s, TV's David Letterman asked me if I was interested in signing Landon to star in *I Was a Teenage Werewolf II*. I answered, "Yes, but if we made a sequel, we'd have to title it *I Was a Middle-Aged Werewolf!*"

Perhaps Michael was watching that show. In 1987, he had apparently gotten over any lingering embarrassment from the thirty-year-old movie, and he revived the werewolf on his NBC series, *Highway to Heaven*. In the episode, Landon's character was on the trail of the teen werewolf, which in fact was Landon himself in his role thirty years earlier. He had obtained our permission to use old footage from the original movie. Appropriately, he titled the episode *I Was a Middle-Aged Werewolf*.

As with most of our early movies, *I Was a Teenage Werewolf* was pretty innocent, particularly by today's standards. (These days, the picture plays on Saturday morning and afternoon TV.) In the film, Landon looked more like he was adorned in a Halloween costume than something designed to really terrorize youthful audiences. Even so, it was a well-made picture by the 1950s standards for special effects, and it still plays quite well.

Nevertheless, that title was too tempting for the conservative, censorship-prone do-gooders to ignore...those vocal folks who proclaim themselves to be guardians of the moral high ground. "Teenagers who go to movies like *Teenage Werewolf* are doomed to a life of decadence and delinquency," they proclaimed.

How ridiculous! Did they think that all teenagers, at the light of the full moon, would turn into werewolves?

Nevertheless, the critics won some influential political leaders to their side, at least for a while. About two weeks after the film's release, I received a letter from Senator Paul Douglas of Illinois. "The kind of picture you have made in *I Was a Teenage Werewolf* is of considerable concern to me. At a time when the country is sensitive to the problem of juvenile delinquency, we need the motion picture industry to take a responsible stand in the movies it makes for young audiences, rather than making movies that are scandalous and immoral."

Scandalous! Immoral! With adjectives like that, Senator Douglas should have been writing advertising copy for AIP.

Although Douglas's letter was off the mark, I knew it required a response to keep the controversy from snowballing. Yes, controversy is good for just about any motion picture. But the senator's letter upset me, in part because I was an admirer of his. I figured that he had probably not seen *Teenage Werewolf*; if he had, I doubted that the letter would have ever rolled through his secretary's typewriter.

"Please do not be overly influenced by the advertisements for the movie," I wrote in my response. "As you know, there is a tendency among American businesses to be enthusiastic about their products. Perfume manufacturers hold out the promise of seduction in their ads, yet every time a woman uses a few drops, she isn't automatically seduced. Keep that in mind when you read the ads for *I Was a Teenage Werewolf*.

"If you have not already seen the picture," I added, "I think a screening will allay your concerns about its content. I would be happy to set up a private screening for you at your convenience."

I never heard from Senator Douglas again. But the controversy surrounding *Teenage Werewolf* in particular and our youth pictures in general certainly didn't die. Senator Estes Kefauver, who had run unsuccessfully for Vice President the previous year on the Democratic ticket with Adlai Stevenson, headed up a congressional subcommittee investigating the causes and cures of juvenile delinquency. And movies like ours were just the kind that the committee singled out.

Fortunately, Kefauver's committee issued its report, *Motion Pictures and Juvenile Delinquency*, before *Teenage Werewolf* was even released. But it gave plenty of ammunition to the hypercritical nitpickers dedicated to "cleaning up America's movie theaters." Although the committee report conceded that serious researchers had found no connection between "bad movies" and delinquency, it nevertheless claimed that social scientists "feel that to allow the indiscriminate showing of scenes depicting violence or brutality constitutes a threat to the development of healthy young personalities."

Senator Kefauver himself seemed as perturbed by the industry's advertising as by the movies themselves. He said that the ads were "supercharged with sex! Purplish prose is keyed to a feverish tempo to celebrate the naturalness of seduction, the condonability of adultery, and the spontaneity of adolescent relations."

Like Douglas, Kefauver should have been writing our ad copy, not criticizing it!

Throughout controversies like this, Jim and I realized that small motion picture companies like AIP took heavier hits than the majors. Whether it was in their depictions of violence or sex, the studios could get away with more because of their own power and the big-name actors, actresses, and directors associated with their movies. Their big budgets and their stable of stars gave their pictures less of an "exploitative" aura, and thus they came under less fire. Of course, because Jim and I were pretty old-fashioned, we weren't necessarily trying to break new ground in areas like violence and sex. But as I said in more than one speech, "It's no surprise that the majors are treated with a gentler hand by the Production Code office—particularly since their dollars are supporting it!"

Back in 1933, in hopes of defusing criticism aimed at the movies, the motion picture industry had set up that Production Code, headed by Will Hays, a former postmaster general under Warren Harding. While Hays was making proclamations like, "Good taste is good business"—and the code itself heralded principles like "No picture shall be produced which will lower the moral standards of those who see it"—the majors consistently got softer treatment than the independents. Under Hays and his successor, Eric Johnston, scripts were reviewed, movies were scanned, and a code seal was awarded to those pictures that passed the "moral standards" test. But there were so many ridiculous rules that needed to be met: For example, if a couple was in bed together, each of them had to have one foot touching the floor. A friend of mine in the Production Code office in those days told me he always got a lascivious sensation whenever he saw a foot artificially planted on the floor; he said it gave him a kinky feeling!

Even though none of AIP's movies was ever rejected by the code, we sometimes had more problems with organizations like the Catholic Legion of Decency, which would assign classifications to motion pictures. And then there were the local rating boards, in cities like Chicago, that were composed of the elderly widows of police sergeants and captains ("It's an honor they give them in lieu of an adequate pension," I used to joke with Chicago exhibitors). Anything that was the least bit sexy used to make the Chicago board very nervous, although violence didn't seem to bother the members at all. But if you wanted your pictures to play and be well received in Chicago, you had to try to keep these self-proclaimed defenders of morality content.

Sometimes, we took some heat from the most unlikely sources. For example, not long after the release of *I Was a Teenage Werewolf* and some of our other teen-oriented pictures, Jim and I were in Miami at the meeting of the Theater Owners Association of America. At these conventions, AIP would host a luncheon for the exhibitors, where we'd show trailers from our upcoming movies, schmooze a little, and generally try to make one-on-one contact with the local merchants in hopes that someday they might give us better percentage deals on the product we screened in their movie houses. In those days, executives from the well-capitalized majors would attend the conventions but not sponsor luncheons of their own. Jim and I used to get a laugh from the exhibitors when we'd say that we would entertain our customers, even if the majors couldn't afford it.

Jerry Wald, a writer-producer for Twentieth Century-Fox, attended the AIP luncheon that year. He was an aggressive producer, who some people said Budd Schulberg had used as a model when he wrote *What Makes Sammy Run?* in 1948. Although Wald wasn't one of the exhibitors we wanted to wine and dine that afternoon, we never had any objections to studio executives sitting in to listen to what we had on our minds. However, we weren't prepared for what Wald had on his agenda.

After lunch, once we had described our schedule of forthcoming releases, Wald stood up and asked for the floor. Under my breath, I mumbled, "Why doesn't he throw his own luncheon if he wants to talk?" But we politely turned the microphone over to him.

"Sam Arkoff and Jim Nicholson are great guys," Wald began. He looked over at us. With a lead-in line like that, I was braced for anything. "But let's face it," he continued, "AIP makes irresponsible movies. They aren't the kinds of pictures you'd want your own kids to see. I've heard that some PTAs have warned parents to keep their kids away from AIP movies like *High School Hellcats* and *Hot Rod Gang*. And I think *I Was a Teenage Werewolf* speaks for itself."

Wald looked at us and then continued. "Jim and Sam, I wish you would think about what you're doing. These aren't the types of pictures that are going to build a market for the future. You may make a few dollars from these movies today, but what about tomorrow? Please think about lifting your horizons!"

As Wald sat down, the audience was silent and obviously uncomfortable. And I was fuming.

"Jerry," I said, rising to my feet, "I want to thank you for being our *uninvited* guest at lunch today. I hope you enjoyed the meal that we paid for."

There were chuckles from the crowd.

"Since we're talking about movies," I continued, "let me remind you of your own latest picture. Perhaps you've forgotten that *Peyton Place* is your most recent film. Now, when I saw *Peyton Place*, Jerry, there was one scene after another of rape, incest, and murder. Rape, incest, and murder! You've heard the cliché about people in glass houses, haven't you? Well, if you're talking about films destroying the fabric of America, Jerry, I think you should first look at your own.

"You mentioned *I Was a Teenage Werewolf*. Jerry, in AIP's movies, our monsters do not smoke, drink, or lust. Can you say the same about the characters in your movies?"

Wald was squirming noticeably in his chair as the crowd roared its approval. He never showed up at our luncheons again.

In the wake of *Teenage Werewolf*, we began looking for ways to capitalize on the movie's success. Soon Jim came up with another classic title: *I Was a Teenage Frankenstein*.

We both looked at each other and nodded our heads.

"I think that's it," I said.

It didn't take us long to make decisions. By the end of the day, we had talked to Herman Cohen. He was interested in the title, hired Aben Kandel (using the pseudonym Kenneth Langtry) to write the screenplay, and *Teenage Frankenstein* was on the fast track toward production.

That fast track, however, accelerated into a frantic pace after a meeting Jim and I had with R. J. O'Donnell in Los Angeles just before Labor Day 1957. O'Donnell was from the Southwest, where he was the head of Texas Interstate, a large theater chain that was once part of the Paramount circuit before the consent decree. During our meeting, he was complaining about the studios.

"I spent all day yesterday arguing with them about percentages and grosses," O'Donnell said. "They want to squeeze every dollar out of us that they can. If we agreed to their terms, we'd almost be losing money with every ticket we sold."

Texas Interstate had booked *I Was a Teenage Werewolf*, but not in its largest and most prestigious theaters like the Majestic, its flagship house in Dallas. The Majestic had always been a single-bill theater that stuck with studio blockbusters like *The Bridge on the River Kwai* and *Around the World in 80 Days*; we had been relegated to the second tier of theaters, the so-called action houses.

During our conversation, Jim mentioned that *I Was a Teenage Frankenstein* was on AIP's drawing boards. And O'Donnell looked interested.

"When will it be ready?" he asked.

"The script will be done soon," I told him. "The picture should be ready for release in January."

O'Donnell thought for a few seconds, then said, "Here's what I have in mind. If you can get me the picture—and a second feature—by Thanksgiving, I'll put them into the Majestic. The majors just assume that I'm going to play their big Thanksgiving pictures without question. I want to show them that I don't need them as much as they think. Get me your pictures by Thanksgiving."

Of course, O'Donnell had no intention of paying us the same rental fees as the majors. The studios were getting 45 to 50 percent of the grosses; he offered us 35 percent. Even so, we jumped at the offer. It would have been a major coup for us to be booked into the Majestic, particularly on a big holiday like Thanksgiving, which was one of the most lucrative moviegoing weekends of the year.

"Are you sure you can do it?" O'Donnell asked. "Because if you can't, I'll book what the majors give me."

Jim and I looked at each other. "Yes," I said. "We'll have both movies ready for you by Thanksgiving." If we had had a rabbit's-foot handy, we would have been rubbing it furiously.

So between Labor Day and Thanksgiving, we set out to do the impossible. As the script for *I Was a Teenage Frankenstein* was being finished, Herbert Strock (whose credits included *The Magnetic Monster* and *Gog* for United Artists) was hired to direct it. In October and November, the film was shot, edited, and mixed. At the same time, we also were feverishly working on a second feature, *Blood of Dracula*.

On Thanksgiving Day, the combination opened at the Majestic, much to the chagrin of the majors. It also opened doors for us, changing the attitude of many exhibitors, who finally recognized that AIP was making movies that could earn money for theater-owners in their prestige houses. And we had a *Teenage Frankenstein* to thank for it.

Almost everywhere it played, *Teenage Frankenstein* did nearly as much business as *Teenage Werewolf*. Whit Bissell, who played the sinister psychologist in *Teenage Werewolf* who catapults Michael Landon back into a "primitive state," returned for an equally evil role in *Teenage Frankenstein*. Bissell, portraying the grandson of the original Professor Frankenstein, is really a chip off the ol' mad scientist. A very demented forerunner to today's transplant surgeons, Bissell's character creates a facially deformed teenage monster (played by Gary Conway), using limbs and tissue from the cadavers of brawny teenagers who have, quite conveniently, died in car and plane crashes. "He's crying!" exclaims Bissell as he examines his ghoulish creation. "Even the tear ducts work!"

The monster, however, doesn't mingle well with people. He begins to terrorize the neighborhood, liquidating one innocent victim after another, finally disposing of the ultimate authoritarian parent, Professor Frankenstein himself, who will never again mutter, "I know what's best for you!" Eventually, as the police close in, the monster electrocutes himself as he stumbles into a control panel.

What would Mary Shelley have thought!? Who knows? But many of the reviews were kind. James Powers of *The Hollywood Reporter* said the movie was "intelligently and imaginatively done." Even so, some squeamish critics recoiled at the on-screen suggestions of body parts being prepared for grafting, with the sound of a buzz saw screeching in the background. Certain people just can't take a joke!

In creating the picture's advertising, we threw caution to the wind. The posters for *Teenage Frankenstein* read, "Body of a Boy! Mind of a Monster! Soul of an Unearthly Thing!" The artwork promised "the most gruesome horror ever shown!...Not for the squeamish!...Free first aid and smelling salts!...Don't come before dinner!"

We didn't leave a single cliché untouched.

I Was a Teenage Frankenstein rang the cash registers so often that we just couldn't give up on the teenage and horror themes. Herman Cohen and Herbert Strock teamed up again for *How to Make a Monster*—a horror film that was supposedly an insider's look at how monster movies are created, complete with reappearances by the teenage Frankenstein and werewolf. In *How to Make a Monster*, however, they ungratefully kill the movie studio executives (I presume that meant us!) who have nurtured their rebirth.

Meanwhile, Roger Corman was harder to sell on the value of teenage themes—and of titles that grabbed audiences and wouldn't let them go. He once approached us with a title that wouldn't end—*The Saga of the Viking Women and Their Voyage to the Waters of the Great Sea Serpent*. Jim and I found it unacceptable.

"Roger," I complained, "*no one's* ever going to be able to remember that title. Even if they did, they'd be out of breath after saying it just once!"

"But Sam," he countered, "it says exactly what I want it to."

"It would keep the marquees working overtime. Forget it!"

We finally agreed upon *Viking Women and the Sea Serpent*—but we should have also kept a closer watch on how the picture was doing in production. Roger had been approached by a team of special effects "experts" who made promises they couldn't keep. "We can create this great scene in which the monster rises from the sea to intimidate the Viking women in their ship," one of them told Roger. "We've got all the techniques to pull it off."

Roger could barely contain his enthusiasm. The scene looked great in the artist's rendition—but it lost something by the time it became the finished product. During the actual shooting, the model of the boat was positioned in front of a rear-projection screen, onto which Roger and his special-effects colleagues projected the image of the serpent emerging from the ocean. Unfortunately, they could never synchronize the elements quite right—and in the finished shot, the boat appears to be riding *above* the water! I was always proud of AIP's innovations, but even I couldn't justify defying the laws of gravity!

Roger realized he had gotten in over his head. "I'm still trying to pull the scene together," he said, as he reshot it again and again. "But this is not my area of expertise." He finally ended up lighting the scene very dimly to try to minimize its obvious shortcomings. If he really wanted to minimize them, I had a better idea—leave the film on the cutting-room floor!

After that picture, we began looking for a project for Roger whose title would take advantage of the word "teenage." Eventually, we settled on *Teenage Caveman*, although it was a choice with which Roger wasn't completely happy. He wanted to call the new picture *Prehistoric World*, which I abhorred.

"Roger," I argued, "there's nothing new or novel about it. Dozens of museums have exhibits called 'prehistoric world.' Also, take a look at the plot. Don't forget that near the end of the movie, the audience realizes that they're not watching a story about prehistoric men at all; it's about survivors of a modern-day atomic holocaust! A title like *Prehistoric World* is just going to confuse them. Besides, I'd like to get the word 'teenage' into the title, too." Roger was still a late convert to fully understanding the teenage market.

Teenage Caveman's story line depicts a different style of youthful rebellion, in which Robert Vaughn stars as a young caveman challenging the rules of his primitive clan, venturing out past the familiar, barren confines into the world beyond, exploring the postapocalyptic earth and looking for lusher pastures. There, moviegoers see evidence of the nuclear blast—in particular, a beast whose human ancestors were mutated into monsters by the bomb, and who carries a rather unlikely piece of evidence of the prenuclear era—a postcard from New York City.

Vaughn, then a twenty-five-year-old struggling actor, was still six years away from the TV hit *The Man From U.N.C.L.E.*, and he was delighted to get the starring role in *Teenage Caveman*. And he got used to the AIP way of making movies very quickly. At one point in the script, he was supposed to shoot a deer. And that presented some problems. First of all, we didn't have a deer. Even if we could find one, it was no longer deer season, particularly in the heart of Los Angeles. Also, the movie was so low-budget ($70,000) that we may not have even been able to afford a single bullet!

Nevertheless, Roger Corman wasn't easily deterred. He sent one of his assistants to either the Elks or the Moose Club, where he unofficially "borrowed" a stuffed deer. And that's what Robert Vaughn took aim at and "killed." In the movie, he beams with the pride of a big-game hunter as he parades the stuffed deer before the cameras. The picture would have played very well at a taxidermists' convention.

Roger, who often insisted that his movies contained subtle, social messages, must have loved the critical reaction to *Teenage Caveman*. For example, the reviewer for *Variety* called it "a plea for international cooperation in terms of the dangers of atomic radiation." That was music to Roger's socially conscious ears.

"Despite its ten-cent title, *Teenage Caveman* is a surprisingly good picture," the critic for the *Los Angeles Times* wrote.

By 1958, with the success of the teenage movies boosting our confidence levels, Jim and I decided that we had outgrown our Sunset Boulevard offices. Perhaps we had let our egos overtake our reason, but we felt we needed a studio of our own. After some shopping around, we took over the master lease of the old Charlie Chaplin Studios on Sunset and La Brea.

The Chaplin Studios may have made us feel more like big-time filmmakers, and we began shooting many of our pictures there. But it was a lot of headaches, too. The studio had enough termites to cast a dozen, insect-infested horror movies. We also built a cheap, two-thousand-square-foot office complex on the lot, which became a building without a bathroom. AIP always did things cheaply, but even I could recognize the usefulness of a bathroom. Nevertheless, the contractors could not find the existing pipes they needed to hook up the plumbing, and we didn't want to pay for an expensive new configuration. As a result, we ended up having to use a bathroom in an old dressing room about one-hundred feet away.

To make matters worse, we found ourselves in the middle of a strike. Throughout Hollywood, motion picture studio craftsmen walked off their jobs. Although we didn't have many union people on the lot—just a few cameramen and stagehands—we found it more comfortable to shoot our films on location away from the studio as the strike dragged on.

Before long, both Jim and I agreed that we really didn't need the studio after all. Yes, studios have a useful purpose for TV series with recurring sets, and for period pictures where realistic sets are easier to create behind studio walls. But we realized that for the youth and action pictures AIP was making, it was almost always less expensive and more realistic to use real houses, buildings, and streets. At the same time, lights, cameras, and sound equipment had become so lightweight, mobile, and high-quality that we could shoot virtually everything on location. It became so much more economical than supporting acres of real estate and sound stages.

We kept our ears open for someone to purchase our master lease, and Red Skelton came to the rescue. Skelton's CBS television show was enjoying enormous popularity, and he and his managers began looking for a site to tape his programs. They were charmed by the fact that this was once Charlie Chaplin's studio. After all, some critics were calling Skelton "a latter-day Chaplin," so what could be more appropriate than for Skelton to move onto the lot on La Brea? Once Red got out the checkbook, we were absolutely delighted to oblige.

Skelton sold some real estate to build up more capital, purchased the studio, bought out our master lease, and then moved his people onto the lot. We shared space with them, however, until an office building we were constructing on Sunset Boulevard was completed. Our contract stipulated that we could remain on the lot rent-free for a year.

Within a couple years, Skelton learned what we had realized many months earlier—that he didn't need a studio lot after all. Red approached the CBS executives, who would do just about anything for him. They bought the Chaplin lot from him, bailing out their comedy star from the quagmire on La Brea.

More recently, I've compared studio lots to medieval castles. Both are extremely expensive to maintain, and don't serve much useful purpose anymore. At least that's how I viewed the lots for the kinds of movies we were making. Others in Hollywood have come to recognize that a physical studio may be obsolete. United Artists, for example, has never had one. Many of today's big production companies, like Morgan Creek, Carolco, and Castle Rock, also have never owned their own lot.

Yes, it may be different for the majors who produce a large quantity of theatrical pictures and TV programming, and who may find a studio lot very useful. But it's still far more expensive to make pictures this way; moviemaking on a major lot inevitably raises costs. Some states have attracted film productions within their borders by pointing to "mini-studios" that have been built as part of subdivisions or shopping center complexes; I can only wish the heads of these studios well—but ask them not to invite me to become a partner in their ventures.

Sure, there is a certain snob appeal in being able to say, "I'm going over to the studio now!... We'll be filming at the studio next week!" But a lot of people in Hollywood say things like that even when they *don't* have a studio to go to. I've told friends in the business, "If you feel the need, just brag about having your own studio; it's a lot cheaper than financially supporting one!"

7

What a difference a few decades make.

In 1958, AIP made a movie called *Machine Gun Kelly*. The budget for the film: $100,000. Charles Bronson, who played the bank robber-kidnapper, was paid $5,000 for his first starring role, the most he had ever earned to date for a picture. At the time, Jim Nicholson and I wondered if we were overpaying him.

At the end of 1991, as this book is being written, my present company is preparing the production of a remake of *Machine Gun Kelly*. But you can't make movies for $100,000 anymore. You can't even make them for $10 million. The budget for the new *Machine Gun Kelly*: in the neighborhood of $20 million! I guess that's progress.

Back in 1958, *Machine Gun Kelly* was a different kind of picture for AIP. Jim and I had been looking for other genres beyond the teenage and horror movies with which AIP had become identified.

"Why not a gangster movie?" Jim proposed one morning. We gave it some thought, discussed some story lines, and eventually brought Roger Corman on board to direct *Machine Gun Kelly*.

Although Charles Bronson was not the stereotypical leading man, he had the look of Kelly, or at least the look that we thought Kelly should have. In fact, we took a lot of poetic license with that script. In the movie, Bronson played a tough, violent criminal who showed little feeling for his victims, although he did become a bit squeamish about the possibility of spilling his own blood. While the real George "Machine Gun" Kelly may not have been the kind of guest you'd want at a formal dinner party, he never killed anyone, and was not nearly as notorious as J. Edgar Hoover tried to paint him.

Kelly went to college for a year during the Depression and might have been nothing worse than a bootlegger were it not for his wife. She was an ambitious, manipulative woman who gave him the nickname "Machine Gun" and helped create his ferocious image ("I gave you the machine gun, the name, the reputation... a backbone," she says). Kelly robbed banks, but he wasn't another Dillinger. In fact, as we depicted it in the movie, before he surrendered rather timidly to FBI agents, he mumbled, "I didn't want to be Public Enemy No. 1." As they took him away, the Feds taunted him with the name "Pop-Gun Kelly."

At the time, Charles Bronson was thirty-six years old and still a relative unknown. Hilda and I both thought Bronson had a terrific face. I focused upon those craggy, rugged features that showed the toughness he had developed working in the Pennsylvania coal mines. One critic, in fact, referred to him as "an ugly type."

Bronson thought *Machine Gun Kelly* was a pretty good picture. But he felt unsettled that Susan Cabot, who was cast as Kelly's love interest, had no resemblance to Kelly's real girlfriend. "Susan is short and dark; the actual girlfriend was a big blonde," he told me. "That really suspends my belief in the story itself. But I can adjust. That's what you have to do as an actor."

I had always felt that actors like Bronson and Jack Nicholson never would have become stars in the heyday of the studio system, when the majors were looking for actors who were handsome in the conventional sense, *à la* Robert Montgomery or Robert Wagner. Bronson just doesn't have traditional good looks; Nicholson also has a sardonic quality that some people find offensive. They were both much more suited to the more rebellious sixties and seventies.

During the filming of the original *Machine Gun Kelly*, Roger Corman discovered just how tough Charles Bronson really was. One afternoon, the two of them were playfully sparring during a break in the shooting. Apparently, Roger didn't know or had overlooked the fact that Bronson was a former semipro boxer.

Corman good-naturedly threw a left hand, which Bronson intercepted. Bronson countered with a right, then a left, then another right, all to Corman's stomach. He kept punching until a flurry of twenty blows had connected with Roger's midsection. Muhammad Ali couldn't have landed them more quickly. Although none was particularly stinging, Roger seemed stunned and he staggered backward, trying to catch his breath as he stumbled. If he had been able to speak, he might have shouted "Cut!" to stop the action; but there was a danger that Bronson may have taken it the wrong way, and opened a six-inch gash on Roger's forehead.

Machine Gun Kelly turned out to be an important picture for Bronson. Both critics and audiences liked *Machine Gun Kelly*, and it won particular acclaim in Europe, where it has been reviewed again and again in festivals. It was a watershed movie for Bronson, the springboard to starring roles in *The Magnificent Seven* and *The Dirty Dozen* in the sixties.

J. Edgar Hoover was a nemesis of more than just the real Machine Gun Kelly. He got on the nerves of a lot of filmmakers, too, when he vilified movies that glorified violent crime and criminals.

Although Hoover never singled out *Machine Gun Kelly* for attack, the movie industry in general took its share of criticism from the FBI chief—while television escaped his wrath almost completely. And that really annoyed me.

In a 1958 speech before a group of exhibitors, I pointed out that *Machine Gun Kelly* and its cofeature, *The Bonnie Parker Story*, had been approved by the Production Code. "None of the leading characters in either of these movies is glorified or put on a pedestal. We're not glamorizing a life of crime."

Then I aimed my remarks directly at J. Edgar Hoover. "If he really wants to get to the source of much of the violence seen by young people, why doesn't he go into people's living rooms? Why doesn't he look at what they're watching on TV? That's where Americans see a lot of violence!"

Unfortunately, there has been violence since the beginning of time. But it was really color movies that produced squeamishness among many people. When blood was depicted in black-and-white films, it looked black and didn't seem quite as offensive. But when action pictures began being shot in color, and pouches of "blood" were pierced and flowed freely, the gooey red hue made some viewers queasy.

Even so, no matter how realistic the film seems, attacking motion pictures as provoking violence is nonsense. If violent pictures were eliminated, there would still be violence. All you have to do is read the history books.

Nevertheless, many of AIP's titles—if not the content of the movies themselves—raised the blood pressure of the self-proclaimed protectors of America's moral fiber. *A Bucket of Blood* was one of those AIP movies that got them waving their American flags and thumping their Bibles.

Despite its title, *A Bucket of Blood* was a comedy brimming with black humor, a witty examination of the beatnik lifestyle of the fifties. Our ads proclaimed, "You'll be *sick, sick, sick*—from LAUGHING!"

Roger Corman directed *A Bucket of Blood*, working faster than he ever had for us—shooting the movie in just five days. To cut costs, Roger even made use of some existing sets that hadn't yet been dismantled from another one of our movies, *Diary of a High School Bride*. That was AIP's style.

Although *A Bucket of Blood* was not our biggest moneymaker, it was almost impossible *not* to make money with a picture that had a $50,000 budget, a good title, good posters, and good action. Still, we were dripping with ideas on how to promote this one, and encouraged exhibitors to pump up their own publicity efforts. Although the movie was a comedy, "blood" seemed to be the best way to attract customers. I must give credit to our enthusiastic promotion department for the following suggestions sent out to theaters (but I confess we may have gone overboard on this):

AIP PROMOTION MATERIAL:

The first thing that should be set up in your lobby is a giant bucket that is tipped to the side and has the appearance of red fluid dripping. This can be done with some art or possibly just filling the bucket with red dye.

Paths of red drippings should lead from various strategic points of the city to your theater.

Make some sort of arrangement with your local Red Cross to have a tie-in with *A Bucket of Blood*, whereby they would get enough volunteers to fill many buckets. This could even be tied in with your local newspapers.

Feature a special "Blood Drink," and for those patrons who might have thin blood, give them a red candy pill, representing a blood builder and energy pill for witnessing *A Bucket of Blood*.

Have contests such as, "How many *Buckets of Blood* would a human be able to fill?" Or, "How many different blood types are there?"

Looking back upon the early history of AIP, one of our most successful pictures was *The Amazing Colossal Man*, which grossed very well after its 1957 release. Universal-International had just issued *The Incredible Shrinking Man*, and we decided to turn the binoculars the other direction, building a story around a pitiful character who experienced the world's most terrifying growth spurt.

The Amazing Colossal Man was a bigger-than-life picture in which we took certain liberties with fact. It was the story of an army officer (played by Glenn Langan) exposed to radiation from a plutonium-bomb blast. Rather than succumbing to the exposure, his body experiences some reckless cell growth and he sprouts into a giant the size of a New York skyscraper, adding about a foot a day to his height. The poor fellow, perhaps unable to locate a big-and-tall men's clothing store, terrorizes the neighborhood wearing only a loin cloth, while being pursued by scientists equipped with the world's largest hypodermic needle, filled with shrinking serum. The giant eventually is cornered and killed at Boulder Dam, but not before he terrorizes Las Vegas, threatening to disrupt blackjack games from one end of the strip to the other. As the critic for *The Hollywood Reporter* wisecracked: "Every girl wants a man she can look up to, but not when he is thirty-six feet tall and still growing!"

Bert I. Gordon had become part of the AIP team, and cowrote, directed, and produced *The Amazing Colossal Man*. He had come to Hollywood from Minnesota, worked on a couple of early TV series (*Cowboy G-Men, Racket Squad*), and then began making movies. He produced *Serpent Island*, a Sonny Tufts film, and then *Beginning of the End*, the story of a swarm of berserk locusts that attacks Chicago.

Unlike a lot of other low-budget filmmakers, Bert insisted upon the best special effects that he himself could assemble. He did a credible job with the modest budgets with which he worked.

For *The Amazing Colossal Man*, Bert could not afford to hire a townful of extras to flee from the giant as it stormed down the streets of Las Vegas. So he did the next best thing: He shot a photograph of an empty Las Vegas street, projected it onto an oversized screen, and had a group of actors stand in front of it, screaming hysterically as if their lives were in jeopardy. Then he superimposed a shot of the colossal man onto this image. It worked remarkably well.

The critics rarely raved about AIP's special effects, but audiences seemed to find them believable. Most of all, they didn't detract from the story itself. Yes, the special effects of the fifties seem amateurish in comparison to those the *Star Wars* era. (Can you imagine a contemporary filmmaker creating his on-screen creatures by putting actors in monster suits?) But in many recent movies, directors have allowed their special effects to overshadow the stories themselves. Too many directors become so enamored with the effects that they forget that, more than anything, moviegoers want an interesting story and likable characters. When producers and directors overlook the characters, they are dooming their movies to failure. That was something we couldn't afford to do.

In the aftermath of *The Amazing Colossal Man*, we made pictures featuring other odd-sized characters. There was *Attack of the Puppet People*, for instance, another Bert Gordon movie, followed by other "attack" pictures—*Attack of the Giant Leeches, Attack of the Mushroom People,* and *Attack of the Monsters*. Once you've found something that works, why not milk it dry?

When Jim and I wanted feedback on our movies, we often turned to some of our toughest critics: our own children! Beginning in the late 1950s, I used to show movies in the living room of my home above Studio City, on a large, 35mm screen I had built just for that purpose. My children, along with nieces, nephews, and a lot of their young friends, would get a preview of the upcoming films of AIP and the other studios, thanks to an arrangement among most motion picture companies to loan their films to others in the business for screenings. And when the youngsters didn't like a picture, they showed no mercy.

Actually, there wasn't any better way to find out what kids really thought about the movies. One of the great mistakes made by studio executives in their forties and fifties is thinking they knew what kids in their teens and twenties wanted to see. That's why so many movies explode on the launching pad. We felt that we needed some honest opinions and real reactions from young people during the tumultuous 1960s—and we got them.

In the early days, we screened three double features each weekend—on Friday, Saturday, and Sunday nights. But my wife soon advised me that while she was sympathetic with my love of movies, "I don't want to live in a theater!" So at her insistence, we dropped the Sunday night screenings.

When the movies were being shown, I would sit in front of the kids, who were scattered behind me on chairs, sofas, and pillows on the floor. I would position myself between them and the screen so I could hear the soundtrack over their frequent chatter; I just didn't want to miss a thing. On occasion, when the lights would go on after the screening, I'd be startled to find that I was sitting all alone; the audience had drifted into the kitchen for a Coke or were outside talking, having voted with their feet if they didn't like the picture. Thirty to fifty young people usually attended these screenings, and my children, Louis and Donna, often led the discussions that followed. I'd heard comments like, "I love those characters. They remind me of my friends. They were real."

Or, "This picture was made by someone who doesn't know teenagers. We don't talk that way and we don't dress that way. Was this movie made for teenagers or for their parents?"

Once the discussion got lively, I'd sometimes jump in with cogent questions. But for the most part, the kids carried it on their own. I found their feedback invaluable, particularly when Jim and I were planning our future projects.

One AIP picture that raised a few eyebrows during those family screenings was *Naked Paradise* (later titled *Thunder Over Hawaii*)—not because of its exotic title but because of one of its actors: Sam Arkoff.

The movie was shot in Hawaii, on the island of Kauai, although I never figured out why we went all the way there just to make one of our low-budget pictures. Elvis Presley had come out with his film, *Blue Hawaii*, so the islands were on everyone's mind. But for all the use we really made of Hawaii, we could have shot it on Catalina Island. Maybe we just wanted a vacation.

Roger Corman, however, convinced us that we would get our money's worth. "While I'm shooting *Naked Paradise* for you and Jim,

I plan to shoot another movie on the same trip," Roger told me. "It's called *She Gods of Shark Reef*, financed by an independent producer named Ludwig Gerber. So you can split costs with him, particularly the expensive transportation bill."

Suddenly, Hawaii was sounding more attractive.

The actors were looking forward to the trip, too, especially Beverly Garland, who was part of Roger's regular acting ensemble. Roger was so preoccupied with moviemaking that when he did occasionally think of girls, he tended to date actresses in his movies, simply because they were close at hand. As we boarded the plane to Hawaii, Beverly Garland was the object of his affection.

"I'm looking forward to this trip so much," Beverly told me on the flight. "Roger works so hard when he's home; at least in Hawaii, we'll get to spend some time together."

Not true. Since Roger was both producing and directing these pictures, I knew that when he wasn't on the set, he'd be preparing for the next day's shooting. While the rest of us were staying at the Cocoa Palms Hotel, Roger cocooned himself down the road so he wouldn't be bothered at night as he planned his camera setups and shots. During our two weeks there, Beverly hardly saw him. For her, Hawaii wasn't the romantic paradise that Elvis had promised.

Beverly should have known that Roger's preplanning was standard operating procedure for AIP pictures. We almost always insisted that directors diagram their shots in advance—before the actual shooting, when it doesn't cost money. I would fume when visiting the sets of other movies and see directors stroll onto the set late, sip a cup of coffee, and ask, "What did we do yesterday? What's planned for today?" No wonder pictures cost so much and take so long to finish!

Both Jim Nicholson and I took our families with us on that Hawaiian trip, and when Roger needed a couple of extras, he approached us. In the story, a sugar plantation is held up on payday. Roger asked me to portray the plantation owner.

"Sam," he said. "You're perfect for the part. This character smokes cigars!" I realized immediately that Roger had done a superb job of casting.

As it materialized, my part certainly didn't require intensive training at the Actors Studio. Nevertheless, once I was on the set, Roger told me that he needed me to speak a line of dialogue, too.

"Roger, this is ridiculous," I said. "I can't act."

"It's just *one* line," Roger argued. "That's it. All you have to do is look at Richard Denning [the film's male lead] and say, 'It's been a very good crop this year; the money is in the safe.'"

It wasn't a particularly demanding request, although it was an important line, since it let the audience know where the money was hidden. But I buckled under the pressure. I blew the line—not once, but three times. On the fourth take, I finally got it right.

Much to my chagrin, I got no critical notices for my acting debut. Even more shocking, Roger never asked me to act for him again. Nor did anyone else.

Roger himself, incidentally, was also in the movie, saving a few more dollars on actors' salaries. He portrayed a plantation worker who is killed during the robbery. He always saved the best parts for himself.

More than a year after we had returned from Hawaii—long after *Naked Paradise* had been released and had earned back its cost and more—Roger called me with an offer.

"Remember that other picture I made in Hawaii?" he asked. "*She Gods of Shark Reef?*"

"Yes," I said, "what ever happened to it?"

"We still haven't found a distributor for it," Roger said. "I'd like you to take a look at it."

She Gods wasn't quite a masterpiece. It was barely even mediocre. Ronald Stein, who wrote the musical score, once told a reporter that it was "one of the worst films ever made."

Maybe so. But Jim and I decided to take it on and see what happened. We released it as part of a combination with *Night of the Blood Beast*, and it made a respectable showing at the box office.

One reason for the success of our combinations was their "saturation booking." Unlike the majors, who at that time would open their movies in just one flagship theater downtown and then slowly move them into outlying theaters and surrounding communities, we would book our pictures into as many neighborhood theaters and drive-ins in a single city as possible, transforming these theaters into our "first run" houses. We rarely played in single flagship theaters in Beverly Hills or on Broadway, but we'd cover a city with multiple screenings in thirty, forty, or more theaters. The reason: to get as much mileage as possible out of our TV advertising.

AIP was one of the first motion picture companies to use TV ads. Jim and I would make special deals with television stations to buy all their unsold ad time late at night. In a small or a medium-sized town, we might spend $1,000 for a burst of thirty to forty TV ads over a one-week period. On many of our films, we spent more on advertising and prints than on producing the movies themselves, but television fit right in with the type of distribution we were doing.

AIP also never took any of its pictures out of release. We'd play them until the prints were in shreds. Even then, we'd extend their lives, resuscitating them for a few more months by cannibalizing the prints—taking one reel from one print and another reel from a second print until we had created a single print from the remains of several of them. Starting out with one hundred prints, a picture might eventually play four to six thousand engagements, moving from city to city, and from the downtown theaters to the outlying movie houses. It often took a year or two for a picture to move through the entire distribution network.

Those were incredibly rewarding—and hectic—times. Fortunately, we had a young staff so enthusiastic about what we were doing that they were willing to work long hours. We also teamed up with inventive directors like Burt Topper, who wrote and directed pictures like *Tank Commandos* and *The Devil's 8*. Burt could do just about anything behind the scenes—take a camera apart, build a camera mount, or produce, write, and direct a picture like *Hell Squad*, which was made for $20,000. For several years, we put him in charge of physical production, as we did later with Norman Herman, who produced some pictures for us, too.

Jimmy Honore began as a gofer ("go for this, go for that") at AIP, working as a mail clerk and a messenger. But his real interest was in editing, and he rapidly moved from an apprentice to a first-class editor. He was one of many young people who we helped get into the motion picture craft unions, which was not easy in those times. Feature production was down, and the only new union members were the sons of individuals already in the unions. But using the Taft-Hartley law as leverage, AIP forced the unions to permit new craftsmen, including Jimmy, to work for us if we guaranteed them work for one year, which opened the doors for them into the unions. Today, Jimmy is senior vice president of post-production at Columbia/Tri-Star.

In the office, we had indefatigable employees like Irene Ramos, who was in charge of our prints. Irene had an extremely important job, keeping track of the prints as we shipped them from one part of the country to another. It was often a mad scramble, moving one hundred prints on a Tuesday from theaters in Texas and ensuring their arrival in New York by Wednesday to play in a circuit there. The studios never had to work under such pressure, since they could afford to make extra prints—often about five hundred per picture compared to our one hundred. But we couldn't play with our budgets as loosely as they could. We'd start those one hundred prints in three territories, and if the movie did well—if it proved itself—we'd have some additional prints made (sometimes up to 500 extra prints) to allow for wider distribution of the film. Every print was always accounted for, and was playing somewhere. In some cases, we even chartered planes to make sure that the pictures reached their destinations on time.

Some of the craziest scheduling occurred on rare instances in the early days when two theaters in a town shared a single print of an AIP movie, due to unexpected problems like a print being delayed in transport. Their starting times would be staggered, and as soon as the first reel was shown at Theater A, it would be driven at breakneck speed to Theater B, which would load it onto the projector, play it, and then rush it back to Theater A. This went on all day, every day. Back in the 1920s, these were called "bicycle prints," since the reels were transported by bicycle messengers. But at AIP, we had progressed to using automobiles. Nevertheless, it was nerve-racking for the exhibitors, who never knew whether the reels were going to arrive on time. On occasion, they didn't, and audiences were treated to an unexpected intermission.

As carefully as we planned our pictures and their distribution, we couldn't control everything. Eventually, as the 1950s drew to a close, our combinations had started to lose their appeal. In 1958 alone, AIP distributed eleven combinations (twenty-two pictures), mostly our own productions, but by the third quarter of that year, we were having difficulty getting them booked into as many theaters as before. We were suddenly facing competition from copycat movies made by independent producers or smaller film companies. Other moviemakers had looked at what we were doing, and began making their own teenage and horror movies. Most had very little originality to them, and could have been AIP clones: *Hot Car Girl* and *Hot Rod Rumble* from Allied Artists; *Life Begins at 17* and *Teenage Crime Wave* from Clover Productions; and *Juvenile Jungle* from Republic Pictures.

None of AIP's pictures, of course, had big budgets, but these imitations were even cheaper. Also, unlike our movies, many of the competing films had parental characters who often gave lectures to their teenagers—an immediate turn-off for young audiences. Most of these pictures were distributed by small organizations that had recently sprung up, but the majors picked up some of them for distribution, and by using their influence with exhibitors, they squeezed us out of bookings.

To further complicate matters for AIP, the majors had finally discovered the summer season. Until the late fifties, they shied away from releasing their big pictures in the summer, convinced that people were just too busy vacationing or having backyard barbecues to go to the movies. They just didn't realize that some drive-ins were capable of grossing $50,000 or better a week during the summer, which was far better than most hardtops. Once the studios had heard about some of AIP's summer box office successes, however, they began rethinking. In the summer of 1958, the majors started releasing some of their biggest movies of the year in the summer making it increasingly harder for us to get into the theaters, even the drive-ins.

And then there were the dollars and cents of it all. Particularly in those early years, many exhibitors kept giving us second-class treatment, becoming stingier with us than with the major companies. I used to complain that the exhibitors had a license to steal, and that wasn't too much of an exaggeration. Most theater chains had their own policies on the types of deals they would make with various distributors, based on the strength of those companies. To some of them, the smaller companies like AIP just didn't count, especially since we were distributing "exploitation" movies. These exhibitors would have a so-called house nut—the amount of money it cost them to operate their theaters and get a fair return on their investment; but they'd negotiate a different house deal with each distributor, and during our early years our deals never became as good as the ones the majors negotiated, forcing us to settle for a smaller percentage of the box office receipts. While the studios would get 50 percent of the gate—sometimes more for a successful major picture—we continued to settle for as little as 25 or 35 percent if the picture didn't gross well. It used to infuriate me when our combinations would bring in grosses larger than the theaters had seen in months—and our young audiences would buy more at the concession stands, too—but we'd still get less than any major. The exhibitors made enormous profits with the concessions, and considered it all theirs, and certainly not open to negotiations with either us or the studios. And they would be smug about it.

"Look at the kinds of pictures you're making, Sam," one exhibitor told me. "Do you really think they deserve to get as much as the costly movies the majors are making?"

"You bet I do!" I said, becoming angrier by the moment. "If our picture earns the same money, it should get the same rental!"

The exhibitors were no more attuned to the teenage audience—and the kinds of movies they liked—than the majors were. At times, the theater owners were simply astounded by the hordes of young people who bought tickets at their hardtop theaters and drive-ins. Some exhibitors were even afraid of the teenage crowds, anxious about "unruly young crowds prone to violence."

In fact, there was a lot of evidence that some theater owners had a poor understanding of their own business. They were slow in moving into shopping centers, convinced that theaters could not be built in the same conventional square or rectangular boxes as a department store or other retail establishment. Even as many theaters struggled during the TV revolution, most exhibitors still swore by the odd shapes, the sloping floors and the unusual ceiling heights of the older movie palaces. It took many years before they recognized the value of multiplexes in neighborhood shopping malls.

The shopping center magnates were also anxious about odd-shaped theaters, fearing that if the movie houses moved out, they'd have difficulty re-renting the space. Eventually, however, they recognized not only that their conventional boxes could be used as theaters, but that movies drew their biggest crowds at night when shopping-center parking was much more available.

To further aggravate our own situation, this was a tense time for exhibitors and distributors. With the new rules in the aftermath of the consent decree, there were numerous lawsuits between exhibitors and distributors, causing bitter feelings to arise. In this environment, we often had trouble collecting the money the exhibitors owed us. (The majors did, too, but their collection problems weren't as serious as those of an independent company like ours.) We would ask that the franchise holders bill the exhibitors in our name, so the checks would be made out to AIP and could be forwarded to us immediately. But more often than not, the checks were made out to the franchise holders instead. So we never knew when the money came in, not to mention whether we were getting a fair accounting.

The big theater circuits like the Stanley Warner chain would routinely take up to six months to pay us. Apparently, they decided to just hold onto the money, either earning interest on it or using it to invest in their other enterprises. With the uncertainty in the theatrical movie business due to the television revolution, some chains were moving into other types of businesses, too, using *our* dollars to finance their entrepreneurial ventures.

That used to really irritate Jim Nicholson and me. Exhibitors would tell us, "The AIP movies are really good for our concession business; the kids who come to see your youth and action pictures buy a lot more popcorn and candy than the ordinary customers." Even so, some of the exhibitors felt no obligation to promptly pay us what they owed us, pleading poverty despite their thriving concession businesses.

"Look," I used to tell them, "we aren't running a charity for theater owners. We need our cut of the box office receipts just to stay in business. As much as I'd like to, we can't subsidize you any longer!"

Operating theaters, of course, is a cash business, and some exhibitors were notorious for inaccurate reporting of the number of tickets they sold. Some, for example, didn't tear tickets at the door, and then they resold them. The majors would have their lawyers and accountants "blind-check" theaters at random, literally conducting head counts of patrons going into a particular theater on a given day and then comparing those figures to the number of tickets the exhibitors claimed had been sold. However, in Texas, the state legislature—under the influence of a governor who had been connected with the theater industry—passed a law banning this "blind" (or unannounced) checking. This Texas statute, of course, was a ridiculous protection of pirates. But the theaters, which were local businesses, had more leverage in the state legislature than even the major motion picture companies, who wielded their influence primarily in Washington, D.C.

To make matters worse, when drive-ins began installing heaters that allowed them to stay open year-round, most exhibitors wanted distributors to give them an additional allowance for the heaters since they cost extra money to install and operate. At first glance, that might have seemed fair. But most exhibitors were already charging an extra twenty-five to fifty cents per ticket for the heater rental—a surcharge on each ticket, even when there was only a single heater keeping a carload of six teenagers warm. They would deduct that twenty-five to fifty cents from each admission price in computing the distributor's share of the box office. In addition, some exhibitors would levy the heater surcharge for nine months a year (omitting only the summer months), even though the heaters were rarely used more than five months a year.

Some drive-in circuits discovered other ways to enhance their bottom line. As part of their admission prices, they gave their customers a twenty-five or fifty cent credit on snacks like pizza from their concession stands—and deducted that amount before calculating our percentage of the gate, even though many theater-goers never bought the pizza or other snacks. Other drive-ins sold "student books," a ten-dollar packet of six tickets that they never included in their accounting of box office receipts.

I remember complaining to one drive-in owner, "This is ridiculous. When those student tickets are used, they should be counted as part of that day's box office. It's unfair to do it any other way."

However, he wouldn't be swayed by logic. "Sam, we never consider them as *real* tickets. They're promotion. They're really a way of advertising."

They were also a way to cheat us out of hundreds of thousands of dollars a year.

It was a constant war, a game of one-upmanship with some exhibitors to get our money, or as much of it as possible. At one time, we were owed literally millions in overdue receipts. Sometimes, the only way the exhibitors would pay was if we agreed to accept less than was really owed to us. Despite our signed agreements on rental terms, certain exhibitors always felt they were open to renegotiation.

Leon Blender used to get the exhibitors on the phone, and complain, "Look, we need our money."

"Well, Leon, maybe we can work something out," they'd typically respond. "How about taking twenty-five percent of the gross instead of thirty-five?"

If a major was offered a deal like that, it could threaten to withhold its next blockbuster until its past-due accounts were paid in full. The studios had so-called stop pictures—those movies that carried the stipulation, "If you don't pay your back bill, we'll stop delivery of the picture to your theaters." But we weren't big enough to wield that kind of leverage. And depending on how badly we needed the money, Leon would sometimes agree to take less than what we were owed.

Leon worked with these exhibitors every day, and would often get into heated arguments with them (although by the next day they would be playing golf together). Jim hated confrontations of any sort—and as an ex-exhibitor himself, was sometimes sympathetic with the problems that the theaters had. I, on the other hand, was pretty consistently pugnacious and considered AIP's differences with theater owners to be my fight.

One day, an exhibitor broke down and gave me a partial victory after a heated fight between the two of us. Afterward, he said, "You enjoyed this fight, didn't you?"

I had to admit that I did. That's when I realized for the first time that I really needed a crisis a day to keep my blood circulating—and I still do.

By the spring of 1959, Jim and I knew we were in trouble. "The market is just inundated with copies of what we're doing," I told him one day over lunch. "We can't go on any longer with these combinations and hope to survive. We've got to change." Both Jim and I recognized that the film business was and is different than most others, in that change is almost perpetual. Unlike many other enterprises, it can't continue along the same successful path indefinitely, even with good management. We were a growing company frequently confronted with obstacles presented by the majors and exhibitors. We knew we'd have to gird our loins from time to time, and keep them girded through periods of transition.

We considered a number of options and then made some hard choices. Our first decision was to produce more expensive pictures, and make them in color. "We can take the money that we would have otherwise spent on two movies and channel those funds into just one," I said. "Rather than making two $150,000 black-and-white features, we can produce one $300,000 color motion picture."

When each of these new movies was distributed, we would send out an older AIP picture as the cofeature, thus saving us the cost of production and prints for a new picture. "Let's say we issue a new movie in September," Jim proposed. "As its second feature, we can reissue the top-of-the-bill picture from three months earlier. Then, when the next new feature is ready in December, we can release it along with the September movie at the bottom of the bill, charging a second-feature price for it. There's a lot of mileage left in these older pictures; a movie can be a hit if it sells two, three, four million tickets the first time around, depending on its cost, but there are still a lot of people who haven't seen it. And even when an individual has already seen the second feature, he'll tolerate it again if he wants to see the top picture."

Our Edgar Allan Poe films helped launch this new venture into more expensive movies. *House of Usher* was made for a budget of $300,000, in color and CinemaScope. As we awaited its production and release, it was a tense time around the company, particularly since many exhibitors weren't happy with our decision, even those we got along well with and who were drawing large crowds with our movies.

"What are you guys trying to prove?" one of them bluntly asked. "Why don't you guys stay small? We like the inexpensive combos you're making. You guys are doing a wonderful job with those little pictures." What he didn't say—and what he really meant—was, "If AIP starts making more costly movies, we might have to pay you the same percentages we give the studios, which we don't want to do." They wanted us to keep delivering pictures on cheap terms; as I told Jim, "It's like they'd prefer to keep us barefoot and pregnant."

As the first Poe picture moved into production, we decided to pursue another new direction as well. We had heard about the revived motion picture industry in Italy, and were familiar with some of the inexpensive Italian action and Biblical features that had been imported for American release. Many of them were attracting large American audiences.

"Money goes a lot further in Italy," people would tell us. "You can acquire pictures for peanuts. Or you can make a big picture for a lot less money in coproduction arrangements."

In 1959, Jim and I decided to test the waters in Italy. We had enjoyed a good run with the combinations, but we recognized we'd have to change.

8

We didn't know exactly what to expect when we decided to try our luck in Italy. As the 1960s evolved, however, Italy turned out to be an incredibly exciting place to make movies. The Italians were producing big action pictures, in part because those kinds of films could still be made there without breaking the bank.

By contrast, the entire American film industry was suffering from a bad case of the economic doldrums, with a dramatic decline in the number of pictures made in Hollywood and growing anxiety over when (or whether) the domestic industry would recover from the television revolution and the other internal changes.

Although AIP arrived in Italy before the majors had fully caught on to the potential there, the studios eventually discovered the ability to make films there much cheaper, particularly big pictures like historical epics or Biblical tales. As a result, throughout the sixties, American productions and coproductions in that country grew significantly. *Cleopatra* was probably the best-known, big-budget American picture made (primarily) in Rome, but there were dozens of others. A flurry of "spaghetti Westerns" took Clint Eastwood, Charles Bronson, Henry Fonda, Lee Van Cleef, and other actors to Italy, where they remained for years.

Not surprisingly, the American film studios always found some way to spend more money than necessary in Italy. The Italians were clever, and somehow always seemed to talk the studio representatives into hiring a few more local workers and spending a lot more lira than they had originally planned to. I wasn't afraid to say no to them, willing to let a picture fall through rather than letting it go over budget. ("Why won't you renegotiate?" the Italians used to ask me. "The studios always do.") The studio representatives didn't want the deal to collapse and to go home without the picture—representing failure on their part—so they agreed to a lot more spending than they should have.

As a result, there were always many more crew members than they could ever use, a phenomenon never more evident than during the filming of *Cleopatra*. I used to see the crew wearing their ID badges that said "Grip #24" or "Electrician #36." Why in the hell would any picture need thirty-six electricians?

I rapidly fell in love with Rome. This was before the era of the one-day strikes in Italy, when everything from theaters to airports would close down for twenty-four hours, plunging the entire country into short-term chaos. During Rome's moviemaking heyday, Jim and I stayed at the Excelsior Hotel, and we could sit at the nearby Cafe Doney or Cafe de Paree on the Via Veneto and watch one American movie star after another walk by. From Henry Fonda to Shelley Winters to Charles Bronson, they were finding much more work in Italy than in the States. Rome had become "Hollywood on the Tiber."

Italy, of course, hadn't always been such an exciting place for filmmaking. The country, in fact, had come a long way since World War II, when there was virtually no legitimate motion picture industry. During the war, Mussolini had used moviemakers to produce primarily propaganda films. The message was monotonous: Crush the allies. Crucify Churchill and Roosevelt.

Once the war was over, the industry struggled to get back on its feet. The neorealists like De Sica and Rossellini were helping to revive the Italian movie business. But Americans and other foreigners also had an open invitation to bring their scripts—and, just as important, their checkbooks—to Rome. Even so, moviemaking was structured differently there by necessity. Unlike the U.S., which had a huge potential moviegoing audience, most major European countries had populations of only thirty to forty million people; that just wasn't enough to support a big-budget picture. So they came up with an idea to increase both the budgets and the box office potential of pictures. Namely, most of the Italian movies in those days were coproductions with other European countries. All the governments actively encouraged these arrangements in order to help resuscitate their own local movie industries, even providing subsidies or low-interest loans for these coproductions.

Thus, when an Italian producer wanted to make a movie, he would put his money into a multinational production. Backers from France, Germany, Spain, and England—or any combination thereof—would toss in financing of their own for the same picture. In return, each country would send one of its own stars to appear in the movie—perhaps a French actress (speaking French) would star opposite a Spanish actor (speaking Spanish) and a German costar (speaking German); the dubbing would have to be taken care of later. Since each country's initial investment was so modest, it had a good chance to be a profitable enterprise. Together, they were building their own Towers of Babel, hoping to reach some kind of financial heaven that they couldn't attain singlehandedly.

I liked what I saw in Italy. Although the United States was never directly a party to these coproductions—the U.S. government didn't have any coproduction or subsidy laws, primarily because the majors didn't want them—AIP could still get involved in some of filmmaking ventures on our own and reap the benefits of these foreign subsidies. We had already done that in England with pictures like *The Cat Girl* and *Black Museum*, which we coproduced with Nat Cohen and his Anglo-Amalgamated Pictures. "This is worth a gamble," I had told Jim Nicholson as the British coproductions began to take shape under the auspices of a corporation we had formed in the U.K. "We can send over a script, a producer or director, an American actor or two, and a portion of the budget, and become part of a coproduction that would get us ownership and the Western Hemisphere distribution rights to the movie, or some alternative."

The possibilities were irresistible. So while we were preparing to make bigger movies in the States, like the Edgar Allan Poe pictures and later the Beach Party movies, we looked toward both England and Italy as new avenues for production that would be a minimal drain on our investment dollar.

Initially, we got our feet wet in Italy by purchasing the U.S. rights to a number of Italian sword-and-sandal spectacles: *Sign of the Gladiator, Goliath and the Barbarians, Samson and the Slave Girls, Goliath and the Sins of Babylon, Goliath and the Vampires* and many more.

Just as important, on our first trip to Italy, we met Fulvio Lucisano, a creative young producer who became our liaison and a wonderful friend there, and with whom we eventually coproduced many pictures. He would introduce us to contacts in Rome and run interference for us. In the evenings, he would escort us to many of Rome's finest restaurants—something which I truly appreciated. He'd lead us not to the expensive tourist traps but to the outdoor restaurants frequented by the locals—where we would socialize and even make deals late into the night, with Fulvio often translating for us in the heat of the negotiations. Unlike in England, where the deal-making ended at five P.M., we could transact business day and night in Italy.

The first picture we acquired was *Sign of Rome* in 1959, a French-Italian coproduction starring Anita Ekberg. Ekberg played a queen of Syria who plotted a revolution against the Roman conquerers. Jim and I liked the picture, although there were some matters to be resolved.

First, the movie had already been dubbed into English for the Southeast Asian market, primarily Hong Kong and Singapore. But it was such a cheap dubbing job and the English was so unintelligible that I couldn't even understand it. "Thank goodness for Fulvio," I told Jim. "Maybe he can translate the *English* for us!"

We also didn't like the title. Since the beginning of AIP, our titles had been one of our biggest drawing cards. And while *Sign of Rome* might have worked in Italy, it probably wouldn't have the same appeal in Oklahoma City or Des Moines.

"How about changing the title to *Sign of the Gladiator*?" Jim asked.

"Well, I like your title better," I told Jim. "But there's a small catch. There's no gladiator in the picture!"

Jim and I pondered the problem for a few minutes, and realized that since we were going to have to redub the picture anyway, we could take care of a change in the plot when we dubbed it in English.

And we did. We adjusted the plot a little and had Ekberg's love interest—a Roman general—utter a few lines about the days when he was a gladiator, and how he might get sent into the ring (and to his death) if he didn't succeed in quelling the impending revolution. On the theory that "one picture is worth a thousand words," we also spliced in a shot of a gladiator from another film. It worked. It was that simple. We had made some minor changes to fit the new title. That's show business!

In typical AIP style, our ads for *Sign of the Gladiator* were not prone to understatement. With the artist's rendition of a gladiator slaying half of the soldiers west of the Nile, the ads promised a 4-*See* picture:

> The Screen Explodes With Wondrous Spectacle Bigger Than Anything You Have Ever Seen!
> See! 10,000 Horsemen Charge the Valley of Blood!
> See! The Amazing Fire Throwing Catapults of War!
> See! The Barbarian Torture Catacombs of Horror!
> See! The Destruction of a Mighty Pagan Empire!

How could anyone stay away?!

Sign of the Gladiator is a crudely made spectacle. The deepest thing about it is Anita Ekberg's cleavage.
—*Variety*

The second picture we brought home from Italy was a Hercules movie starring Steve Reeves. Reeves was an American who used to frequent Muscle Beach in Santa Monica before becoming the biggest strongman in the movies, thanks in large part to the success of an early Hercules picture picked up by Joe Levine, who had gone to Italy before us. When we first saw the rough cut of the new picture, it was only about three-quarters completed, but we liked what was there. Reeves played the leader of a group of peasants successfully battling an army of invaders who, from the film's beginning to end, shouted threats like, "Kill! Burn! Take their women!" We thought it had potential, although because we did not want to seem as though we were trying to exploit Levine's success with his Hercules movies, we eventually changed its name to *Goliath and the Barbarians*.

Actually, Jim and I took a real chance on *Goliath and the Barbarians*. The picture wasn't finished when Fulvio first told us about it. The producer, who was a friend of Fulvio's, was continually running short of money, like most Italian producers, and he desperately needed some additional cash to wrap up the shooting. Each time a foreign distributor came to Rome, he would screen the rushes to try to make a sale to that country to raise more money.

"The producer is a wonderful guy," Fulvio told us, "and the picture is pretty good. But he hasn't paid his crew and his actors in a while; instead of cash, some of them have been given chits that are being accepted by local merchants. It's getting to be a desperate situation."

We looked at the rushes and liked what we saw, and decided to trust our instincts (which was not always the wisest thing to do). Jim and I met with the producer while the cast was waiting impatiently on the set, anxious to see if a deal was going to be made with AIP. If our negotiations had fallen through, the production would have shut the doors and everyone would have gone home.

But at ten o'clock on a Saturday night, we shook hands and wrote out the terms of the deal on a tablecloth at the Café Doney. I signed a check for $20,000, handed it over to the Italian producer, and we went down to the studio with him. As we entered the stage, we were greeted with cheers and shouts as though we were war heroes. The producer waved the check in triumph, as some of the cast members walked over to inspect it, perhaps suspicious that it might be fool's gold. We had some beer and wine brought in, and we celebrated with the cast and crew until one in the morning. Maybe they had trouble financing movies, but the Italians sure knew how to celebrate. On Monday morning the movie went back into production.

Goliath and the Barbarians became a huge hit for AIP, more successful than *Sign of the Gladiator*, and thus launched us into the "spaghetti era" at full throttle. When *Goliath* opened at the Palms Theater in Detroit on Christmas Eve, the theater manager didn't expect much of an audience. He allowed most of his employees to go home early to spend the holiday evening with their families—and that's when the crowds arrived. His box office receipts for the night were more than the Palms had taken in during any single day in more than five years.

We received a telegram from Joe Jackson, the head buyer of the Interstate circuit in Texas:

"*Goliath and the Barbarians* opened in Dallas, Houston, San Antonio, Fort Worth, and Galveston on Friday, December 18, to the biggest grosses of any picture in the history of our company's pre-

Christmas playing time. Thanks to American International for the availability of this attraction at this particular season."

Nationwide, by the time all the tickets were sold, *Goliath and the Barbarians* had grossed enough in the U.S. to put AIP back on firm financial footing. We knew we were in Italy for the long haul.

In the early days before AIP started our own productions in Italy, I (and sometimes Jim) would fly to Rome, and Fulvio would set up a series of screenings for us in labs throughout the city. The screening rooms were paid for by the producers of the films we were viewing. We would watch rough cuts and unfinished prints, literally from dawn to the point of collapse.

The projector at the first lab would start up at eight in the morning, and we usually viewed pictures until ten at night. Sometimes, after a reel or two, Jim and I would look at each other and shake our heads. Once the projectionist would turn on the lights, we'd head for the door to go to the next lab and the next screening on our schedule.

We would see about four movies a day this way. But that wasn't enough, since there were literally dozens we wanted to watch. Finally, we found a way to accelerate the schedule.

One day, I asked Fulvio, "For God's sake, can you arrange to get all the films we want to see together in one location? We'll pay for the screening room, which I'm sure the producers will love. But we have to stop wasting so much time moving from one lab to the next, and feeling obligated to watch each picture from beginning to end since someone else is paying for the screening."

On our next trip to Rome, Fulvio did just that. We watched as many as ten to fifteen movies a day. When the pictures were good, we watched them from beginning to end. But sometimes we needed to preview just a single reel to make our decision. Or we'd watch only the first and the last reel. On occasion, if the last reel piqued our interest, I'd put on the next-to-the-last reel and then the one before that, in effect running the picture backward. Or we had two projectors going at the same time, each showing a different movie. One summer, we screened so many movies that I brought over Stan Dudelson, the head of our television department, to help us watch the pictures; a couple years later, Harold Brown, Stan's successor, joined us for the screenings. We were looking for production value, and it often didn't take long to figure out which pictures had it and which didn't.

Paul Maslansky, who produced the enormously successful *Police Academy* movies in the 1980s, had just started to make horror pictures in Rome when we were there in the 1960s. He was a musician who had become interested in motion pictures after making a documentary about a European composer. Paul knew that Jim and I were buying a lot of product in Europe during this time, so he talked us into looking at his first movie, *Castle of the Living Dead*, hoping that we would finance its completion and pick it up for distribution in the Western Hemisphere, which we eventually did.

One afternoon, I invited Maslansky down to our screening room, and he later told me that he had never seen anything quite like what was taking place there. I was sitting near the front of the small room, smoking my cigar and munching on some fruit, and Fulvio was next to me. We had removed the sliding door separating two screening rooms, and I was watching different movies on each of the two screens, while shouting out instructions to the projectionist:

"Put on the last reel on the right screen.... Change the left screen to the next movie."

All the while, I was controlling the volume, adjusting it for the picture I wanted to see. Mostly I was looking for adventurous scenes, scary moments, and pretty girls. The fact that I couldn't understand the foreign languages didn't matter that much, although Fulvio would translate some of the dialogue so I could understand the plot.

"This is the most amazing thing I've ever seen," Paul said. I never knew whether that was a compliment or not. But the Italians thought I was crazy watching two pictures at the same time.

One cold spring morning in Rome in 1960, Jim and I watched a movie called *La Maschera del Demonio (The Mask of the Demon)*, a film by director Mario Bava. The screening room was almost unbearably chilly. The Italians couldn't have both the heat and the air conditioning usable at the same time, so they would shut down the heating at the beginning of spring, and wouldn't start it up again until the late fall. So in the midst of this unseasonable cold spell, as we sat watching this movie at eight in the morning, we had no heat. Jim and I had on overcoats and our teeth were still chattering.

But when *La Maschera del Demonio* came on, we almost forgot just how miserable we felt. It was one of the best horror pictures I had ever seen. Mario Bava was a brilliant horror director who, as a former cameraman, could create wonderful special effects right in the camera. Ironically, he was never as appreciated in Italy as he was in other parts of Europe, since Italians weren't as addicted to horror pictures as people were in England, for example. We retitled the movie *Black Sunday* and released it in the United States.

British actress Barbara Steele starred in *Black Sunday*, cast as a vampire revived from the dead seeking vengeance on the descendants of the brother who put her to death two hundred years earlier. We advertised it as "the most frightening motion picture you've ever seen!" It came close to living up to its billing.

As AIP continued to pick up completed Italian pictures for theatrical release in America, Jim and I recognized that we'd have to devote some of our energies to obtaining as high a quality of dubbing as possible. And in Rome, we found that this was no easy undertaking, simply because of technical and talent problems we unexpectedly encountered.

As we had learned when we first previewed *Sign of Rome*, the Italians just didn't take dubbing as seriously—and approach it as carefully—as we would have wanted. Fulvio explained to us, "Since every international picture requires dubbing, the Italians have grown up with it. We've never demanded that the lip synching be perfect. The dubbing studios here are probably not as careful as you Americans would like them to be."

Because of the market for Italian pictures in the Far East, they were all dubbed in English—at a dubious quality level. For the nearly one hundred smaller Italian pictures that we intended to market only to American television, the more primitive Italian dubbing was frequently acceptable. But we needed higher quality dubbing for the pictures that were going into American theaters.

In Italy, we simply couldn't find the range of voices we felt we needed. There were a lot of talented Italian actors and actresses, but so many of them read English words phonetically. When I listened to their work—and then listened again and again—their cadence just never sounded right.

At one point, a dubbing specialist from England arrived in Italy, and I thought he might be our savior. But the male voices he brought with him from London had a strikingly effeminate sound. It just didn't seem to work, especially when these fellows would dub the voices of tough-looking Roman gladiators or spaghetti-Western cowboys!

Technical problems in Rome simply compounded the difficulties with the actors. Except for one facility, Cinecittà, the Italian studios were not soundproof. There were always airplane or traffic noises that would end up on the sound track. It was pretty amateurish, and not up to our standards.

"This is so ridiculous," I once complained to Fulvio. "We're working with period pictures that are set in the gladiator days. If my reading of history is accurate, it was rare in those times to hear a roar of a 747 flying overhead or the blaring of an automobile horn in the distance! Some viewers are liable to notice the distractions!"

I finally told Jim, "We're going to have to take these pictures to the States with us and have them dubbed or revoiced in English back home." In the States, at studios like the Titra Sound Corporation in New York, we could find exactly what we wanted—a variety of professional voices speaking good English.

The film "purists," of course, considered dubbing into a different language to be a bastardization of motion pictures. They insisted on feeling the blood, sweat, tears—and every other basic bodily fluid—in the original movie, and not have it tainted by "tampering" in the dubbing studio. When I was in college, I was just like them, watching art films and talking like a pseudointellectual with my friends. I wanted to hear languages that I couldn't understand; I wanted to savor every morsel and nuance of the filmmaker's work, even if the foreign tongue chased away 90 percent of the potential viewing audience.

So I wasn't surprised by the letters I used to get from time to time at AIP. People would write things like: "How dare you not use the original voices?! If you were really serious filmmakers, you would use subtitles instead!"

Most of these individuals didn't realize that even filmmakers whom they idolized routinely dubbed voices in their features. Fellini, Rossellini, and De Sica would give roles to people they saw on the streets—particularly the minor roles—because these common folks had a certain look that they wanted. Then in the studio, these directors would dub in other voices in the same Italian language. Sophia Loren's own voice was seldom used in her early movies.

When we contracted for the American distribution of the classic picture, *La Dolce Vita*, it originally played on Broadway and in a handful of American cities in Italian with subtitles. Thereafter, we hired Salvatore Billittari, an Italian-American, to dub it in English in

New York—and we waited for the critics' attacks. However, those verbal assaults were never forthcoming. *New York Times* critic Bosley Crowther, in fact, called our version of *La Dolce Vita* the best dubbing job he had ever seen. He said that he enjoyed the picture much more than if we had relied on subtitles. Coming from Crowther, that was quite a compliment. He and others have realized that dubbing *can* be done right, and Europeans who have grown up with it are not as adverse to it as Americans. We brought Salvatore to Hollywood to work as the head of our post-production.

After the success of *Goliath and the Barbarians*, Jim and I decided we needed another "Goliath" movie, and we signed contracts in Italy to coproduce a new film, *Goliath and the Dragon*. Lou Rusoff wrote a script for us, and we flew Debra Paget, who had starred with Elvis Presley in *Love Me Tender*, to Italy as one of the leads in the new picture. When Lou flew to Rome, he brought over parts of the dragon that would be used in the film, like a giant claw that would throttle its human victims. The special effects involving the entire monster would be shot later.

Just days before production was set to begin, however, the movie was put on hold. The Italian filmmakers decided they needed to make some changes—most significantly, they wanted to double the budget of the film. "Sorry," I told them, "we have a signed contract. I'm not budging from the original financial arrangement."

The Italians were shocked. "Some of these guys think that a signed contract is just the first step in the negotiations!" Fulvio warned me.

To the Italians, American moviemakers continued to have deep pockets and were always willing to pay more money. However, AIP was not MGM or Twentieth Century-Fox. "We're willing to abide by our signed deal," I said. "Take it or leave it."

It was a stalemate, and after days of the deadlock, I decided to bail out, leaving the Italians stunned at my willingness to walk away. I told Fulvio, "Sorry this one didn't work out. Tell them we don't care what other companies do; we're not going to be blackmailed. I'm going to Japan. AIP has a Godzilla production in the works over there. And I'll take some time for a vacation, too."

I spent a week in Japan, where we were coproducing a picture called *Frankenstein Conquers the World*. Then I flew to India. While I was there, I received a telegram from Fulvio:

"Come to Rome. There's a partially produced picture available that could become your *Goliath and the Dragon*."

With no more information than that, I flew back to Italy. Apparently, a Hercules movie in its fourth week of production had run out of money. Film Finance of Italy, a new Italian bond company (and a franchisee of an English bond company), had been contracted to guarantee that the picture would be finished. But in the excitement of getting started, the film hadn't received the production funds they were supposed to dispense. Suddenly, they were desperately searching for financing.

I looked at the footage that had already been shot. "Fulvio," I said, "I think we can rework the remainder of the script to make it presentable, and even use the dragon parts that we already have over here." We got involved in the project, and it became *Goliath and the Dragon*.

The star of that movie was Lou Degni, an American gymnast in his late twenties whose muscles made him the 1960s forerunner to Arnold Schwarzenegger. Degni's physique propelled him into a short-lived career as a hero of Italian epic movies, although his name almost undermined those plans. "Degni" didn't sound American enough for our audiences, so we insisted that he change his name to something more all-American.

"It's ironic," Jim chuckled, "that we have this American actor with an Italian name—making a picture in Italy—and we change his name to something more American!"

Degni agreed on the name Mark Forest. He used it for a dozen more sword-and-sandal movies, including AIP's *Goliath and the Sins of Babylon*.

A few years later, we encountered a similar situation with Peter Lupus, who had appeared in *Muscle Beach Party*, one of our early "beach party" movies. Lupus subsequently starred in the *Mission Impossible* TV series, but we thought he could be our next Italian strongman hero.

We flew Lupus to Rome after calling Fulvio. "When Peter Lupus arrives, can you arrange to have news crews there waiting to meet him at the airport?" I asked him. "He'll be wearing strongman garb when he comes off the plane. Just have some cameras and a lot of pretty girls there."

Fulvio got on the phone to the Italian press. "This guy is the next big American superstar," he told them. He didn't mention that Lupus's biggest credit was AIP's *Muscle Beach Party*, in which he had played a character named "Flex" Martin.

As we had done earlier with Lou Degni, we talked Lupus into changing his name—at least for the short term—to Rock Stevens, which was more "acceptable" for international audiences. "Lupus sounds more like a disease than a movie star," one of my Italian friends advised us.

When Lupus arrived at the airport in Rome, the press was waiting. As he disembarked from the plane, he lifted up two attractive, buxom models whom Fulvio had positioned at the bottom of the stairs, and he posed for pictures with one girl on each bulging arm.

Lupus was scheduled to star in two movies we had agreed to coproduce with Fortunato Misiano, an Italian producer known for his action pictures. Before we had a deal, Fortunato and I had argued for days, trying to iron out the details. I had proposed that he put up $25,000 per picture for Lupus's services as part of our coproduction agreement; he insisted that he wouldn't go higher than $15,000.

Fulvio had told me that Fortunato owned race horses and gambled on the races. So one morning I made a proposal to Fortunato as we debated his financial stake in the movie. "Let's settle this right now," I said. "We'll just flip a coin. You call it. If you win, I'll agree to your terms; if I win, you'll agree to mine."

He had a startled look on his face. "I've never heard of doing business like this."

"Well," I said, "if you're not a gambler, let's forget it."

Of course, I knew that Fortunato couldn't pass up a wager, particularly one at even odds. He contemplated it for a few seconds. "Okay, why not?"

"I'll tell you what," I said. "The person who wins has to take the loser out to lunch."

Fulvio flipped the coin skyward, and while it was in the air, Fortunato called heads.

The coin landed tails.

In a matter of seconds, Fortunato had lost $20,000. And he was beside himself.

As we walked over to a restaurant near the Excelsior Hotel,

Fortunato was fuming, cursing in Italian under his breath. We were in the restaurant for four hours, and he ordered and ate enough food to feed most of the Italian army. If his stomach and an antacid had allowed it, Fortunato would have eaten $20,000 worth of lunch that day.

Fortunato didn't know that, over the years, I had used coin flips to settle a number of disputes related to making motion pictures—and usually ended up winning them. When both parties would become stubborn and unwilling to bulge, these coin tosses resolved the matters quickly, usually with little or no lingering resentment. I flipped with Roger Corman a number of times—he won the first toss, but never again. Ultimately, Roger decided he didn't want to settle our disagreements that way anymore. Fortunato probably would have backed out of any future coin flips, too.

Generally, things seemed to go our way in Italy—although a pasta dish once got the better of me in Rome. There was a restaurant that served great dishes with rich toppings—such as wild boar with chocolate sauce and nuts—and I'd usually overeat there. One night, after devouring some pasta with wild hare sauce, I got an extremely painful attack of gout in my left foot, leaving it swollen and tender.

The next day, I had to make an appearance at the Venice Film Festival. I was supposed to wear a black tuxedo to the event, and escort a buxom blonde actress named Eva Six, who appeared in a picture that AIP had entered in the festival. But because of the gout, I couldn't fit into the black shoes that went with my tuxedo.

As I was getting desperate, Fulvio had an idea. "Come down to the shoeshop near the Excelsior Hotel, and buy the biggest pair of shoes they have," he said "Your feet will be more comfortable with them on."

Unfortunately, the biggest pair were *brown* suede shoes. Even worse, they still weren't big enough for my swollen foot. So in my hotel room, Fulvio and I cut out part of the leather, thus exposing the portion of my foot that was inflamed.

The next night, I showed up at the Venice festival limping, wearing a tuxedo and brown suede shoes with part of the leather cut away, while escorting Eva, the actress with the large chest. Both the shoes and the girl were quite a sight.

"Everyone's looking at your feet," Fulvio whispered to me.

"Forget it," I said. "I know they're looking at the girl."

Swollen feet aside, these trips to Italy were exciting. I sometimes made a dozen trips a year to Rome and London, often mixing business and pleasure by continuing to negotiate deals over late-night dinners. On occasion, I would scribble down the terms of the agreement on the tablecloth, and then take it with me the next day to the office of my Italian lawyer, Mario Belatramo, and have the details transferred to a formal contract. Occasionally, when Belatramo would linger over the notes on the tablecloth for what seemed like an inordinate amount of time, I'd quip, "What are you doing? Trying to figure out what I had for dinner last night?" He sometimes could.

Getting to Belatramo's office wasn't always easy. He was a partner in Gracia Dey, a prominent law firm with important clients, whose offices were in a building across the street from the Excelsior. To reach his fourth-floor office, however, you had to put ten lira in a slot in the building's elevator to make it run. Ten lira, of course, wasn't much money—it translated to about two cents American money—and I didn't carry that kind of change with me. So I frequently had to climb three double flights of stairs to get to the law offices.

"Why don't you pull out that damn meter?" I once asked Belatramo. "You're the best law firm in Rome! Why do you need to collect ten lira per ride?"

Belatramo was apologetic. "It's the landlord," he said. "We don't have any control over it. I'd like to get rid of it, too."

Over the years, although Jim and I continued to keep our ears open for Italian productions that we could get involved in, there were certain types of pictures of which I was particularly wary. At the top of the list: Movies that were made on ships. There were just too many things that could go wrong on the bounding waves.

The Rizzoli Company in Rome was coordinating an Italian-Spanish coproduction in which they invited AIP's participation. They were going to make a pirate picture in South America, and were building two ships that would be anchored near the shore for an on-screen battle. I liked the script, and made a deal with Rizzoli, putting up one-third of the production costs in return for a portion of the world distribution rights, including the full rights to the Western Hemisphere.

Even so, I was worried about the problems that can occur at sea. There was a completion bond that would supposedly protect us if something went awry, but I still insisted on the following: "Other than a token down payment, AIP's share of the financing will be paid upon the delivery of the final film—not before." Rizzoli agreed, and I kept my fingers crossed, letting its crew oversee the day-to-day shooting.

During much of the filming, the two ships remained near the dock, since neither had been certified as seaworthy and thus couldn't get insurance. Eventually, however, the director became exasperated. "I'm tired of shooting the ships from just one angle," he complained. "Everything is being shot from the dock! Get the crew to move the ships out into the ocean. I need some more creative shots!"

He had visions of *Mutiny on the Bounty*; after I got a report of what he had planned, I had visions of disaster.

Within an hour after the ships left the dock, both had sunk.

As a result of that nightmare at sea, the picture was never finished. Fortunately, it cost AIP very little. That was one picture I was glad to see sink into the horizon.

I kept traveling to London, Rome and Cannes throughout most of the 1960s and even into the 1970s. AIP coproduced pictures with Fulvio for many years, and to this day he is one of my best friends.

Whenever I could drag my wife, Hilda, away from our children, she would accompany me on those trips to Italy. While I had learned a few words in Italian—enough to get along—Hilda relished learning and speaking foreign tongues, and even when she made mistakes in her choice or pronunciation of words, she made friends wherever she went. AIP ultimately was involved in coproductions in much of the world—including Spain, Yugoslavia, Denmark, Germany, Sweden, Japan, Hong Kong, Australia, Ireland, and Czechoslovakia—and Hilda always managed to get us by.

In country after country, I also proved my fondness for both good food and a wide variety of it. I could never turn down a new delicacy, whether it was roast boar or certain types of fried insects. In the interest of periodic dieting, I deposited a Teflon pan in my name in the kitchens of the great hotels throughout Europe, and along the way, my weight fluctuated greatly. In order to accommodate my various weight plateaus, I have at least three sets of clothes of different sizes, including one wardrobe that I bought at my wife's urging after I had lost sixty-five pounds and reduced to 178 pounds; at that point, she dragged me to the most expensive tailor she could find for six new suits, two new sport coats and assorted trousers, figuring that my pride would keep my weight down. Six months later, I couldn't fit into any of them anymore, and they've hung in my closet for decades. Like the old saw, I have taken off 2,000 pounds in my life—and added 2,001.

Eventually, the Italian market dried up for AIP. By that time, however, it had served its purpose many times over. AIP had produced and coproduced more pictures in Italy than any other foreign company. Our assistance to the Italian film industry led the Italian government to bestow upon me its Commendatore of the Order of Merit Award. The Italian pictures also had helped make AIP financially solvent. Along with the Edgar Allan Poe pictures and our beach party movies, they turned the 1960s into an enormously successful decade.

Incidentally, when I go to Italy today, I often wear my Commendatore pen. When I do, my Italian friends call me "Commendatore"—which means I probably have to pick up the check!

9

At times, the press treated American International Pictures with the same respect that Babe Ruth showed major league pitchers. Take the *New York Times*, for example. In one of its less charitable moments, the paper referred to the early days of AIP as having about as much status in the American film industry as the fellow who sweeps up the elephant droppings after a circus parade. Mind you, it was nice to even have the *New York Times* acknowledge us, although we would have preferred some gentler recognition.

Fortunately, however, many of our movies eventually won the respect of the media, if not their hearts. *I Was a Teenage Werewolf* made critics take notice. Three years later, the Edgar Allan Poe movies elicited the kinds of adjectives usually reserved for the studio blockbusters.

In 1960, when the first Poe picture, *House of Usher*, was released, we were up against some impressive movies from the majors. Despite the competition, however, the critics didn't shortchange us.

In fact, Jim Nicholson and I were so proud of *House of Usher* that we decided to unleash it on the press, confident of a positive reception. Until then, we rarely held media screenings, convinced that we'd be better off if the pseudointellectual film critics saw our pictures in a theater glutted with teenagers and other loyalists who paid their own money to cheer us on. At the same time, if the critics didn't see the pictures until they opened in the theaters, a bad review wouldn't be printed until it was too late to interfere with the first weekend's business.

Still, as we were preparing for the release of *House of Usher*, Jim said, "Let's see what happens if we really court the critics. I think we should throw them a party."

I was initially hesitant. In the past, I sometimes felt that we were like Hansel and Gretel, waiting for the press to shove us into the witch's oven. I also abhor Hollywood cocktail parties in general, where the "creative" people in this town talk about books they haven't read and movies they haven't seen. There's a lot of phoniness in Hollywood.

Nevertheless, Jim and I finally agreed to invite the media to a preview screening of *House of Usher* in Palm Springs, followed by an elegant party, complete with red carpets, kleig lights, and enough food and drink to tranquilize even the most hostile critic.

The movie reviewers, including the ones who had once sneered at us—even those who believed AIP could never produce anything but low-budget, blood-and-thunder flicks—were suddenly gushing with enthusiasm. That evening, one critic told me, "It's so wonderful that AIP is making pictures based on great literature."

Another raved, "Sam, Edgar Allan Poe would be proud. You were so faithful to the novel!"

Faithful to the novel! I could barely restrain my laughter. "You fool," I mumbled under my breath. "The Poe horror stores are only a few pages long. This picture would have to be a five-minute short if we were 'faithful to the novel.'"

Even so, I politely accepted the compliment. To me, *House of Usher* was, more than anything, just a good horror story. We didn't mind bringing great literature to the masses, but more than anything, we were trying to find a new niche for AIP—higher budget movies that would bring in higher profits.

Although we eventually made thirteen Poe movies, I wondered in the beginning whether they would ever find an audience. We were launching into making more expensive movies than ever before, and unlike earlier pictures, the Poe films would have big-name stars (most notably, Vincent Price). But frankly, I was uncertain whether the Poe name and the Poe stories were enough of a hook to entice the public to the box office. Would these period pieces attract the young people who had become AIP's primary audience? British and French producers had been making period pictures—including Poe movies—for years, but most of these films were aimed at adult audiences, and were brimming with sexual innuendo and necrophilia. Not exactly kids' stuff. Not exactly a perfect fit in the AIP mold.

When I sat down with Jim Nicholson and Roger Corman to talk about making *House of Usher*, I was probably more of a Poe fan than either of them. And although Poe's tales were engaging and fascinating—just what AIP was always looking for—I had concerns. While French and British filmmakers had molded their own versions of Poe's *Fall of the House of Usher* (in 1927 and 1950), the American studios hadn't touched it, and I could understand why.

"Here are my worries," I said. "How can we turn Poe's stories into full scripts? They're just too short. The literati are going to be screaming that we've taken too many liberties with Poe if we stretch it into an eighty-minute picture."

In fact, few critics ever appreciated how difficult it was to take a Poe short story or poem, and turn it into a full-length feature. Of course, Poe's mind was so fertile and his vision so graphic that he provided us with some powerful works to adapt; no wonder he's still so widely read today.

The brevity of Poe's work wasn't my only concern. "AIP has always had a monster or a beast in its pictures to bring the audiences in," I added. "Poe didn't have them in his stories. So where's the monster?"

Roger had an answer. "In *House of Usher*," he said, "the *house* is the monster! Can't you see it? It's the house!"

I thought Roger was reaching a bit for an answer. But I was willing to see if his concept would work. In the middle of shooting, Roger made sure he had covered his bases. He asked Vincent Price to utter a couple of lines that he had written into the script at the last minute—"The house lives! The house breathes!" Vincent had no idea what the lines meant.

"It doesn't matter what the lines mean!" Roger told him. "We've got to include them to make Sam happy."

What really made me happy, of course, were the picture's box office receipts. *House of Usher* cost us $300,000 to make, by far the biggest budget and the biggest gamble in AIP's history. But it became one of

Hollywood's hit movies of 1960. In some theaters, *House of Usher* was paired with *Psycho* as part of a double bill; those jittery audiences probably didn't sleep for days.

House of Usher was shot in color and with a longer shooting schedule than AIP had ever had before—fifteen days! With the extra time, Roger did a remarkable job, making a film that one critic called "elegant" and "remarkably sensitive to the spirit of Poe." In this and his later Poe efforts, there was something to draw a scream out of just about everyone... from a bloody hand opening a casket to mysteriously slamming doors... from blood-red candles to blasts of thunder that must have kept audiences peering toward the sky at America's drive-ins.

We paid Vincent Price $50,000 for *House of Usher*, and by his last Poe movie, he was making $80,000 per picture. That was a lot of money for AIP, and I wasn't sure that we could afford Vincent. But I sat down with him, and we negotiated an agreement that we both could live with.

"Here's my offer, Vincent," I told him. "You're already doing quite well financially, not only from your movies, but from your art lectures and from your contract with Sears to help them choose art for their department stores. But what about the future? Why not let us hold on to the money we're paying you for the AIP pictures, and we'll give it to you sometime down the road? It will be like an annuity that will come due in a few years."

Vincent agreed to my proposal. I guaranteed him a series of AIP pictures, and we deferred his payments. That made him affordable to us—and we clearly got our money's worth. Vincent was the consummate professional. He would become irritable at times, particularly if other actors couldn't rise to his standards. Or he'd want changes in the script—requests that we usually tried to accommodate. But Vincent was always prepared, and he had his own fans—a built-in audience he brought to AIP with him. That was the kind of actor we liked.

Earlier in his career, Vincent had enjoyed substantial success as a character actor on the New York stage and in motion pictures, but got much more attention as the star of horror movies. The horror picture buffs loved him, thanks to films like *House of Wax* and *The House on Haunted Hill*. We gave him one more house as a costar, although as the Poe pictures became an AIP series, he had many other costars, too. Over the years, he shared the billing with Boris Karloff, Lon Chaney

Jr., Basil Rathbone, and Peter Lorre. Not a bad lineup for a small motion picture company. Along with Lon Chaney Sr. (who came before my time) and Bela Lugosi (with whom I was associated in his last picture before my AIP days), the stars we brought into the AIP stable were the great horror actors of our time. Until *Silence of the Lambs* was released in 1991—in which Anthony Hopkins gave a remarkable and memorable performance—no actor had emerged as a challenger to the horror actors with whom we were associated.

Despite myths to the contrary, none of the horror stars at AIP were themselves violent men, from Price to Lorre to Karloff. But as much as I appreciated all those veteran actors for their talent in front of the camera, I particularly enjoyed being around Vincent. He was much more intelligent, sophisticated, and cultured than some people might expect from a horror movie star. He had studied art history at Yale and had an impressive art collection of his own. He sometimes allowed the public to tour his home and view his works of art in order to raise money for various art projects. Whenever he had some extra cash, he would spend it on art before just about anything else.

During the filming of the later Poe movies, many of which we made in England, I visited Vincent in the London hotel where he was staying in what struck me as the worst section of the city. And I was shocked at how simple both the hotel itself and Vincent's own room were. No elaborate suite with comfortable sofas. No room service. Instead, it was a small, bare single room—just large enough for Vincent's lanky six-foot-four frame—that didn't even have a toilet of its own. When he had to use the bathroom, he walked down the hall.

"I don't get it," I told Vincent. "We're paying you $80,000 for fifteen days' work, and we've increased your expense money to $1,000 a week. With that kind of money, can't you afford something better than this room?"

"Sam, if you loved art as much as I do, maybe you *would* get it," he explained. "I'm buying art with the $1,000 a week. Who needs a toilet?"

Van Gogh and Rembrandt would have loved this man!

Vincent also adored Edgar Allan Poe, so in my negotiations with him, it really didn't take much arm-twisting to convince him to star in *House of Usher*. We had already hired Richard Matheson, a well-known science-fiction novelist who had also written several scripts for

The Twilight Zone, to pen the screenplay for *Usher*. Designer Danny Haller also was an invaluable team player, working around the clock, sketching out sets on paper napkins and then building them through the night, sometimes finishing them just minutes before the cameras began rolling.

Although we had never started out to make a series of Poe movies, after the success of *House of Usher*, we were delighted to see that it could lead to more. Inasmuch as AIP was producing about twenty pictures a year, we were always eager to find a movie that could lead to sequels. As always, we looked for a vein to mine, and we found it in the Poe pictures.

We talked with Roger about making a second Poe movie and eventually decided upon *The Pit and the Pendulum*. We pulled together the same team, including Vincent Price, Richard Matheson, and Danny Haller. When the picture was released in 1961, it became an even bigger box office hit than *House of Usher*, earning a place as the most successful Poe picture of them all. The screams of *House of Usher* had not only breathed new life into horror pictures, but they had helped lift AIP itself up from the grave.

If you like torture chambers, you would have loved *The Pit and the Pendulum*. John Kerr had the good fortune to play the character who comes looking for the cause of his sister's death, only to end up in the basement of a castle with Vincent Price, a Spanish nobleman whose hobby is experimenting with various devices that would have made the Marquis de Sade look like Mother Teresa. Kerr was chained beneath the eighteen-foot "pendulum of fate" that inched closer to him with each swing.

The pendulum set filled up a complete soundstage. Danny Haller did a wonderful job designing the pendulum itself, although he had to do some improvising when problems developed with the original model. It initially had a rubberized blade, which would graze Kerr's chest as it swung from side to side, sometimes even getting stuck against his body. That's when Danny made a suggestion. "Let's try using a sharp, metal blade instead," he said. "It will look remarkably realistic in the close-ups." John Kerr gulped.

The trick, of course, was to have the blade swing close enough to slice Kerr's shirt—without drawing blood. I had nightmares of trying to explain this one to our Blue Cross insurance agent.

"Don't worry," Roger told John. "We have this steel band you can wear around your midsection. Even if the pendulum drops a little too low, you're not going to get hurt."

As the pendulum swung, of course, Roger was at least fifteen feet away, securely positioned behind the camera, out of the line of the pendulum's swing. Despite the heavy makeup, John seemed to be sweating a little more than usual during that scene. After five takes, he had perspired enough to melt away a few pounds.

With its blade in place, the pendulum was eighteen feet long, and it took four men—all of them big enough to play on the defensive line of the Pittsburgh Steelers—to operate it. Even so, they could never get it moving fast enough to satisfy Roger. "The pendulum has gotta swing quicker," he would say with exasperation. "What's wrong? Why is it going so slow?"

Finally, in the cutting room, Roger came up with a solution. He spliced out every second frame of the pendulum scenes, thus giving the appearance that the blade was moving at twice its actual speed.

With the success of *The Pit and the Pendulum*, Jim and I began planning still another Poe picture—although Roger almost beat us to the jugular. Roger was making pictures for other companies—including his own—as well as for AIP, often making the more expensive ($300,000–$400,000) pictures for us and the cheaper ($100,000) ones for himself. At about this time, executives at Pathe Laboratories approached Roger about directing a Poe picture for them. We already were having all our lab work done at Pathe, so when we heard that they had made the decision to get into production—and decided to latch onto the Poe idea, too—I was livid.

"I don't get it," I told Jim. "If Pathe wants to make movies, the least they can do is come up with an original idea, not one that they've stolen from one of their best customers."

I was also upset with Roger. After all, I felt that, in a real sense, the Poe pictures belonged to AIP. We had labored hard to raise the public consciousness about Poe, and in the motion picture industry, it was widely recognized that *we* were making the Poe movies. Nevertheless, both Roger and Pathe seemed to be trying to capitalize on the groundwork we had laid. And although I had become accustomed to

Roger's occasional peccadilloes, I was still surprised when he moved ahead with his plans with Pathe.

By this time, however, AIP already had Vincent Price under contract, with our agreement stating that Vincent couldn't make a horror picture for anyone but us. So Roger hired Ray Milland instead, casting him as the star of Pathe's first Poe film, *Premature Burial*. Pathe immediately began to publicize its new venture, running numerous ads in the trades. And that made me even more furious. I finally flew to New York for a meeting with William Zeckendorf, the real estate baron who owned Pathe. During a thirty-minute meeting, I let off enough steam to power James Watt's first engine from Glasgow to Hollywood.

"This movie you're going to make is a direct rip-off of what AIP is doing," I told Zeckendorf. "If you want to make movies, find a niche of your own."

Zeckendorf didn't even flinch. "You don't have a patent on Edgar Allan Poe, Sam."

"It's still reprehensible," I said. "And what makes it even worse is that we do our laboratory work with you, and now you're going into competition with us."

"It's a free country, Sam. I'm just trying to earn a few dollars, too."

Then I hit him with my trump card. "If you make this new movie, I'll cancel all our lab work with you. That's several million dollars of business a year!"

I had struck a nerve. Zeckendorf suddenly seemed willing to negotiate. Thanks to the almighty bottom line, he instantly became much less interested in producing Poe pictures. In fact, he ultimately agreed to turn over production and ownership of *Premature Burial* to AIP, settling for a payback of his investment from the producers' share of the movie's receipts.

On the first day of shooting, Roger looked up and saw Jim and me walking onto the set. Roger told me later, "I thought to myself, 'That's so nice; they've come to wish me well.'"

Between takes, Roger said to us, "I'm so happy to have you here, fellas. Pour yourselves a cup of coffee."

Then he realized that we were smiling more than he was. "What's happening?" Roger asked.

"Welcome back to AIP!" I told him. "We got Pathe to turn the picture over to us. We're partners again, Roger!"

At first, Roger thought we were kidding. We said we'd honor the terms of his contract with Pathe. Frankly, he seemed delighted with the news.

When *Premature Burial* was finally ready for release, we recommended that exhibitors publicize the movie by staging "an actual burial alive demonstration by a man or pretty girl." Harry Houdini, of course, was no longer available, and in many parts of America, it's a bit tricky to find volunteers to be buried alive. So in a memo, we suggested to theater owners, "Should you have difficulty contacting a stuntman or woman in your area for this purpose, get in touch with [AIP's] publicity department." If things had unfolded differently, I might have volunteered Zeckendorf for the underground stunt.

Even though *Premature Burial* did well at the box office, it did not reach the heights of the earlier Poe movies. The critics and the film historians had fun with it, too. In *Roger Corman: The Millennic Vision*, David Pirie called the picture "a self-evident disaster," insisting that part of the problem was replacing Vincent Price with Ray Milland (*Premature Burial* was one of only two Poe pictures without Vincent; the other was *Murders in the Rue Morgue*). The *New York Times*, which had labeled *The Pit and the Pendulum* as "Hollywood's most effective Poe-style horror flavoring to date," had a far different opinion of *Premature Burial*, which it called "static" and "starchily written."

Nevertheless, the Poe pictures continued to be successful, and we persevered with more of them. We reteamed Vincent Price and Roger Corman for *Tales of Terror*, a trilogy of three Poe stories ("Morella," "The Black Cat," "The Facts in the Case of M. Valdemar"). The cast also included two other veterans of the horror genre: Peter Lorre and Basil Rathbone.

Since one of the segments of *Tales of Terror* was called "The Black Cat," Milt Moritz (our advertising and promotion chief) came up with an appropriate promotional stunt. He ran small ads in the trade papers, announcing a black cat contest. We told people to bring their black cats down to the old Producers Studio on Bronson Street, and we'd select one of the cats to appear in the movie.

We didn't know what we were getting ourselves into. That morning, nearly every black cat in Los Angeles must have shown up. We had

Samuel Z. Arkoff

1926: In those days, there was a photographer with a camera and a pony. At that time there were only three of us. Brother Abe and sister Edith are on the pony, and the boy who would grow up to make *Muscle Beach Party* is standing in front.

(Above) A 1929 family portrait: young Harold, Edith, Sam, and Abe with our parents. (Below) The Arkoffs circa 1933: my mother and father with (front row, from left) brothers Abe, Bob, and Harold. Sam and sister Edith are standing in the rear.

Sam Arkoff (second from left in back row) in basic training at Kearns Air Base, a short distance from Salt Lake City, July 1942.

Sam and Hilda Arkoff, circa 1950.

With partner James Nicholson around the birth of American International Pictures in 1954.

Some of the early films that put AIP on the map.

Adele Jergens and friend in Roger Corman's *Day the World Ended* (1955).

(Below) Early AIP horror: Ed Nelson being menaced in *Invasion of the Saucer-Men* (1957).

(Above) At an AIP luncheon at the Texas National Drive-In Convention in 1955, that's me standing next to the flag and Jim at the podium.

AIP gave Michael Landon one of his first roles in *I Was a Teenage Werewolf*. Here he is with and without his monster makeup in that 1957 classic. The blonde is Yvonne Lime; the damsel in distress, Dawn Richard.

These are the AIP double-bills that brought the kids into the drive-ins.

One of AIP's terror hits: *The Spider* (1958), directed by Bert I. Gordon.

One of the greatest of AIP's Poe movies and the extravagant set (1961)

Jim and I showing off our AIP wares in 1960 (left photo) and joining one of our stars, Basil Rathbone, and, at right, Leon Blender, AIP's vice president in charge of sales, at a 1962 luncheon. (Photos courtesy Academy of Motion Picture Arts and Sciences)

AIP's "other" Nicholson, Jack, with Boris Karloff in *The Terror* (1963).

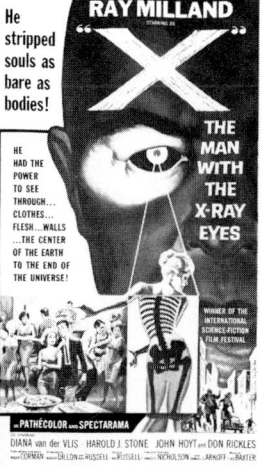 

Ray Milland in the cult favorite, "X"--*The Man With the X-Ray Eyes*, that Roger Corman produced and directed in 1963.

Frankie and Annette in *Muscle Beach Party* in 1964 ...

... and paying their regards to the boss. (Photo courtesy Academy of Motion Picture Arts and Sciences)

over seven hundred people and their cats at the studio gate, in a line extending for two blocks. And before long, the situation became pretty chaotic. Some of the cats began fighting with and clawing at one another.

Today, you wouldn't dare do a stunt like that because of the liability concerns. But in those days, we just did it! Our ignorance was probably our greatest asset.

Incidentally, the stunt paid off. A shot of the cats and their owners became *Life*'s "picture of the week." That was the kind of publicity we had wanted.

After *Tales of Terror*, we moved forward with *The Raven*, which took AIP's Poe movies to a new plateau—comedy. *The Raven*, of course, is a mere eighteen-stanza poem. Although it is one of the most famous poems of all time—"Once upon a midnight dreary, while I pondered, weak and weary"—eighteen stanzas are not normally the stuff of which great feature-film scripts are made. So we turned loose Richard Matheson's imagination, suggesting that he think in terms of humor as well as terror. "We've been doing these Poe movies long enough that it's time to spoof or satirize them a little," we told Matheson. The actors themselves wanted to play it differently, too.

Matheson was delighted, having become weary of turning out straitlaced Poe thrillers. With tongue firmly in cheek, he fleshed out an eighty-six-minute script that was witty, yet still had moments of real terror. Price and Lorre were joined in the picture by Boris Karloff, who had starred in the 1935 Universal version of *The Raven*.

Jim and I felt that with *The Raven*, we had assembled one of our most interesting casts. Like Vincent, Boris was several rungs above the average actor in terms of intelligence and culture. Boris was a soft-spoken, dignified man who might have been happy spending his life going to cricket matches. He loved acting, too, once claiming that he would die wearing his greasepaint.

Lorre was a likable fellow, but he was also a troubled, sensitive man. His marriage had disintegrated, he didn't see his daughter as much as he would have liked, he lived by himself in a modest apartment on Hollywood Boulevard, and he didn't really enjoy doing the horror roles he was being offered. While Vincent and Boris were proud of being stars in horror pictures, Peter saw himself as a dramatic actor, often looking back to one of his first starring roles playing a psychopath in the 1930 German film, *M*. He still yearned for a greater variety of parts.

Peter ad-libbed his way through *The Raven*. It would have been a waste of time to attempt to restrain him, so after a while, we didn't even try. Lorre played the raven—a sorcerer whom Boris Karloff had partially transformed into a bird. And Peter sometimes found it hard to keep to the script while dressed like an oversize black bird with four-foot-long wings. At one point, as the cameras rolled, he peered around a cobweb-strewn dungeon and quipped, "Hard place to keep clean, huh?"

In a later scene, Vincent said to Peter, "My wife's body is buried in a crypt beneath the house." Having seen the other Poe pictures, in which the coffin was *always* buried in a crypt under the house, Peter exclaimed, "Where else?!"

At first, Jim and I were disturbed by the ad-libbing, and insisted on filming these scenes two ways—with and without the improvisations. But, in fact, most of the ad libs worked, and they made it into the movie. In particular, Roger and Vincent were able to appreciate Peter's improvisation. Boris, however, perhaps because of his formal theatrical training, was a perfectionist, and sometimes seemed flustered by Lorre's ad-libbing.

Vincent added his own brand of humor to *The Raven*. He persuaded Roger to insert a running gag that would leave no doubt that this movie was something more than just a horror picture. So every time Vincent walked through his study, he "accidentally" bumped his head into a telescope. It was a joke that got more laughs each time it appeared on screen.

As funny as *The Raven* turned out to be, Vincent found little humor in Roger's announcement that a boa constrictor was being brought in to play a scene with the actor.

"Roger, I don't like snakes," Vincent said matter-of-factly. "To tell the truth, I'm terrified of them. Especially big snakes. How big is this one?"

"Not that big," Roger told him. "Only about eleven feet long."

"Eleven feet!"

"Don't worry," Roger said. "I don't think it's poisonous. And it'll only be wrapped around you for a few minutes."

"Did you say the snake would be *wrapped around me*?!"

The snake trainer tried to reassure Vincent. "It's really well trained, Vincent," he said.

"I'm well trained, too, but unexpected things happen on movie sets."

With his knees knocking, Vincent finally agreed to proceed with the scene, figuring it would be over in just a few minutes. In fact, it dragged on for more than an hour and a half. Whenever Roger wanted the snake to slink to its right, it wouldn't move at all. Whenever the snake became overactive, Vincent needed a moment to catch his breath. Once the entire scene had finally been shot, the trainer required the help of two burly crew members to pull the snake off Vincent.

During the calmer moments on the set of *The Raven*, Vincent often chatted with a young, unknown actor named Jack Nicholson, who played the son of Peter Lorre. The name "Nicholson" really hit home with Vincent, and he and Boris figured that Jack Nicholson must be Jim Nicholson's son. They eventually found out that the two weren't related, but for a while, they just assumed that Jack had gotten the part because of family ties. Vincent and Boris used to joke among themselves, "Nepotism! Nepotism!" and roar with laughter.

In publicizing *The Raven*, we didn't let the audiences forget that we had spared no expense bringing together motion pictures' biggest horror stars. One promotion line read, "See the Great Triumvirate of Terror—Boris Karloff, Peter Lorre, and Vincent Price!" One cynical critic exclaimed that we "might just as well have utilized the Three Stooges."

The Raven was a big financial success. And despite an occasional negative ruffling of the feathers, the picture won most of the critics to its side. No one seemed to notice that the movie was based on an eighteen-stanza poem.

Of all the horror pictures, *The Raven* flaps the wildest wings.
—*Newsweek*

A sappy little parody of a horror picture cutely calculated to make the children scream with terror while their parents scream with glee.
—*Time*

Price, Lorre and Karloff perform singly and in tandem like what they are, three seasoned pros who can take a gentle burlesque and play it to the end of its value without stretching it past the entertainment point. They are performances, in their own way, that are virtuoso.
—James Powers, *The Hollywood Reporter*

Most directors can't pass a pretty woman without wanting to put her into a picture, let alone wanting to do anything else with her. On the other hand, Roger Corman also seemed to have an equally powerful inability to pass a terrific motion picture set without wanting to shoot a film on it. So once he had seen the cemetery sets for *The Raven*—"It's the best cemetery set I've ever seen," he said—he figured it was a shame not to get more use out of them. So he ordered the crew not to dismantle them.

At the Friday evening wrap party for *The Raven*, my wife and sister-in-law, Bess Wexler, had prepared a veritable feast for the actors and crew, knowing that Roger's actors always ate more than their share. "These people are eating like they're not going to see food again until the next wrap party," I told my wife.

During the party, I noticed that Danny Haller's Gothic cemetery set hadn't been taken down, and I got suspicious. "Those sets are normally dismantled right away," I told Jim. "Something's fishy here."

Weeks earlier, even before he had started shooting *The Raven*, Roger had talked to me several times about using the set for a second picture, although I couldn't pin him down on what movie he might have in mind. Then he came back later, claiming that he had two days of a script, and he was going to try to get Boris Karloff for those two days of shooting. "Two days, Roger," I said, "that doesn't make much sense. What can you pull together in two days?" That was the last time we talked about it; since Roger never mentioned it again, I assumed he had dropped the idea.

On Monday morning after the wrap party, I drove back to the sets. I suspected I'd find Roger there, and I was right. He was busily shooting, using a clapboard that read, "American International Pictures: *The Raven*." I realized he was not only shooting another movie on our set, but charging it to *The Raven*'s production costs!

Roger was in the middle of a scene with Boris Karloff. I waited patiently in the wings until he was done with that particular shot. Roger spotted me and I noticed a flicker of surprise in his eyes. Finally, he walked toward me.

"Roger, what picture are *we* making now?" Of course, I knew the answer to my own question. Roger was shooting his second picture using AIP's set. If it was anybody but Roger, I might have called the police. But Roger is Roger.

He was noticeably embarrassed but still kept his poise. He pointed at Boris Karloff, who was having some makeup applied to his face. Forcing a smile, he exclaimed, "It's that second movie, Sam. Don't you remember?"

Roger explained that he had finally decided to use the graveyard scene in his own picture. He had rounded up most of the same crew who had worked on *The Raven*. Leo Gordon, a character actor turned screenwriter who had written *Attack of the Giant Leeches* for AIP in 1959, began turning out the first few pages of the script, stealing from some of his own unsold screenplays that he had stored in a trunk at home.

Meanwhile, Roger had called Karloff's agent and began negotiating. Roger was going to try to make the movie on his own for about $100,000, and tried to hire the actor for less than his normal $40,000 fee. "I only need him for two days," Roger pleaded. "He will play the lord of a medieval castle, and he's perfect for the role."

"Perfect for the role?" the agent said skeptically. "You just want him for his name, don't you, Roger? You'll have to pay full price."

Roger finally spoke to Boris himself, and although not having much of a script pulled together yet, he convinced the actor to give him those two days.

In fact, they turned into a rather harrowing forty-eight hours. Actors were running in all directions, trying to figure out where they belonged, what they were supposed to wear, what they were supposed to say. On the second day, the seventy-six-year-old Karloff was submerged in cold water for most of the afternoon. The chilling experience didn't do much for Karloff's health—in fact, his wife later told me that he caught a bad cold and was forced to take to bed.

With Karloff on his way back to London to recuperate, and with the sets finally being torn down, Roger took a hiatus from the shooting of what would later be called *The Terror*, while the rest of the script was written around the scenes that were already in the can. The remainder of the picture became somewhat of an adventure for Roger, eventually shot over the better part of the next calendar year. The story ultimately was a complicated one, difficult to follow, and one that several editors took a stab at, but were unable to piece together into a coherent story. Roger recruited some help in directing the remainder of the film, drawing upon the talents of Francis Ford Coppola, Monte Hellman, Jack Hill, and Dennis Jakob. It evolved into a "stepchild" picture, with different people working on it at different times. But as each of these aspiring directors added his own input, the story line became even more convoluted.

Jack Nicholson was Karloff's costar in *The Terror*, but even though the two actors were in the same scenes, they were never in the same shots. After those initial two days of shooting, Karloff never returned to the set; Nicholson shot his scenes later, so skillful editing was needed to make it appear that Boris and Jack were in front of the cameras at the same time.

Jack later recalled almost drowning as Francis filmed some scenes in the Big Sur for the movie. Jack was a strong swimmer, but Francis had him swim out to some rocks, then waved him out farther and then farther still. To make matters worse, Jack was wearing a Napoleonic uniform and boots—costume that might have tested even Mark Spitz's survival skills. In the middle of shooting, Jack was struck by some waves and he started to panic. While frantically treading water, he quickly began disrobing as his uniform was becoming waterlogged and as heavy as an anchor. By the time Jack reached shore, he was half naked. When I heard that story, I better understood the value of stunt doubles, and how they really earn their paychecks.

As the story goes, Coppola took almost two weeks shooting that brief scene in the Big Sur—a time period in which Roger Corman himself probably could have shot two entire films.

Finally, even Jack Nicholson—who also rewrote the script—got his turn behind the camera. "Roger," he said, "you've let everybody west of the Rockies direct a scene in this picture. Give me a chance." Roger agreed, and Nicholson tried directing for the day.

The Terror was never intended to be a Poe picture. It was one of more than 150 horror, fantasy, and/or science fiction movies that AIP made over the years. We advertised *The Terror* as a horror picture to capitalize on the craze we had created. Our promotional materials proclaimed, "From the depths of an evil mind came a diabolical plan of torture... Inconceivable... Unbelievable."

Apparently, the critics found it unbelievable, too. Years later, Peter Bogdanovich joked with Jack Nicholson, claiming that if *The Terror* were ever rereleased, it could ruin Jack's career.

Perhaps *The Terror* wasn't a great picture, but it does illustrate Roger's ability to put a movie together on the spur of the moment. I don't know anyone else who can do it as well.

It is something, in color, called *The Terror*, which it most certainly is.

—Bosley Crowther, *New York Times*

During the early 1960s, we made other Poe movies, including *The Haunted Palace*. We were very proud of the Poes, and most critics said they were the best pictures Roger ever made. Even today, they stand up well. Because we were producing them so fast, Roger, on occasion, would transplant a scene from one Poe picture to another—most noticeably, the fire scenes in which flames engulfed a house or some other edifice. Roger once said that if he had known that people would someday rent those movies and watch them, one after another, on their VCRs, he might have been a little more careful about splicing shots from one movie into the next.

Ultimately, Jim and I decided to shift the production of the Poe pictures to Great Britain. Not only was it cheaper to make the movies there, but by making them U.S.-British coproductions, we could qualify for a British government subsidy under the Eady Plan, thus helping to underwrite the movies. After World War II, the British government's Eady Plan encouraged the production of motion pictures by imposing a box office tax that was used to finance the makeup of films. Of course, we had already had some good experiences coproducing pictures (like *The Cat Girl* and *Circus of Horrors*) in England with Nat Cohen and his Anglo-Amalgamated Pictures. And we were convinced that we could move some of our productions, including the Poe pictures, to England and make them profitably.

One of the continuing appeals of the Poe pictures was that their titles were all in the public domain, and so we didn't have to drain the AIP bank accounts to obtain the rights to make *The Raven, The Pit and the Pendulum*, or any of the others. True, because the movies were such a success, we gladly would have paid if we had to, but the poems and the short stories were available without any fee.

For a while, David Selznick fumed, insisting that he had registered all the Poe titles with the motion picture title-registration bureau, and he threatened to take legal action if we used them. But I had always believed that the title bureau was a paper tiger and nothing but a tool of the majors, in which they had routinely registered literally thousands of titles and traded them among themselves. We had nothing to trade, so AIP never joined the bureau. I just ignored Selznick, and went ahead and made our movies, and we were never legally hassled.

AIP had a similar experience back in 1957, when we were about to release *Blood of Dracula*. Universal's lawyers sent us bullying letters, insisting that the studio owned all the rights to the Dracula name and characters. They tried to intimidate me, not realizing that I was the kind of guy who enjoyed intimidating back. I argued that the original "Dracula" story was in the public domain, and that any Universal copyright related only to the *new* elements that the studio had added to the original work. Naturally, we couldn't utilize any of Universal's adaptation, but everything else was fair game. AIP eventually made and released *Blood of Dracula* without Universal ever doing anything more than making threats.

Other filmmakers, however, buckled under the studio pressure, not willing to run the risk or bear the expense of legally tussling with the studios. James Carreras, the chairman of Hammer Films in England, paid fees to Universal for the rights to use the names Dracula and Frankenstein in his pictures. A lot of other independents did the same thing.

The horror genre was incredibly good to AIP, and we stuck with it until we had squeezed out every blood-curdling scream that we could—including variations that combined horror with comedy and ultimately even horror with science fiction. In 1979, we struck gold with *Love at First Bite*, a vampire comedy, and I'm convinced that variations of horror pictures will go on forever. With the original Edgar Allan Poe material, of course, we had a terrific author. And he certainly came at the right price.

10

When AIP slipped Annette Funicello into a two-piece bathing suit and had Frankie Avalon chase her around the lifeguard stations in *Beach Party*, the major studios snickered. That was their standard response whenever we created a new genre that the studios just couldn't understand.

But the laughter subsided when we turned that picture into an assembly line of beach movies that kept AIP busily counting its growing receipts during the 1960s.

Amid all the reactions, no one seemed more puzzled, irritated—and, at times, absolutely furious—over our beach movies than Walt Disney. Disney, of course, was one of Hollywood's true geniuses, and I certainly don't minimize his contributions. But he was a product of his own time and background. A Midwesterner, he was the purveyor of all-American innocence, the man who had brought *Peter Pan* and *Sleeping Beauty* to the screen. If you had looked up the word "wholesome" in a thesaurus, you just might have found Walt Disney listed there as a synonym.

Disney may have been upset that AIP was making movies showing pretty young girls frolicking in bikinis. But we also took it one step further: AIP had been contacted by Jack Gilardi, the agent (and later the husband) of Annette Funicello—the former Mouseketeer, the "dutiful Disney daughter." Jack was a great help in casting some of our movies and we signed Annette as the female lead in our beach films. That pushed Disney overboard.

In 1963, before *Beach Party* was ever released, Disney had seen a "glossy" for the picture—that is, the artwork and the taglines that we showed to exhibitors. The glossy showed a girl in a revealing bikini, and Walt was worried that it depicted Annette, and that we would ask her to wear the skimpy bathing suit.

"How could you?" he roared. "Sam, what are you doing to my little girl?"

After *The Mickey Mouse Club*, Annette had appeared in a series of Disney feature films like *The Shaggy Dog* and *Babes in Toyland*. She had a contract with Disney, with a clause that required approval from Disney's attorneys before she could work for anyone else. She had matured into a voluptuous young woman, and AIP offered her a beach party she couldn't refuse. The Disney lawyers went along, with the caveat that Annette couldn't appear in a bikini. But Walt still was upset that his subordinates had let her appear in *Beach Party* at all. I imagine the heads of those attorneys are still rolling down the streets of Burbank.

"Walt, she very much wants to do this movie for us," I explained to Disney when he called. "And I don't have any intention of putting her in a bikini."

"I nurtured Annette's image for years," Walt argued, raising his voice almost to a shout. "Sam, she's my little girl!"

"Little girl!" I exclaimed. "Annette is twenty years old. We're going to let her mature, Walt. She's entitled to breathe a little! Let her grow up!"

Disney continued to cling to those old-fashioned values that he was raised with, making it hard for him to visualize Annette wearing anything more daring than Mickey Mouse ears.

Although AIP's offices were only a few miles from Malibu Beach, where many of our beach movies were filmed, the idea for the first of the series had actually surfaced six thousand miles away in a screening room in Rome. Whenever Jim Nicholson and I traveled to Italy, we would preview dozens of Italian movies, and we'd always pick up a few of them for U.S. distribution. In the summer of 1962, we screened a picture about a middle-aged man who falls in love with a woman in her twenties who is spending time with her friends at a beach resort. There was a lot of drinking and dancing on the beach, and the characters were too old for AIP's target audience. But there was something about the movie that I found intriguing.

"I don't like the film itself that much," I told Jim. "There's not enough there that American teenagers can identify with. But the beach is a wonderful setting for a teenage movie. And it doesn't hurt to show some girls in skimpy bathing suits."

We sent Lou Rusoff to spend a few days at the beaches of Los Angeles, observing adolescent life on the sand. By the end of the week, he was working on the script of *Beach Party*, a picture he also produced.

Once we had cast Annette as the female lead for the picture, we searched for her male costar. We first considered Fabian, one of the hottest teenage idols of the time. But he was under contract to Fox, where he was making movies like *Hound-Dog Man* and *North to Alaska*. So instead we offered the part to Frankie Avalon, another teen heartthrob who had already acted in one of our 1962 pictures (*Panic in the Year Zero*), and whose voice appeared in a AIP animated feature (*Alakazam The Great*) in 1961.

The beach movies also gave a regular paycheck to William Asher. Bill was an Emmy-winning TV director (for *I Love Lucy* and *The Dinah Shore Show*), and was excited about making a splash in motion pictures as director of our beach pictures. He had grown up on the beach himself and envisioned telling the story of young people on the brink of adulthood, whose summer on the sand is an unforgettable rite of passage. We gave him a budget of from $350,000 (for the first picture) to $600,000 (for the last), and turned him loose. He recruited most of the bikini-clad girls with the Pepsodent smiles right on the beaches of Malibu.

In a sense, Jim Nicholson and I were taking a gamble with the beach movies. After all, there were no beaches in Iowa, Idaho, Kansas, or many of the other places where our movies played. But we felt that kids across America needed a change from the films about hot rods and juvenile delinquents, and that no matter where they lived they fantasized about romping on the beach. The idea of having fun on the sand, where kids were exposing as much skin as the law would allow, seemed like it would appeal to just about every young person.

Nevertheless, when *Beach Party* was ready for release, there was no tidal wave of confidence around the AIP offices. We decided to release the picture in only three cities, and waited nervously to see how it would be accepted. Even though the Poe movies were doing quite well by this time, we never really felt that we could afford a major flop. And with a budget of $350,000, plus a costly advertising campaign, we had a lot riding on *Beach Party*.

It was a stressful time around the AIP offices for another reason, too. Lou Rusoff had become seriously ill with brain cancer. Even though his eyesight had become impaired, his wife, Suzanne, would push him around in a wheelchair on the set of *Beach Party* and take him to screen the dailies, although we never knew if he could really see them. Lou was a superb screenwriter, thoroughly understanding the types of pictures we made and how to write to our specifications. Even in those final weeks of his life, he remained cheerful.

Lou died while *Beach Party* was being edited. In his honor, we held a benefit premiere of the picture for the Variety Club children's charities in Winnepeg, Lou's home town.

When *Beach Party* was finally released nationwide in the summer of 1963, we put on one of the most aggressive publicity campaigns in our history. Frankie, Annette, and a dozen bikini-clad starlets guested on TV talk shows in big and small cities. They made appearances on beaches, at public swimming pools, and in theater lobbies. Department stores sponsored bikini dance parties. Drive-ins had beach sand trucked to their theaters and dumped in front of their concession stands, where "beach parties" were held just before sundown. Hardtop theaters offered free admission to girls who showed up in bikinis, and sponsored "Miss Bikini" contests.

As a result, there was a flood of ticket sales. By the time the sun had finally set on the picture, we had sold millions of tickets to *Beach Party*, making it an enormous hit. Some kids saw it again and again until they had committed every song, every corny joke, and every shapely body to memory.

Four of our Houston drive-in theaters opened your *Beach Party* first run multiple to such outstanding business that the first five day grosses were well ahead of such outstanding grossing pictures as *Hud, Tammy and the Doctor, The Nutty Professor* and *The Birds*.
   —Memo from Stanley Warner theater management official

The story lines of our beach movies weren't particularly memorable, and the dialogue and the songs wouldn't have made Shakespeare or Cole Porter nervous about the competition ("Surf's up!" Frankie exclaims before he sings "Beach Party Tonight"). But the combination of bikinis, rock music, and surfboards, and the sights of kids letting their inhibitions down at the beach struck a chord. The pictures provided a welcome escape from newspaper headlines that were screaming with news about social turmoil and the battle against racial segregation.

In spite of Walt Disney's anxiety, there wasn't anything much more wholesome on the screen than our beach movies. We gave the illusion of being daring, but there was a lot of teasing with no real payoff. The girls looked delicious and the boys were fun-loving, and although the swimsuits were provocative, the kids didn't do anything that would have shocked their grandmothers. They drank nothing stronger than soft drinks and an occasional beer. They didn't smoke cigarettes, much less marijuana. There was no delinquency. They were as interested in suntans as sex. They even talked about (gasp!) getting married. And there was certainly no on-camera nudity.

Beach Party was the innocent story of a professor (played by Bob Cummings) studying the sexual behavior of adolescents who hang out at the beach. In this and the subsequent beach movies, no one talked about school, grades, financial worries, and parental problems. In fact, there were almost no adults in the pictures at all...definitely no mothers and fathers giving kids their most monotonous Judge Hardy-type lectures about cleaning up their rooms, doing their homework, and leading lives of morality and chastity. The adult characters—played by Cummings, Morey Amsterdam, Mickey Rooney, Buddy Hackett, Buster Keaton, and Dorothy Lamour—were little more than parodies, and they certainly didn't get in the way of young people having a life of their own. A decade later, *American Graffiti* used the same approach—leaving parents out of the script. It's the ultimate teenage fantasy!

The running gags in the beach movies weren't going to challenge Robert Benchley or Will Rogers, but they consistently got laughs. Frankie might say, "This is a wild, crazy beach!" to which Annette would respond, "You can say that again." On cue, Frankie would repeat his line.

At times, Frankie would deliver asides directly into the camera, as if conversing one-on-one with the audience. Putting on a deadpan expression, he might turn to the camera and say, "Do you believe this?!" Or, "You win some, you lose some!" Not particularly profound, but somehow they worked.

During the 1960s, AIP produced thirteen surf-and-suntan pictures—a breeding frenzy in which *Beach Party* gave birth to *Muscle Beach Party* which begat *Bikini Beach, Beach Blanket Bingo, How to Stuff a Wild Bikini*, and so on. There were a few related but meandering departures along the way—pictures like *Ski Party* (a beach party on skis) and the British import, *Summer Holiday*—which took us away from Malibu Beach, but we kept coming back to the sand.

One after the other, these pictures were fast-paced, with almost no fades or dissolves to interfere with the rapid tempo. They were short on plot but long on provocative beach scenes brimming with girls with endless body English, into which we tossed outdoor barbecues, pie-throwing fights, Zen Buddhism, pajama parties, karate, rock and roll, skydiving, uninhibited dancing, and just about anything else with which we thought adolescent moviegoers might identify. We didn't invent the American teenager, but the beach movies made them feel as though they and AIP were as inseparable as Frankie and Annette.

In those movies, we showcased an array of young actors who later went on to more prominent roles in TV and motion pictures: Linda Evans, Nancy Sinatra, Meredith MacRae, Raquel Welch, Gary Crosby, and Pamela Tiffin. Bill Asher called the 1960s the longest summer in history. So did some of the less friendly critics.

No one can blame Nicholson and Arkoff for continuing a pattern that has made them money, but this [*Beach Blanket Bingo*] is ridiculous.

—*Variety*

As the months and years passed, and Walt Disney continued to see our newspaper ads for the beach movies, he somehow convinced himself that everything he had worked for was being swept out to sea. He became outraged by promotional lines like, "Bare As You Dare!" But the one that really sent him lunging for his phone was in an ad for *Beach Blanket Bingo*: "When 10,000 Bodies Hit 5,000 Blankets..."

To Walt, that was a sign that the moral fabric of America was unraveling, and to him, I was the point man in the revolution.

"How dare you subject Annette to this sort of degradation!" Disney yelled as I picked up the phone.

"You're looking at the ads and the artwork, Walt," I tried to explain. "I would love you to see these pictures. I don't think you'd find anything offensive at all."

"You've really gone too far," Walt said. "Think about what you're doing, Sam. What kind of effect do these movies have on young people?"

It seemed to me that Disney never recognized that teenagers had different interests—and were attracted to different types of movies—than grade school kids. *The Mickey Mouse Club* was fine for young kids, but by adolescence, youngsters had outgrown *Old Yeller* and *Son of Flubber*. Still, Disney was not alone in his discomfort with the rapid changes occurring around him: Millions of adult Americans felt unsettled and outraged by the social revolution that began in the sixties, with its rock 'n' roll music, uninhibited dancing, and longer hair.

After a while, I stopped hearing from Disney. Maybe he had grown weary of trying to rescue Annette from the evil riptides of AIP and all the social changes around him. Once we had turned Annette, this maturing twenty-year-old, into a modern young woman, Disney recognized that he could no longer cast her as the obedient fifteen-year-old daughter, the role she had been playing in his movies. She never made another picture for Disney after that.

Walt Disney may have been our most emotional critic, but he wasn't the only one who was upset. Our newspaper ads for the beach movies not only depicted bikini-clad girls surfing, dancing, and flirting, but it also showed their navels! Editors of more than two hundred newspapers across America were offended and refused to run the ads.

"This is so ridiculous," I told one newspaper editor. *"Everybody's* got a navel! I don't think you're going to shock anyone by printing a photograph of a girl in a bikini!"

But the editors didn't agree. They ultimately ran the ads, but not until they had airbrushed out the navels. I imagined young people across America looking at those photos and wondering where in the hell we had found all those actresses without belly buttons! Maybe it could have been fodder for another AIP movie: *The Beach Girls Who Lost Their Navels!*

As absurd as the airbrushing was, AIP still would usually welcome controversy, since it helped us get publicity. I'd make frequent appearances on TV shows, defending AIP against questions like, "Why do you feel the need to make these beach movies?"

On a television program in Los Angeles, I pointed out that, unlike the studios, we thought it was common sense to make movies that appealed directly to our audiences. "Unfortunately," I said, "most of our critics are closer to the menopause and don't understand that teenagers love our pictures. Kids can't identify with the forty-year-old heroines and the fifty-year-old heroes who the majors put into their movies. Our films are important to young people, and there's nothing corrupting about the pictures. Nothing."

Jim used to compare the beach movies to the Mack Sennett bathing beauty silent films. "We're paying our actors more than Sennett did," he said, "but our wardrobe costs are a lot less."

As they had done with our hot rod and teenage movies of the fifties, the majors gradually recognized just how successful AIP's beach movies were and eventually began making some copycat films of their own. Some of these celluloid clones were big-budget films like *Girl Happy*, which starred Elvis Presley. But there were plenty of other imitations—nearly one hundred of them in all: Columbia made *Ride the Wild Surf* (with Fabian and Shelley Fabares); Fox produced *Surf Party* (with Bobby Vinton); Warners chimed in with *Palm Springs Weekend* (with Troy Donahue and Connie Stevens); and Paramount made *The Girls on the Beach* (with Noreen Corcoran) and *Beach Ball* (with Edd Byrnes and Chris Noel).

Except for the Presley pictures, however, none of the imitators enjoyed the success of the AIP beach films. They were using the same beach as AIP. And the same ocean. The girls were clad just as skimpily. And the advertising mimicked AIP's ("When Beach Boys Meet Surf Sweeties—It's a Real Swingin' Splash of Fun Fun Fun!" promoted *Surf Party*). But they overlooked some of the key elements of our movies. There were parents in their pictures, which tended to make them lectures to some degree. And their teenage characters had to deal with serious crises in their lives (like parental problems) that detracted from their fun.

The studios also spent so much money producing these pictures that it was difficult for them just to break even, much less make a few dollars. None of AIP's beach pictures ever lost money, although the later movies did not gross as well as the early ones. As happens with most pictures that are part of a series, each subsequent movie tends to cost more than the previous one, as both actors and crews demand more money. Ultimately, as the costs rise and the box office receipts dip, it becomes time to move on to a new genre.

Near the end of the beach party cycle, as we could see the trend fading, Jim and I decided to mix genres, altering the focus of the beach movies and making comedy almost as important as the daring bathing suits and the fun-loving teenage antics. We still had a contractual commitment to Vincent Price to cast him in a couple of movies a year, so we put him in *Dr. Goldfoot and the Bikini Machine*—a satirical movie in which he played a berserk scientist. Frankie Avalon and Dwayne Hickman shared the billing with Vincent, along with a cameo role from Annette. As the title indicates, the movie was designed to capitalize on the popularity of the James Bond superspy movie *Goldfinger*, while also luring the teenage guys whose heartbeats would accelerate to 180 at the mere sight of bikini-clad girls.

In the picture, Vincent's character invents a way to duplicate female robots in his lab, all of whom are attired in (what else!) golden bikinis. (One of the golden girls was Susan Hart, who later became Jim Nicholson's second wife.) These girls are assigned the mission of trapping wealthy men so that Vincent (Dr. Goldfoot) can lay his hands on their riches.

Vincent played the role magnificently and thoroughly tongue-in-cheek, particularly the scenes in which he spoofed the Poe movies while holding Avalon and Hickman captive in his torture chamber. The *New York Herald-Tribune* wrote that Vincent had "played past the hilt."

Dr. Goldfoot and the Bikini Machine did quite well at the box office—good enough to encourage us to capitalize on the *Goldfoot* name with a sequel. I had talked to Fulvio Lucisano, who coproduced many of our Italian productions, and he felt that if we made the next *Goldfoot* a U.S.-Italian coproduction, he might be able to lure Mario Bava to direct it. This arrangement would also allow us to split the costs of making the movie, as well as take advantage of a substantial subsidy from the Italian government.

Bava, of course, was the great horror director whose *Black Sunday* was an AIP release in 1961. And we thought we had scored a coup when he finally agreed to direct *Dr. Goldfoot and the Girl Bombs* in Italy.

We talked Vincent Price into reprising his starring role as Dr. Goldfoot. Vincent played a lunatic scientist who, with the support of China, devises a plot to provoke a war between the United States and Russia. In his scheme, Vincent implants bombs in the belly buttons of female robots, and they are set to detonate whenever the girls make love to NATO generals. "Meet the Girls with the Thermo-Nuclear Navels!" as our ad copy read. It was a story that even G. Gordon Liddy or the most creative minds in the CIA couldn't have fabricated.

Two Italian comics, Franco Franchi and Ciccio Ingrassia, were cast in the movie as doormen hired by Fabian Forte (a secret agent) to subdue the Dr. Goldfoot character. But, in fact, they overpowered everything Vincent was trying to do on screen. Unfortunately, although they stole nearly every scene, they weren't funny. Neither was the movie.

Dr. Goldfoot and the Girl Bombs might have been saved but for some unusual "heroics" by my own nephew, Ted Rusoff. I had sent Ted to Rome to do some work for us, and when he first met Laura Antonelli, the female star of the new *Dr. Goldfoot* picture, he was swept off his feet. Antonelli was a beautiful young woman, and Fulvio and I figured that the picture would have a lot more box office appeal if she removed her clothing while the cameras rolled, and she appeared quite willing. But Ted seemed shocked that we would even suggest that she disrobe. Overcome by his newly developed crush, he became very protective of her and told me, "She's a serious actress, Sam. It would be insulting to ask her to take her clothes off!"

Ted sat Antonelli down and pleaded his case. "You don't have to take off your clothes. If you tell them no, they're not going to force you. I don't think you should do it."

Antonelli gave it some thought, and then followed Ted's advice. Her clothes stayed on. If Ted weren't my own flesh and blood, I might have fired him on the spot.

The real irony is that Antonelli later became a big star in Italy, and one of the reasons was that she was willing to take off her clothes at the drop of a clapboard. She starred in movies like *The Innocent* by

Visconti and *The Divine Nymph* with Marcello Mastroianni. She didn't seem to have any inhibitions at all, except when Ted Rusoff was around.

Years later, when I talked to Vincent about the picture, he called it "the most dreadful movie I've ever been in. Just about everything that could go wrong did. At one point, they even lost the sound track to the whole movie! They literally lost it!"

With a vanished soundtrack, the entire picture had to be dubbed. Unfortunately, however, the actors had done so much ad-libbing during the filming that they couldn't use the script as a guide, and none of them really remembered what they had said. They did the best lipreading they could. It was a real nightmare.

Dr. Goldfoot and the Girl Bombs was Mario Bava's first—and last—comedy. It didn't make any money for either AIP or Fulvio. In retrospect, perhaps we should have titled it *A Comedy of Errors*.

During the early sixties, the beach movies gave America's teenagers pure escapism—something that was fun in a fast-changing and sometimes confusing world. Those thirteen movies touched a lot of young lives. But as the hippie movement, with its long hair, illegal drug use, and antiwar protests, took hold, the beach movies became an anachronism.

In the early 1970s, in the midst of the Vietnam war, we rereleased five of the beach movies on a single bill, figuring that even in a time of social turmoil, a beach party marathon still might find an audience. The newspaper ads for the quintet of movies played up the campiness of the entire series. ("See! Actual Simulated Hand Holding!... Shown Intact and Uncut! Totally Uncensored!") And in that pre-home-video era, many thousands of people paid to get another look at AIP's beach phenomenon.

Incidentally, Walt Disney never really had anything to worry about. Even if AIP hadn't been contractually bound to keep Annette out of a revealing bikini, we wouldn't have put her in anything but a more conservative two-piece bathing suit. Annette just didn't have the figure to provocatively fill out a bikini.

America's newspapers must have breathed a collective sigh of relief at that decision. They didn't have to airbrush out her navel!

11

Jim Nicholson and I never left too much to chance.

In an uncertain business, we would try to sneak around the land mines and wade past the icebergs by analyzing the market, dissecting the social and political trends, and reflecting upon where the motion picture industry was headed. At the beginning of every year, we would sit down and plan the upcoming twelve months. How many teenage movies did we want to make? How many horror pictures? How many science fiction films? How many movies would we try to import from abroad? Through a series of calculated judgments and educated guesses, we attempted to minimize our risks in an industry where unpredictability is the name of the game.

We not only had to plan the pictures we wanted, but we had to make sure they were completed and ready for release by the promised dates, with all the advertising set to go. A reality of distribution was that there were a specific number of slots (release dates) a year that had to be filled. Our pictures were often playing in theaters only three months after they were shot.

Throughout AIP's history, before raw film was ever loaded into the camera for a new movie, Jim and I knew precisely who our audience for that picture would be. We weren't making movies for elderly matrons, although some of them may have bought tickets to AIP movies. Our audiences were not necessarily the same for a beach picture as they were for a Poe movie. If a film had a political message, like *Why Must I Die?* (an anti-capital punishment picture), we didn't expect it to appeal to the same people who might stand in line to see *The Brain That Wouldn't Die*.

When Larry Buchanan directed *Free, White and 21* for us, the story of a black businessman accused of raping a white Freedom Rider, we tried to broaden the appeal by literally making the audience the jury, giving them sixty seconds to decide if the accused was innocent or guilty, with the clock literally ticking off the seconds on the screen; we actually filmed two endings for the picture—one guilty, one innocent—and depending on the audience response we expected in a particular neighborhood, we'd send one or the other version out to each theater. Creativity was always on our mind—but so was the bottom line. We never forgot that if today's films didn't make money, then we might not be able to make new ones tomorrow.

Although AIP never stopped making pictures in the United States, the economic appeal of foreign productions in Europe grew as the sixties progressed. In the early sixties, we coproduced a few pictures in England and many more in Italy. By 1963, we found that we could transplant the Poe movies five thousand miles from home, too, and not leave any of the terror behind.

In the fall of 1963, we took Roger Corman to England and, in consecutive years, made two Poe pictures, *The Masque of the Red Death* and *Tomb of Ligeia*. We simply found it easier to cut corners and pinch pennies in England, particularly with Roger, whose own instincts kept him frugal anyway. If there was a way to save a few dollars, he could figure out how.

Roger shot *The Masque of the Red Death* at the Elstree Studios, next to a sound stage where Roger Moore was taping the TV series, *The Saint*. Shortly after arriving, Corman and Danny Haller discovered some disassembled sets that had just been used in the filming of *Becket*. Corman must have figured, "If they're good enough for Henry II and Thomas Becket, they're good enough for Vincent Price and AIP." He and Danny put the sets back together, and they became backdrops for the very lavish look of *The Masque of the Red Death*. To round things out, Danny built a few other items for Vincent's torture chambers—racks, flails, thumbscrews, iron maidens, mantraps, and chains. Absolutely everything the well-equipped sadist would ever want.

The Masque of the Red Death was the story of a medieval prince (played by Vincent) who is a disciple of Satan. In the film, there is a big party scene—a Masque Ball—where the actors celebrate the Dance of Death. Roger hired a professional dance troupe to bring the scene alive.

On the last day of shooting, I happened to be in London, and was on the set as they wound down to within thirty minutes of the end of the eight-hour shooting day. Roger still needed to put the dance scene on film, and he was worried about whether the crew would cooperate. Unlike the U.S., where you'd just load the camera and start shooting, all the British unions needed to agree to work overtime or none of them would. Both of us had heard rumblings that led us to believe that the unions would not go along with any overtime.

This was Roger's last day working with the dance troupe, since they were about to leave for another city and a series of Christmas pantomime shows. So he quickly called for a rehearsal of the dancers, and the next thing I knew, he actually began filming the rehearsal itself!

"I knew we were short on time, and might not be able to have as many takes as I had hoped for," Roger told me at the end of the day. "So I shot the rehearsal, figuring I needed to get something on film."

The unions were outraged when they realized what had happened. By that time, however, the film was in the can. Leave it to Roger.

For *The Masque of the Red Death*, Roger had a lengthier shooting schedule—five weeks—than either he or AIP was accustomed to. However, in typical Corman fashion, he didn't waste a moment. The Kennedy assassination occurred in the middle of the production, and on the day of JFK's funeral, Roger told his assistants, "I really feel that I should give the cast and crew a little time off to mourn the President—but I don't want to fall behind schedule, either." So on that Monday, he closed down production—but for only a few minutes. He just couldn't bear to lose any more time in the production schedule.

We ran into a lot more serious problems, however, when the British bluenoses came out of the London fog and decided to make *The Masque of the Red Death* their target. Both government and non-government censors previewed the picture, and seemed particularly repulsed by scenes of a "black mass" involving Hazel Court, a redheaded British actress who portrayed Vincent's mistress. Court's character offers herself to Satan and is sliced up by a blade that shows no mercy.

"Those scenes are much too sacrilegious for our tastes," one of the censors told me. "The Church of England officials won't stand for that kind of devil worship."

I watched the scenes a half-dozen times and tried to remain open-minded. But I never really understood why they were so offensive to certain people. Sometimes, however, you have to make compromises for expediency's sake. I gave the order: "Let's make the deletions of the 'offensive' scenes. We need to get this picture released in the United Kingdom." I wasn't completely pleased with my decision, but I kicked myself all the way to the bank.

The Masque of the Red Death turned out to be one of the best Poe movies. Nicolas Roeg did some wonderful cinematography work, and the movie was a visual delight. Thanks to the recognition Roeg earned for his work behind the camera, he later moved into the director's chair on pictures like *Don't Look Now* and *The Man Who Fell to Earth*. Roger Corman sometimes thought back to all the crew members he had worked with who later became directors, and asked himself, "Have they become directors because they learned so much from me? Or are they looking at me and saying to themselves, 'If Roger can do it, anybody can do it!'?"

Tomb of Ligeia was Roger's last Poe movie, and it may have been his most lavish picture for us. It was brimming with wide-screen tracking shots and stunning color schemes that enhanced a strong script from Robert Towne, who later wrote the screenplays for *Chinatown* and *The Last Detail*.

Most of the movie was shot outdoors at a sixteenth-century English monastery and in a quaint English church. But when we moved indoors for some shooting at the Shepperton Studios, we almost lost our leading man and his costar.

Vincent had told me that he was absolutely terrified of fire. "I've done so many pictures with fire, but I've never gotten used to it," he said. So naturally, he was not particularly pleased that the script for *Tomb of Ligeia* included a scene in which he was supposed to set fire to the abbey and die in the flames. When I had joked with him that the picture was "a hot property," this wasn't exactly what he had in mind.

The crew painted the set with liquid cement that covered the walls and gave out a gas. There were signs all over that said, "No smoking on the set." Vincent walked onto the set with Elizabeth Shepherd, the British actress, but as they were getting prepared for the shot amid all this debris, a crew member walked by with a cigarette. In an instant, everything blew up!

For the next few seconds, it was pandemonium. There were screams from the crew, who frantically tried to douse the flames. Elizabeth was wearing a chiffon negligee, and Vincent grabbed her by the panties and dragged her to safety. For a few minutes, it was a life-threatening situation.

When the fire was out and everyone calmed down, Roger realized he still had a movie to shoot. "OK, everyone," he shouted. "The excitement's over. We've got a set to rebuild and a movie to make." Within minutes, the crew was at work, disposing of the smoldering debris, reconstructing the set, painting it, spraying it, and setting up for the next shot. The whole incident was a near disaster, but to Roger, it was just a minor inconvenience in the whole scheme of things. He wasn't going to let a two-alarm fire make him fall behind schedule.

I thought *Tomb of Ligeia* was a good picture, with enough sadomasochism, necrophilia, and black magic to appeal to the tastes of even the most aberrant moviegoers (Roger never did believe in underplaying things!). But because some critics had let their vitriolic pens run wild for many of our earlier AIP movies, I was stunned by just how positive the reviews for *Ligeia* were.

The *Times* of London commented: "Here at last Mr. Corman has done what it always seemed he might be able sometime to do: make a film which could without absurdity be spoken of in the same breath as Cocteau's *Orphee*."

We made more Poe pictures in England, but before we had exhausted the genre, Roger said he had had his fill of pits, pendulums, and premature burials. He just wanted to do something different, and so when we made plans for additional Poe pictures, we turned to other directors. Some of these movies weren't pure Poe, but they captured the mood, atmosphere and mystery associated with the American poet and short-story writer.

The Witchfinder General was one of these Poe-like pieces. I had been approached by a young director named Michael Reeves, a promising twenty-five-year-old who already had a couple of pictures to his credit (*Sister of Satan, The Sorcerers* with Boris Karloff). He had cowritten a script based on a novel called *The Witchfinder General* by Ronald Bassett, a book that had sold quite well in the United Kingdom.

The story itself was set in England in Oliver Cromwell's time, and recounted the escapades of a witchburner named Matthew Hopkins, portrayed by Vincent Price. Over a two-year period, Hopkins had become the consummate serial killer, shedding the blood of a couple hundred people who he claimed were witches. Along the way, he seduced and raped women who often submitted to his demands in hopes of saving their own loved ones from the witch-hunting butchery.

Although the story had a Poe flavor to it, we had worried that *The Witchfinder General* was an English tale that wouldn't have much appeal on this side of the Atlantic. Bassett's novel had never been published in the States, and the question was, "Would Americans give a damn about Cromwell—or even know who he was?" To make matters worse, I felt that audiences might find witchburning a particular unappetizing theme to go along with their buttered popcorn and bonbons.

However, we came across an Edgar Allan Poe verse which included a line that spoke of a "conquerer worm." We weren't exactly sure what it meant, but it was pure Poe and seemed to fit with *The Witchfinder General*'s story line. We felt if we had Vincent recite the poem at the beginning of the film, we could legitimately call the picture a Poe movie.

That's what we did, and when the movie was released in the U.S. (as well as in most of the world), it carried *The Conqueror Worm* title. It had audiences holding on to their seats from the moment the curtain rose to the closing credits. By far, it was our most violent—and least humorous—Poe picture. There wasn't much funny about torture, hangings, and burnings at the stake. But it was effective.

On *The Conqueror Worm*'s release, some reviewers were disturbed by the level of violence in the movie. But that certainly wasn't a universal reaction. Other critics sounded as though they had seen a thoroughly different movie: They praised the work of Michael Reeves, insisted that it was Vincent Price's best performance, and labeled the film as the most compelling and Poe-like of all our pictures of this genre. Comments like that drove people to their local movie houses; the picture did well throughout the world.

On one bizarre night in Hong Kong, the violence of the movie poured over into the audience as well—and all because of the title itself. A group of British sailors had gone to see *The Conqueror Worm* in a downtown theater, where it had been booked by AIP's foreign sales department. Coincidentally, the same picture had been playing on British military bases and ships under the title *Witchfinder General*, where these same sailors had seen it just a week earlier, booked there by our British distributor. They bought tickets at the Hong Kong theater, not realizing they were paying to see a movie they had already watched for free.

The sailors were pretty intoxicated, and didn't catch on right away that they were seeing the same picture for the second time. Eventually, however, after watching Vincent Price cackle at his stake-burning exploits once too often, they realized that they might have been had.

"We want our money back," one of them screamed, pounding on the window of the ticket booth. But the theater owner refused.

The sailors' fury grew. For the next hour, they systematically created chaos in the theater. They threw popcorn boxes at the screen. They shouted loud enough to drown out the soundtrack of the picture. They tipped over trash cans and even threw a few punches at one another. They continued to try to intimidate the manager into refunding their money, and when he finally realized what had happened, he gave them back their admission price. But we had to pay for the damages.

In 1969, we put Edgar Allan Poe's name on still another movie, *Histories Extraordinaires (Tales of Mystery and Imagination)*, even though the picture had been completed before AIP ever bought the distribution rights. Two years earlier, I had been at Cannes, where *Histoires Extraordinaires* had been entered in the film festival by its French and Italian producers. It was actually three short films in one, each based on a Poe short story, and each directed by an important director: Roger Vadim, Louis Malle, and Federico Fellini.

I contacted the producers, who were looking for an American distributor for the film.

"This is a high-class picture," one of them said. "We can get more money from someone other than AIP."

Disparaging comments like that never bothered me. "I'm willing to offer you $200,000 for the U.S. and Canadian distribution rights," I told them. "My money is just as green as MGM's or Twentieth Century-Fox's."

Their ears seemed to perk up, and they saw no problem when I suggested retitling the picture. But then I mentioned, "I'll want Fellini to reedit some of his part of the film. There's a scene that spoofs the Academy Awards, and it seems like a private joke on Fellini's part. It just doesn't fit in the midst of a horror picture. The movie's a little too long, too."

They were shocked. The thought of asking an auteur like Fellini to doctor his movie was more than they could handle. The deal was dead.

The next year, I was back at Cannes. Even by this time, however, *Histoires Extraordinaires* still hadn't found an American distributor. I again contacted the producers, and made them the same offer. After a full year of struggling to sell their picture, and disappointing box office grosses in Europe, they were more receptive to AIP.

"I think we can make a deal," one of them said.

Then I reminded them that I wanted Fellini to reedit the film. They instantly became very anxious again, although not enough to back out of the deal.

"Sam, we can't ask him to do that," one of them pleaded. "We're talking about Federico Fellini, not Gary Glutz. We wouldn't dare approach him ourselves. You'll have to talk to him."

So I contacted Fellini, for whom I had the utmost respect. "When I saw the picture, I thought you had perhaps interjected the scene of the Academy Awards ceremony for your own amusement. But it really has nothing to do with the rest of the picture. If you agree, we'd like you to edit that part out."

Fellini was very gracious. "Sure, I understand," he said in his broken English. "I'm a realist. I'd like this film to be seen by American audiences, even if it means cutting a few minutes out of it."

In less than a month, Fellini delivered his portion of the film, cutting out the unnecessary scene and thus editing the picture down to the length we had wanted. We retitled it *Spirits of the Dead*, added some narration by Vincent Price and a song by Ray Charles, and released it in the U.S.

With the big-name directors, and some well-known actors (Jane and Peter Fonda, Brigitte Bardot, Terence Stamp, Alain Delon) who were cast in various portions of the trilogy, *Spirits of the Dead* was a satisfactory grosser, particularly in view of the small price we had paid. It was the most expensive of the Poe pictures (although we bore only a small portion of the costs), but it wasn't the type of Poe feature that our own audiences were used to. It had more of a European flavor to it, which didn't have the same broad domestic appeal that our own Poe pictures had. All our Poe movies did well, and in fact, no AIP picture that we produced ever lost money in our first decade, and very few were money-losers after that.

Vadim's *Metzengerstein* [in the trilogy] was made apparently because he had some kinky costumes left over from *Barbarella* and an undaunted desire to continue his campaign of publicly degrading his wife, Jane Fonda.

—Richard Schickel

Although Europe became home for other Poe movies (including *The Oblong Box*) in the 1960s, we relied on it for much more. It was also a place where Francis Ford Coppola made his first picture, *Dementia 13*, for AIP, with the help of Roger Corman.

Mike Frankovich, a good friend of mine and head of world production for Columbia Pictures, had heard me speak highly of Roger, and the two of them signed a deal for Roger to make a Western in Utah. But after shooting had started, Frankovich began developing some concerns. He would look at the daily rushes and simply wasn't impressed with the locations Corman had selected.

Frankovich began sending messages to Roger: "You've got to find different places to shoot. These locations just aren't good enough."

Roger was furious. "AIP never told me where to shoot," he said. "I'm not going to waste time looking for new locations. These will work out just fine."

Roger kept on filming on his own terms. Unfortunately for him, however, Frankovich didn't retreat, sending more messages that Roger continued to ignore. Finally, Mike summoned the director to come in from Utah on the weekend to discuss the shooting. That angered Roger.

"I'm not accustomed to being treated this way," Roger told me. "You and Jim Nicholson always left me alone once the script and the budget were approved."

Roger was convinced that Frankovich was going to fire him, which wasn't the case at all. But figuring it was better to quit than be fired, he decided to remove himself from the picture and return to L.A.

The next morning, Roger showed up in my office, looking tired and weary.

"I need a break, Sam," he said. "I'm thinking of taking a year off, and spending the time in Europe. I want to get away from cameras, actors, and studios for a while."

Roger seemed burned out. Since 1954, he had been producing and directing at least four pictures a year, so the hiatus made sense. But a day later, in typical Corman style, he told me, "As long as I'm taking time off, I'm thinking of making a movie in Europe."

"Roger, that's ridiculous. If you need time off, then take it! There'll be projects waiting for you when you get back."

"I've wanted to make a picture about the Grand Prix racing circuit for a while, and this would be a good chance to do it," Roger reasoned. "I'll get to see Monaco, France, and England, too."

After twenty minutes of talking, I could see that I wasn't going to change his mind. So several days later, Roger returned to my office to talk about his idea for a new picture—an AIP film eventually called *The Young Racers*.

Roger had an incredible scheme to get his regular crew to accompany him overseas. He promised them a European vacation—with a small catch. "Just pay your own way over," he told them, "and then you'll make some money for working there. Once the picture is done, you can do some sightseeing."

Roger's strategy worked. Though the movie was a change of pace for both Roger and AIP, he took most of his usual crew over with him, including a young aspiring filmmaker I had referred to him—an Israeli named Menachem Golan, who later with his cousin, Yoram Globus, built Cannon Films into a large film company. He also brought along Francis Coppola, a graduate of the UCLA film school who had previously worked with us in various capacities. Francis was one of the directors who took his turn shooting portions of *The Terror*, and he also worked in our editing room.

When Corman was preparing to leave for Europe to make *The Young Racers*, he asked Francis if he could recommend a sound man. "I'm a sound man," Francis said. Coppola got the job, and spent the next few days studying the instruction book on how to use a Perfectone sound recorder.

Francis soon became Roger's first assistant on *The Young Racers*, and would travel ahead of the rest of the crew, making arrangements for the filming that would follow. From Los Angeles, I was keeping in contact with Roger and with my own London office, and at one point, I had heard that Francis was in Ireland. It occurred to me that Francis might be shooting another picture for Roger, partly on our time and expense.

"Roger," I told him during one of our long-distance calls. "I'm no expert on automobile racing, but I don't think there's any Grand Prix racing in Ireland. Why in the hell would you be shooting there?"

Roger confessed that Francis had traveled to Ireland for a different reason. "I promised to help Francis make his first picture, and I even put up $20,000 for it," said Roger. "He's also going to be using my crew when *The Young Racers* is finished."

According to Roger, Francis had flown to Ireland to make preparations for the filming of *Dementia 13*. So I told Roger, "Well, since AIP is paying for part of it, I guess this is another picture we're doing together!"

Maybe it was Roger's influence, but Coppola was much more frugal in those days than in more recent years. He made *Dementia 13* for under $50,000—a bit less than Francis's big movie budgets of today.

Dementia 13 was a *Psycho*-like picture, a movie complete with an obligatory ax murder. All through the filming, Francis was sending dailies to Los Angeles, and when the first rough cut was ready, Roger invited Jim and me to watch it with him. Both of us were disappointed. "His talent is enormous," we told Roger, "but we wish the story line was easier to follow."

Corman had a few meetings with Coppola back in Los Angeles, and Francis agreed to write some new scenes. Coppola took a crew to Griffith Park for some additional, final shooting.

AIP ultimately paid half of *Dementia 13*'s production costs, and when the picture was released in 1963, we handled all of its distribution, except in England. As the reviews trickled in, Francis was delighted with some of them. One afternoon, he called his brother, August, beaming that Howard Thompson, writing in the *New York Times*, had described the "solid direction of Francis Coppola." August had read the review, too, and corrected his younger brother. "No, Francis, it doesn't say 'solid direction,' it says '*stolid*!'" Even so, it was a good first effort, particularly in view of its limited budget, and it made money for everyone.

Before Roger Corman had returned to Los Angeles after completing *The Young Racers*, he traveled to Yugoslavia to join Jim, Fulvio Lucisano, and me at the Pula Film Festival, at a beach resort about one hundred miles south of Trieste. It was an unusual festival, where the movies were shown in a Colosseum-like outdoor amphitheater that could have been time-machined out of ancient Rome.

Even though Yugoslavia was a Communist country, it was different than most Iron Curtain nations in that foreign filmmakers were encouraged to bring their foreign productions—and their dollars—there. When Yugoslavia's filmmakers had come home from World War II, they found that their companies had been nationalized and they were now working for the Tito government. But while most Communist countries had one central government film operation, Yugoslavia had a number of small movie production and service companies. And they generally rolled out their "red" carpets for anyone with a camera on his shoulders and money to spend.

We had not been aware of just how many of these small Yugoslav companies existed. But they were quite competitive, even when it came to playing host to foreign filmmakers. Roger had been invited to the Pula Festival by a Yugoslav film service company in New York; the rest of us had received invitations not only from the same company, but also from a production company in Zagreb.

Jim, Fulvio, and I had arrived by train from Rome, and we met Roger in Trieste, right on the Italian–Yugoslav border. A big jeep was waiting for us at the border but the Yugoslav driver—who had been sent by our production-company hosts—had strict instructions.

"I'm supposed to pick up three passengers," he said in his broken English. "Just three, not four." He looked over the names on his passenger list. "Sorry," he said. "Nobody named Roger Corman."

I didn't have much fluency in any of the Yugoslavian tongues like Serbo-Croatian; they just were never offered at the University of Iowa. But fortunately, the driver spoke a little Italian, and Fulvio took over the conversation. "Mr. Corman is a member of our party," he explained in Italian. "We're not leaving without him. If you expect us to get into the jeep, you'll have to take Mr. Corman, too." Eventually, the driver gave in.

Once in Pula, we lost touch with Roger for a few days. The driver dropped Roger off at the film service company's hotel without fully stopping the jeep, making sure we didn't exit the vehicle until we had reached his employer's headquarters. On the last day of the festival, we reunited with Roger at a big party that had brought everyone together. At that event, Roger's host—who we found out had also invited us as well—came up to me at the party and pressed three envelopes into my hand.

"Sam," he said, "here's some money for you, Jim, and Fulvio. It's money for your hotel and food."

"Wait a minute," I said. "We were the guests here of a production company. They picked up all our expenses."

"I know," he replied. "But we had invited you, too. I can't go back to my bosses and tell them you weren't my guests. They won't be happy that I was superseded by one of our Yugoslav competitors."

I didn't feel right about accepting the money, but he was insistent. "OK," I finally told him, "but the next time we're all in New York, we'll use this money to go out for a good time." And we did.

During the 1960s, we coproduced several movies in Yugoslavia, mostly war pictures using some of the battle paraphernalia left over from World War II. Yugoslavia, in fact, had the largest collection of World War II tanks anywhere in the world. One of our Yugoslav-produced films was *Warriors 5*, starring Jack Palance and a cast of Italian and Yugoslav actors. Palance played an American paratrooper captured by the Germans during the war, but who escapes along with four Italian prisoners.

The film was directed by Leopoldo Savona, an Italian director. Fulvio and I traveled to Trieste to keep an eye on the picture, although technically it was an Italian-Yugoslav coproduction. If the Yugoslavs had known Americans were involved, too, the local crews would have charged us much more money. They were quite skilled at taking advantage of "the ugly American" whenever possible.

Actually, Jack Palance fared better than any of us. Most of us were staying at a second-class hotel, where the staff was always eager to help—until you needed them for anything. We had to carry our own luggage to and from our rooms—a burden that Jack never had to bear since he was staying up the road in a much nicer, first-class hotel.

"How did you get someone there to help you with the luggage, Jack?" I finally asked him.

"You just have to look at them the right way," he said, with a glimmer in his eye. With that craggy face and that piercing stare, he may have literally frightened the bellhops into carrying his luggage to his room.

AIP also, during the 1960s, would occasionally buy some Russian or Czechoslovakian pictures and transform them for American distribution. We would strip out the political propaganda, occasionally shoot some additional footage, and then completely rewrite the story lines before dubbing them in English. The Soviet film, *Red Planet of Storms*, became *Voyage to the Planet of Prehistoric Women*. Peter Bogdanovich, long before *The Last Picture Show*, worked in the editing room (and occasionally did additional shooting) on some of these movies. So did Francis Coppola.

In his pre-*Dementia 13* days, Coppola helped us do a transformation with a Soviet picture called *Nebo Zovyot (The Heavens Call)* that we eventually released under the title *Battle Beyond the Sun*. But it was an exhausting project. Francis actually spent months changing the Russian into English, laboring endlessly over the film and somehow trying to work some sex and violence into the dialogue of a story that was essentially a space adventure.

Francis shot some new footage for *Battle Beyond the Sun*, including some scenes of crowds cheering and waving flags. For those shots, Francis woke up early on New Year's Day, drove to Pasadena before the Rose Parade started, and handed out flags to the crowds waiting along the parade route. "When I give you a cue, cheer and wave the flags!" he instructed the people. They were delighted to cooperate as a way to break the boredom of waiting for the parade to begin. The cameras rolled and the footage made it into the movie.

In true AIP style, Francis had obtained the shot he wanted without having to pay a penny for a crowd of extras. When I heard that story, I knew that he could always find a home at AIP. And I was forever indebted to Pasadena for holding a Rose Parade that morning.

In the sixties, we continued to import Italian pictures and coproductions. They ranged from slightly pretentious ventures such as *Prisoner of the Iron Mask*, a movie with ties to the Dumas novel, to more commercial projects like *The War of the Zombies*, which starred John Drew Barrymore, the son of the famous actor. We also coproduced pictures from the Philippines, Japan, and Denmark.

In Denmark, we occasionally worked with Sidney Pink, a theater operator in Los Angeles, who was a relative of Joseph Moritz, one of the original investors in AIP. Sidney got into film production and direction, eventually in Denmark, where he could make pictures for less money than in the States.

In 1960, we began our relationship with Sidney by distributing *The Angry Red Planet*, a good science fiction film he had made in the U.S. with Ib Melchior, and which did quite well at the box office. Later, we made a deal with Sidney for a movie called *Reptilicus*. It was the story of a prehistoric reptile excavated by mining engineers, and which begins an attack on humanity, overrunning armies and repelling artillery, flamethrowers, and an array of bombs.

On one of my European trips, I flew to Denmark to look at a rough cut of *Reptilicus*. By that point, AIP had already given Sidney $100,000 to help him make the picture. But after seeing not much more than a reel of the rough cut, I shut off the projector. I leaned back in my seat with a horrified expression on my face—and not because the prehistoric reptile was so frightening.

"My God, Sidney, what have you done? You're going to have to loop this entire picture!"

"What do you mean, Sam?" he said. "It's already in English."

"Well, you've got these Danes speaking English, and they've all got that sing-song Scandanavian accent! That will never fly in the U.S. This is a science fiction film—but those voices have turned it into a comedy. If we showed it in the States the way it is now, audiences would laugh themselves silly until they got enough energy to demand their money back!"

Sidney had been in Denmark for so long that he didn't even hear the Scandanavian accents anymore. He was so proud of his movie—much prouder than it really warranted. "Sam, you're kidding me on this one, aren't you? These actors are speaking just fine. Just fine."

"Look," I said, "we have to distribute this picture in the States. Science-fiction aficionados are serious people. We can't run the movie with the existing sound track. You'll have to get some American voices and loop it."

Before I had left the screening room, we were both furious at each other. Sidney threatened to sue AIP if we didn't release the picture as it was. But I refused to budge.

"Sidney, it says right in our contract that the movie has to be shot in

English!" I said. "Right now, it's in a form of English that American audiences aren't even going to recognize!"

Three months later, Sidney filed his lawsuit against AIP for not accepting the picture. But I figured it would never stand up in court. "First of all, the suit will drag on for two or three years just waiting for a trial date, and that will hold up the release of the picture," I warned Sidney's lawyer. "Then when we show it to an American jury, they won't be able to understand half of the dialogue in the movie. Sidney will be the laughingstock of Hollywood."

Sidney arranged for his lawyer and a few industry friends to see the film. A week after that screening, the suit was dropped, apparently at the attorney's urging. Sidney agreed to have the picture looped with American voices at Titra studios in New York. The picture was not a big hit but no one questioned the English.

A few years later, clips from *Reptilicus* were used as a running gag in *The Monkees* television show. If the Monkees' own singing on that series wasn't painful enough, the bizarre antics of the prehistoric monster was there to drive the TV audiences into submission.

We promoted *Reptilicus* in our standard but invariably successful "3-See" way:

Invincible!
Indestructible!
What Was This Beast Born 50 Million Years Out of Time?
See! Missiles and Atom Bombs Powerless!
See! Civilization Rioting With Fear!
See! A Mighty City Trampled to Destruction!

One of our more interesting foreign imports during the 1960s was a Japanese spy picture called *Kagi No Kagi*. We had already had several interesting experiences—some more pleasant than others—with Japanese movies. One of the most unsettling was with *Alakazam the Great*, an animation film which we dubbed in English using the voices of Jonathan Winters, Frankie Avalon, Arnold Stang, and Sterling Holloway.

The story of *Alakazam* revolved around a shy monkey, and in a weak moment, we agreed to our publicity department's idea of a series of publicity stunts in which we actually shipped live monkeys to theaters across the country. Some of the exhibitors gave the monkeys away in contests; others handed them to the first ten moviegoers showing up for a Saturday matinee. We got a lot of publicity out of that campaign; we also got a lot of headaches.

For two months, the monkey caper created chaos for us. Nearly every day, we'd get a phone call or a telegram: "Three Monkeys Have Escaped"... "Two Monkeys Died in Shipment." For years thereafter, I'd flinch whenever I'd get within a mile of the monkey cages at a zoo.

As for *Kagi No Kagi*, it was produced by Toho, a Japanese production company whose pictures we sometimes distributed in the U.S. During a trip to Japan, Henry Saperstein, a producer with whom we had dealt on several movies, brought *Kagi No Kagi* back with him. It had already been dubbed into English, but it was not a great movie.

Saperstein believed the picture was ripe for some type of satire, and asked an up-and-coming stand-up comedian, Woody Allen, to take a look at it. At the time, Woody was eager to get his foot in the door as a filmmaker. He had made an appearance in *What's New, Pussycat?*, a film that he had also written, but was looking for a breakthrough movie project.

Immediately, Woody saw the comedic possibilities of *Kagi No Kagi*. In fact, during that first screening, he watched the movie with the soundtrack turned off, and his mind was already creating hilarious dialogue over the moving lips of the actors.

"Here's my idea," Woody told us. "I'll strip off the dialogue, reedit the picture, put my own English dialogue in, and change it from a spy picture to a comedy."

We gave Woody the green light, and over the next few months, he transformed it into *What's Up, Tiger Lily?*, the first picture over which he really exercised creative control. He turned *Kagi No Kagi* into a spoof about an attempted theft of the world's greatest chicken salad recipe. Some footage from other Japanese adventure movies were spliced into it, as well as scenes featuring the Lovin' Spoonful rock group.

AIP released the picture with its fingers crossed. It was difficult to book, and in its first few weeks of release, it did very little business. Most filmgoers didn't know Woody Allen. I don't think they understood the concept of what he was trying to do, either, and they stayed away when they learned it was a redubbed Japanese movie. At the time, it was just too hip for almost everyone but the college crowd. Even so, many of the critics loved it.

I found myself not only pleased but grateful to comedian Woody Allen for a marvelously unpretentious little movie that sets its sights modestly, then scores bull's-eye after bull's-eye all the way... Allen's sense of fun is at once low-keyed, far-out, and hip.
—Arthur Knight, *Saturday Review*

Woody's filmmaking habits were remarkable. He worked around the clock, able to improvise witty dialogue no matter how tired he became. Throughout the project, he survived mostly on Hershey bars and peanuts.

Ironically, once Woody Allen became a full-fledged movie star, *What's Up, Tiger Lily?* was greeted by a much more receptive American public. We never really took our movies out of release, and overnight, the same people who had stood in line for *Take the Money and Run, Bananas,* and *Play It Again, Sam* were suddenly eager to see a 1967 movie that had flopped (except on the college circuit) its first time around. We were only too happy to accommodate them.

Five years after its original release, we finally made back our investment on *What's Up, Tiger Lily?*

As the 1960s progressed, Jim and I received a number of awards: Producer of the Year from the Allied States Association of Motion Picture Theatre Owners; Master Showman of the Decade from the Theatre Owners of America; and two awards as Producer of the Year from the Independent Theatre Owners. As flattering as those honors were, they were more important for what they represented—our growing status among exhibitors in particular and the industry in general. In AIP's early years, we were sometimes treated like a "last-resort" film company; theaters would book our pictures only if nothing else was available. But with our increasing contributions to the business—for instance, turning last-run theaters and drive-ins into first-run, and creating new film genres (like the beach movies)—we evolved into more highly-esteemed members of the film community.

Throughout these years, recognizing my own good fortune—a loving family and friends, and a career that I enjoyed—I felt a need to give something back. I became increasingly involved in the Variety Clubs children's charites, which I was introduced to by Jim Nicholson, Mike Frankovich, and Monty Hall. I found that my volunteer work with the charities, which aid handicapped and underprivileged youngsters, greatly enriched my life. In the course of my travels throughout the world in the pursuit of producing and acquiring motion pictures, I helped establish chapters of the Variety Clubs in many corners of the globe, from Israel to France. As an international vice president for Variety, I met an array of dignitaries and heads of state—including England's Prince Philip and Monaco's Princess Grace and Prince Ranier—as I helped establish chapters in their countries. (To this day, I remain active in the Variety Clubs, as does Monty Hall, who devotes so many hours each year, chairing telethons and otherwise helping Variety in dozens of ways. Monty is a wonderful man—even if he is my wife's cousin!)

Meanwhile, as AIP continued to become even more production-oriented, Jim and I decided that I would assume the new title of Chairman of the Board of AIP, while he would retain the title of President. This change, however, did not alter our equal partnership in the operations and management of AIP. And with our growing status—and those new plaques on our office walls—we both felt very optimistic about the future.

12

Controversy and AIP pictures were as inseparable as Laurel and Hardy or Burns and Allen. It just came with the territory.

Nevertheless, looking back, I'm amazed that we ruffled so many feathers over the years. By today's standards, so many of our movies were quite innocent. As I've written, our "beach party" films, which became such a phenomenon beginning in 1963, were about sweet, sanitized "good kids" right out of the pages of *Seventeen* and *Boy's Life*. These pictures began reaching out to audiences during the John Kennedy era and in the pre-Vietnam war days, an optimistic time when we decided that movies about fun-loving teenagers would be extremely marketable. At the same time, however, we had to deal with the criticism from adults horrified that we were showing kids partying on the beach rather than studying in the library. Even worse, these young people wore bathing suits so revealing that their navels were exposed!

In 1965, the year AIP released *Beach Blanket Bingo* and months before the debut of *How to Stuff a Wild Bikini*, we found another film genre to mine—and another area of controversy. It was the protest/rebellion movie, which we capitalized upon throughout the remainder of the 1960s, at times competing with the simplicity of our own beach movies.

The sixties were gradually evolving into a revolutionary period, different than any decade in American history. From mild alienation between parents and their children, the times were quickly transformed into an era of dramatic change and violence, aided by the civil rights movement, the Vietnam war, and the draft. Several social observers claimed that, with AIP's evolving standards, we had helped lead the sixties rebellion. But I never felt that was true. The fact is that we made society aware of what young people were thinking by trying to stay one step ahead of the social changes and reflecting them in our pictures.

Throughout this era, I continued to keep my pulse on America's youth right in my own living room by screening movies on Saturdays and Sundays for my own children and many of their friends. After the screenings, the kids would give me their reactions and insights into movies like *The Graduate* and *The Strawberry Statement*. I heard their opinions about the hippie movement, rebellious music, uninhibited dancing, long hair, drug use, and youthful alienation. With that kind of information, AIP could see the revolution unfolding, and it was prepared to respond to it. Far ahead of the majors, we created pictures (*The Trip, Wild in the Streets, 3 in the Attic*) that got to the core of the teenage psyche, as well or better than anyone else ever did.

Some critics and older Americans didn't know quite what to make of those AIP pictures of the sixties. Of course, many adults never saw an AIP picture, drawing conclusions only from our ads and promotions. But if they found the political and social revolution in the streets to be offensive, they typically objected to our pictures, too.

One of our biggest sixties rebellion movies evolved from a cover story on the Hell's Angels in *Life* in 1965. Four of our employees spotted the magazine cover, told me about it, and placed that issue on my desk. I took it to Jim—"We've got to make a movie built around this story," I said—and the same day, we called Roger Corman. We discussed some ideas, and I could see that Roger's interest was growing. Before that meeting ended, we agreed to follow the headlines and make a picture about a rebellious group of motorcycle riders, calling it *All the Fallen Angels* (later changed by Jim to *The Wild Angels*), with Roger directing, aided by his new assistant, Peter Bogdanovich, who ended up rewriting much of Charles Griffith's script. ("Wild" was always a great adjective that we used frequently in titles.)

The Wild Angels was a bold picture for AIP. It depicted a disillusioned and alienated motorcycle gang who invade a desert town where they battle a group of Mexicans. There really wasn't much of plot to it—it was more a series of scenes about the bikers' experiences. But the alienation was impossible to ignore. At the end of the picture, the bikers urge their leader (Peter Fonda) to flee with them from the approaching cops; but he just stares blankly into space and mumbles a nihilistic anthem: "There's nowhere to go." It wasn't Proust or Hemingway, but it was the kind of dialogue with which our young, drive-in audiences could identify.

As with most AIP pictures, we were in a hurry to get *The Wild Angels* into the theaters, hoping to release it before anyone else could cash in on the *Life* cover. Fortunately, with Roger's ability to work at a breakneck pace, we really didn't have anything to worry about. Within days, we had cast Peter Fonda in the movie's starring role, although Peter never knew that he really wasn't our first choice—George Chakiris was.

Chakiris had enjoyed enormous success in *West Side Story*, playing the leader of a gang of Puerto Ricans. He won an Academy Award for that performance, and we thought he'd be perfect for *The Wild Angels*. So we signed him to a contract.

But it never worked out. Chakiris, basically a dancer from the musical stage, just didn't have the constitution to slip into a leather jacket and maneuver a bike à la Marlon Brando or Steve McQueen. Just before the shooting started, Chakiris climbed onto the seat of a motorcycle for the first time, knowing that was where he'd have to reside for much of the picture. He rode for a couple minutes, trying hard to steady his trembling hands. When he finally got off the bike, he was noticeably shaken.

"That's it!" Chakiris said. "I'm sorry, but I just can't get back on that bike. I'll still do the film. But you'll have to get a double to do the motorcycle riding for me."

We were stunned. Motorcycle riding was as integral to *The Wild Angels* as singing was to Elvis' *Viva Las Vegas* or *Jailhouse Rock*—and Presley had never asked for a double to do his singing for him. We stood firm, telling Chakiris, "All the actors—including you—have to do their own riding."

Chakiris refused to give in and so did we. We immediately got on the phone and offered the lead to Peter Fonda, who was already cast in a lesser role in the movie. Peter was in New York trying to raise money to produce a script of his own, *The Yin and The Yang*, that he and Dennis Hopper had written. And he jumped at our offer, even though at that point, playing malcontents wasn't Peter's forte (he had previously starred in pictures like *Tammy and the Doctor* and *Lilith*). Nevertheless, Peter seemed to dress the part of the rebel off-camera—hair that flowed down to his shoulders, a three-day growth of beard, tattered leather jackets, hexagonal glasses with mirrored lenses that barely concealed his eyes. He often attached a sheriff's badge to his jacket, which read, "I Belong to Navy Intelligence."

We paid Peter $10,000 to play the role, fitted him with a new leather jacket, and perched him on the back of a motorcycle. At Peter's request, Roger agreed to change the name of the lead character from Jack Black to Heavenly Blues. Why Heavenly Blues? According to Peter, "That's the name of a drug made from morning glory seeds. If you grind a few hundred morning glory seeds in a peppermill, you can get quite a high!"

In typical AIP style, the movie was shot in fifteen days, mostly on location in a little town in Southern California called Mecca. But it was a tough fifteen days. Roger had hired some Hell's Angels as extras—the real thing—and paid each of them $35 a day. That got the attention of the police, who warned us that we weren't dealing with choirboys. Apparently, warrants were out for the arrest of most of these bikers.

At one point, the state police contacted Jack Bohrer, our production manager, on the set, and simply said, "Here are the facts. Almost every one of these guys is wanted. We're thinking of moving in and taking them all away."

Jack pleaded for patience. "Hey, they're working for a living. Why arrest them now? This is the only legitimate job these guys have ever had!"

The cops finally agreed not to make any arrests—at least not yet. But they told us, "Just be careful. you're working with guys who may be more dangerous than you think they are."

The script of *The Wild Angels* was brimming with fight scenes involving the motorcycle gang. It also included the assault of a nurse, the rape of a minister's wife, and ultimately an orgy in a church. We never expected the endorsement of the PTA or the Catholic Church, but the picture was right up the Hell's Angels' alley.

Actually, the Angels themselves were generally pretty affable fellows—unless they had too much to drink. That's what happened near the end of filming when chaos broke out on the set. Roger was short on extras, so once the cameras were rolling during a fight scene, Roger yelled at Bogdanovich, "Jump into the scene! Get in there!" Bogdanovich followed orders, and was instantly portraying one of the townspeople in a brawl with the bikers. As the filming progressed, however, the Angels got carried away, apparently forgetting—or ignoring—that it was just a movie. In the middle of the free-for-all, Bogdanovich became their punching bag. He ended up curled on the ground, absorbing some hard blows to the body. By the time the scene was over, Bogdanovich probably wondered if there was an easier, less bloody way to become the next Cecil B. DeMille.

When *The Wild Angels* was completed, we previewed it at the National Association of Theater Owners (NATO) convention in Miami. The exhibitors and their spouses who attended the screening—mostly conservative, elderly folks—didn't know quite what they were getting themselves into. No, this picture wasn't a fantasy about a group of white-robed, winged angels. Nor was it excessively violent, although we knew it would shock some people. So we added the following on-screen "disclaimer" to inform the audience that this wasn't going to be *The Sound of Music* or *Mary Poppins*:

> The picture you are about to see will shock and perhaps anger you. Although the events and characters are fictitious, the story is a reflection of our times.

Not long after the screening began, Jim and I realized we were in trouble. As the motorcycle gang was creating havoc on the screen, we could see members of the audience squirming in their seats, looking at one another with disgruntled expressions on their faces.

Unfortunately, things only got worse. About thirty minutes into the screening, a few people began to trickle out, two by two, looking as though they were part of a lynch mob. By that time, Jim and I had decided to seek cover in the lobby, gingerly greeting the exhibitors who were exiting the theater. Most of them were content just to glare. But others couldn't wait to let us have it.

"Fellas, it'll make a lot of money, but I could never show it in my theater."

"It'll never play in my town."

"Sorry, I can't book it."

Those were the kindest comments. One woman was absolutely seething. "No one should ever see this picture!" she ranted. "No respectable person would ever make a movie like that. I'm ashamed of you!"

By the time the orgy scene began, people were stampeding for the exits. An exhibitor from Texas came up to me and said, "Sam I didn't know that you boys were starting to make dirty pictures!" Not a single person said he liked it.

Fonda, who attended a preview with his stepmother, didn't have any more luck. As he walked toward his car, he was accosted by an elderly woman who flailed her umbrella at him. "You're a Nazi," she exclaimed. "What kind of pictures are you making? Nazi! Nazi!"

Many of the critics weren't any friendlier, and were sometimes downright brutal. *Newsweek* called the movie an "ugly piece of trash." In the *New York Times*, Bosley Crowther labeled it "an embarrassment all right—a vicious account of the boozing, fighting, 'pot' smoking, vandalizing, and raping done by a gang of 'sickle' riders."

Fortunately, not all the reviews were harsh, with both the movie and Roger himself being showered with praise by some critics. Vincent Canby, in fact, called *The Wild Angels* "the best work to date of the newest cinema *auteur*—the work of a filmmaker with a vigorous, highly personal cinematic style." As delighted as I was to see Roger receive such high praise, any mention of an *auteur* working for AIP still made me shudder.

As with so many of our pictures, while some critics panned *The Wild Angels*, young people stood in line to see it two and three times on a single Saturday afternoon. Cars filled with teenagers were turned away at drive-ins because of capacity crowds. In only a few weeks, *The Wild Angels* had become AIP's most commercially successful film to date.

Just days after its release, many exhibitors who had originally shunned *The Wild Angels* suddenly were frantically trying to book it. As they saw the box office receipts soar at their competitors' theaters, they had a financially-inspired change of heart and pleaded for the movie in their own theaters. Leon Blender, our vice president in charge of sales and distribution, came into my office one morning, faced with an enviable dilemma.

"Sam, I've got a longtime customer on the phone," Leon said. "He's desperate to book *The Wild Angels*."

"So let him book it," I said.

"But he's one of the guys who told you he'd *never* book that movie. His competitor down the street has it now. What should I tell him?"

I picked up the phone, and savored the conversation that followed.

"Now, I distinctly recall you saying that you weren't going to play this movie," I said. "I remember that, don't you?"

There was a long pause, and then finally the somber voice at the other end of the line responded. "I know, Sam, but we all make mistakes. This is a movie I want now."

"Well, get in line," I said. "Hopefully, we'll get to you before too long."

The Wild Angels eventually made over $10 million. That was a huge amount of money in those days, particularly for a low-budget picture that cost just $360,000 to make. But when the film was released in 1966, young people were ready for this kind of antiestablishment picture. Also, our promotional campaign didn't hurt, either, with advertising that called it "the most terrifying film of our time!" Many people were probably lured into buying a ticket on the ad campaign alone.

In the meantime, Peter Fonda's personal problems were bringing notoriety to the picture. He had been arrested in Los Angeles for marijuana possession, and his trial began within days after the release of *The Wild Angels*. The courtroom proceedings were covered on the front pages of dozens of newspapers nationwide. Peter was no altar boy, but he wasn't an enemy of the state, either, which was almost the image the district attorney painted of him. Nevertheless, the prosecutor couldn't have been nicer to AIP; he repeatedly referred to *The Wild Angels* as "proof positive" that Peter was a drug addict, giving the picture enormous amounts of free publicity. We should have sent him a lifetime pass to our movies.

Peter insisted all along that he was innocent. And ultimately, a jury agreed with him. At the end of the three-month-long trial, it came back with a "not guilty" verdict. By that time, we already had a major hit on our hands.

Peter, however, created other problems for us, rocking the boat—quite literally—when *The Wild Angels* premiered as the American entry at the Venice International Film Festival, where our picture debuted in the prestigious opening night position. Jim Nicholson and I flew to Venice for the festival, accompanied by Peter and Roger. The picture was extremely well received there by an overflow crowd standing in the aisles and sitting on arm rests. Festival sponsors had to schedule a second screening of the movie for those people who couldn't get in for the premiere.

Without Peter's knowledge, Jim, Roger, and I made the decision that we wouldn't invite Peter to attend a special morning screening for the media. Typically, after the picture is shown, reporters interview the director and sometimes the producer, and if there's a big-name actor in the film, they might interview him, too, although actors are usually left out of the process unless they've also directed the movie. It's great publicity for the film, and generates a lot of excitement for foreign distribution sales. But I was worried, telling Jim, "If Peter finds out about the screening, he'll probably want to come."

Peter has always been a good friend and a guy you'd love to have a beer with at your favorite pub, but not necessarily the fellow you'd choose to project your best corporate image. *The Wild Angels* was already controversial, and we really didn't need any more.

As a result, Peter slept through the screening and the media interviews. And that absolutely incensed him. He felt he was one of the picture's creators, and that we should have asked him to be there. Since we didn't, he felt we had snubbed him. When we saw him later that day, we let him blow off steam for a few minutes, and figured that he had gotten it out of his system. But he hadn't. Peter decided there would be more to come.

That night, AIP had chartered a ferry to take a large group of dignitaries from the Lido (the island where the screening was held) to the Palace on St. Mark's Square, where the festival was sponsoring a lavish ball. It was a black-tie affair, the first and biggest party of the festival. But Peter had other ideas. He snuck onto the ferry just before our guests arrived at the dock to board. He told the captain, "Arkoff is already on the mainland; he wants you to take the boat over there." In essence, he hijacked the ferry, stranding three hundred VIPs—including judges and actors—on the wharf.

At first, I didn't realize what had happened. We were in such a festive mood after the screening that I just assumed that the ferry hadn't arrived yet. But after a thirty-minute wait on the dock, I went to a phone and called the captain.

"Where the hell are you?" I shouted.

He told me what had happened with Peter. I was outraged, but quickly arranged for another boat to meet us, although it took another hour for it to arrive. In the meantime, I had this image of Peter, standing elegantly on the bow of that ship as it glided across the channel, tucking his right hand into his coat à la Napoleon, convinced that he had gotten the last laugh at Sam Arkoff's expense.

Peter wasn't our only source of problems in Venice. Shortly before we had left Los Angeles for Italy, I received a phone call from the State Department. "Here's our concern," the government official said. "For a foreign film festival like this, we believe that we should only export pictures that reflect the U.S. in a favorable light."

More than anything, the State Department was worried that Soviets would get their hands on the picture and show it to both Communist officials and the public alike. And the thought of Russians watching a movie depicting rowdy motorcyclists, orgies, and marijuana smoking was more than the U.S. government could take. Even so, we politely declined their request to keep the picture home.

However, we never got a general release of *The Wild Angels* in the United Kingdom. John Travelian, head of the British film review board, was adamant about keeping our picture away from the British isles. "I know your movie isn't as violent as *The Wild Bunch* or some of the war or gangster pictures I've seen recently," Travelian told me. "But yours is a movie that some of the violent kids in England—like the Teddy Boys—are going to relate to. We just can't approve a picture that's liable to give us more trouble in the streets."

I was fuming. "This is the country of the Magna Carta," I roared. "How can you so blatantly censor a picture like this?" But we were never able to get the movie passed in the United Kingdom.

Even without the film board's seal of approval, however, it could still be shown at film festivals in the UK. Not long after my run-in with Travelian, *The Wild Angels* was screened at the Edinburgh Film Festival. I attended the event, and took the opportunity to berate Travelian's decision. "I find it so offensive that something like this could happen in a country with such a rich history of freedom. You English should not tolerate it!"

I pounded my fist on the podium and looked out upon the crowd, expecting to be greeted by rousing cheers. Instead, there was a sea of faces as stern and as animated as Stonehenge. I suddenly realized that I had committed the ultimate sacrilege—referring to an audience of Scots as Englishmen. I quickly apologized, and the crowd good-naturedly gave me a big cheer.

Curiously, after the picture's release in the U.S., some of our biggest problems were with the Hell's Angels themselves. They actually sued AIP for defamation of character, as if their image could get any worse. They claimed that the movie had unfairly portrayed them as an outlaw gang, and their lawsuit asked for $4 million in damages. In the press, one of the bikers claimed that they were really a "social organization" whose only purpose was to spread "technical information about motorcycles." To him, the Hell's Angels were on a par with the 4-H Club. Our picture, he insisted, had grossly misrepresented the motorcycle gang.

That was the somewhat amusing, public side of the quarrel with the Hell's Angels. But behind the scenes, the situation was much more ominous. To be precise, an Angels leader named Big Otto warned Roger that "we're gonna snuff you out."

Roger, who had studied engineering at Stanford, tried some logic on this newfound tormentor. "But Otto," he reasoned, "if you kill me, how are you going to get the money you want from your lawsuit?"

Big Otto, hardly a scholar, apparently bought it. "Yeah," he said, "I see your point." From that moment on, he seemed content just to snarl.

Nevertheless, all our concerns didn't end overnight. In fact, Jim and I got word that the Angels might be after us, too. It was the first time I had been on anyone's "hit list." Jim hired some private security to monitor our homes at night. Fortunately, neither the threats nor the lawsuit ever went anywhere. Our insurance company, which considered the Angels' suit to be nuisance litigation, eventually settled out of court for $2,000.

With the success of *The Wild Angels*, Jim and I decided to produce other pictures reflecting the restless, antiestablishment tenor of the times. In 1967, we made and released *Devil's Angels*, with Roger Corman producing and Danny Haller, who created the wonderful sets for our Poe movies, directing. In the film, John Cassavetes starred as the leader of an outlaw motorcycle gang called The Skulls; the movie grossed about $4 million. Cassavetes didn't really want to make the picture, but he needed the money in order to produce one of his own movies. He was a real professional, and produced some very individualistic pictures, mostly with his own funds.

Also in 1967, Dennis Hopper starred in *The Glory Stompers*, another motorcycle movie which was coproduced by disc jockey Casey Kasem and record executive Mike Curb. *Riot on Sunset Strip* was also released that year, depicting the turmoil that occurred on Sunset Boulevard when protesting young people took to the streets.

One afternoon in 1967, Jim and I sat down with Roger to talk about future projects. And the conversation kept coming back to the drug culture. The headlines were saturated with news about drugs—marijuana, LSD, speed, and at least a dozen others. Timothy Leary was telling kids to "Turn on, tune in, drop out," while author Ken Kesey was asking, "Can you pass the acid test?" No one had ever made a sixties movie tackling drugs head-on. It was a timely subject, yet almost too sensitive to touch. But we decided to try it anyway.

The movie we made was called *The Trip*, and Jack Nicholson was engaged to write the script. Jack was in need of money in those days, so he was doing more and more writing. I also suspect that since his acting career seemed stalled at that time, he figured he might have a bigger future in writing and directing.

While Jack pored over his typewriter, Roger conducted some unconventional research for the picture. Although I've always perceived Roger as a moralist and an old-fashioned capitalist, he decided to take LSD as part of his plan to collect background for the project.

Years later, Roger told me that he had read a book by Timothy Leary, and decided to caravan up to Big Sur to have a "good" drug experience. He checked into the Big Sur Inn, bravely swallowed some "acid"—but nothing happened. At least not for a while. He complained to those with him, "What a ripoff! Something must have been wrong with the LSD." But then the drug gradually started to take effect. For the next seven hours, Roger sprawled on his stomach in the dirt in the shadow of a tree, doing "research" for our movie. He insisted that his LSD trip had "unleashed his mind" and expanded his creativity.

Meanwhile, if nothing else, the first draft of Jack's script turned out to be immense—about three inches thick. He had crammed something about nearly every social and political concern of the sixties into it. He also had included so many special effects that it would have challenged the creative talents and the budgets of George Lucas. The script underwent some revisions, and then we began filming, shooting the entire movie in three weeks. In 1967, when the film was released, it became the first Hollywood feature that dealt with LSD.

In *The Trip*, Peter Fonda played a director of TV commercials who is having problems with his career and his marriage to Susan Strasberg. On the verge of a nervous breakdown, he asks a friend (Bruce Dern) to be his guide on an LSD "trip" to help him understand himself better. The rest of the picture is built around that drug experience. The movie also had something else not common in AIP pictures—nudity. We felt it was necessary to show a little more skin than usual because of the sexual content of the LSD-induced hallucinations.

When *The Trip* was released, it created a major uproar. Some film reviewers reacted with shock. There were several derogatory newspaper editorials. The picture was condemned by Catholic organizations and a number of conservative groups who were upset about portrayals of "reckless" young people. We were deluged by critical mail. The major complaint was that the picture did *not* make an antidrug statement. A lot of people had wanted us to *preach* that drugs were morally wrong or a criminal act. But from the beginning, that just never made sense to me.

The "anti-sin" forces weren't going to go see a movie like this anyway; they were already antidrug and wanted no part of these kinds of movies. As for young people who had an open mind about drugs, they'd stay away, too, if the word went out that we were preaching or lecturing them. We felt that we should let the audience make up their own mind. But in a subtle way, we did try to influence them.

In the editing room, when Roger was already in Europe working on his next picture, and virtually unavailable for consultation, Jim and I were told about problems with footage at the end of *The Trip*. To resolve the difficulties, Jim (with my approval) made the decision to put in a series of fast cuts at the end of the film, and then optically insert cracked glass over Peter's face, feeling it would leave the impression that Peter's life was still confused and shattered, and that the LSD trip didn't solve his personal problems.

When Roger heard about the changes, he was not happy, feeling that the ending should leave open the question of whether Fonda had a good "trip" or a bad one.

Roger's anxieties about his name being attached to an "antidrug" film turned out to be unfounded. I remember waking up one morning and seeing Judith Crist review *The Trip* on one of the morning network news shows. She called it "an hour and a half commercial for LSD." And that was the nicest thing she said about it.

Critics, however, don't buy tickets. And fortunately, moviegoers didn't take Crist's advice. *The Trip* became a big money-maker for us. Hollis Alpert, another film critic, praised it as the best Corman picture to date.

The Trip pulls no punches. This is a smash commercial picture on the national youth problem of taking psychedelic drugs.
—*Boxoffice*

With the success of *The Trip*, we issued another picture on the same subject matter in 1968. It was called *Psych-Out*, was produced by Dick Clark, directed by Richard Rush (who later did *Getting Straight* and *Freebie and the Bean*) and starred Jack Nicholson, Susan Strasberg, Dean Stockwell, and Bruce Dern. Nicholson played a laid-back musician, and the movie gave his career a real boost. The advertising promised, "These are the PLEASURE LOVERS! They'll ask you for a dime with hungry eyes...but they'll give you love—for NOTHING!"

At that point, the major studios finally jumped on the bandwagon, trying to cash in by producing their own "psychedelic movies." Although they made a few films about the drug culture, none was ever particularly successful. I think the studios made a big mistake in the way they put those pictures together. Yes, they got some big names such as Al Pacino to star in movies like *The Panic in Needle Park*. But in film after film—from *The Man with the Golden Arm* to *Needle Park*—the protagonist/drug user came to a bad end. That was a fatal mistake for the majors. The last things young audiences want is a heavy-handed morality lecture, and they certainly won't pay for one.

13

Throughout AIP's history, Hollywood's film reviewers often used our pictures as target practice for their hypercriticism. But in 1968, upon the release of *Wild in the Streets*, one of our toughest assailants wasn't a movie critic at all. It was the mayor of Chicago, Richard Daley.

Although *Wild in the Streets* was clearly a counterculture film, I hadn't realized how many nerves it would ultimately frazzle. It was the story of a wealthy, twenty-four-year-old, pot-smoking, rock-and-roll singer named Max Frost (played by Christopher Jones) who performs at a rally for a liberal politician (Hal Holbrook) and begins to recognize the power of flexing his own political muscle. He gets his girlfriend (Diane Varsi) elected to Congress, and then proceeds to contaminate the District of Columbia water supply with LSD. While her fellow lawmakers are under the influence of the drug, Varsi convinces them to pass a law lowering the voting age to fourteen, and before long, Jones is elected President. He immediately ships everyone over the age of thirty-five to concentration camps where they are sedated with LSD. Holbrook, who has become a disgruntled congressman, tries unsuccessfully to assassinate Jones, and is incarcerated at one of the camps, where he commits suicide. At the end of the movie, the President's small child turns to the camera and says, "Everybody over ten ought to be put out of business."

The screenplay, written by Robert Thom, was based on a novella that originally appeared in *Esquire*. The majors, particularly Paramount and MGM, had pursued the story for a while, but we eventually won the film rights and cast some well-known stars in the picture, including Holbrook, Jones, Shelley Winters, Ed Begley, Millie Perkins, and in his first featured role, Richard Pryor. The movie was shot in twenty days for a budget of $700,000.

Shelley was really something to work with, which we did on several occasions over the years in pictures like *Bloody Mama*, *Who Slew Auntie Roo?*, and *Tentacles*. In every movie, she tried to rewrite portions of the script, not only her role but the dialogue of other actors interacting with her character. As much as possible, we tried to keep those creative efforts to a minimum. Shelley also complained about her wardrobe, although I simply told her that we didn't have the budget to spend extravagantly on it. In *Wild in the Streets*, she ended up wearing some of the clothes she had worn in *Time of Indifference*. "They're pretty classy, Sam, so why not use them again?" she explained. On balance, Shelley meant well, and she was certainly a terrific woman and a very good actress.

As it turned out, *Wild in the Streets* wasn't a movie destined to win any Academy Awards. But in terms of box office receipts, it became our biggest money-maker of the antiestablishment pictures, thanks in part to good timing. The movie was released nationally on May 29, 1968, just a week before the assassination of Robert Kennedy and barely two months prior to the violent Democratic National Convention in Chicago. Kennedy and Eugene McCarthy had waged a strong Presidential campaign highly critical of the Vietnam war, and millions of young people—viewing themselves as potential fodder for a conflict thousands of miles away—couldn't have been in a more rebellious mood.

Chicago's Mayor Daley, always outspoken and often belligerent, was among those honestly frightened by *Wild in the Streets*. In television appearances, Daley pointed to the scene in which the water supply is polluted with LSD; Daley was afraid of copycat behavior, and he directed that a barbed-wire fence and around-the-clock security be put in place at the city's reservoirs to prevent any oddballs from trying to contaminate the water system. To the mayor, AIP was helping to provoke the insurrection.

Nevertheless, Daley's comments helped us at the box office. More important, so did the signs we were able to sneak inside the convention hall, emblazoned with the message, "Max Frost for President." The security at the convention hall was extremely tight, but Milt Moritz, AIP's vice president in charge of advertising, and his staff were able to smuggle in those signs, along with people who were willing to mingle on the convention floor and proudly hoist the placards as the network TV cameras panned the crowd. There, amid the "Humphrey for President" and the "McCarthy for President" banners, dozens of "Max Frost for President" signs were competing for media attention. More than one puzzled commentator asked, "Who the hell is Max Frost?!"

Wild in the Streets got more than its share of good reviews. In early summer, Renata Adler of the *New York Times* even called it "by far the best American film of the year so far." The *Times* management must have cringed, however, when Adler singled out an antiestablishment picture for that kind of praise. At the end of the calendar year, not only was our movie passed over when the *Times* selected its "pictures of the year," but Adler herself was out of a job.

I had always thought that *Wild in the Streets* was ahead of its time. Perhaps Renata Adler was as well.

In the late 1960s, AIP stayed on the antiestablishment bandwagon, thanks to a picture which introduced Tom Laughlin in his role as Billy Jack. When I first met Tom, he and his wife ran a Montessori school in Santa Monica. But he yearned to break into the movies, and was independently making a biker movie that would eventually be called *Born Losers*. One afternoon, he called us and lamented, "I've run out of money, and my investors don't have any more to give. Can you guys help me out?"

There was something about Laughlin that we found appealing. Not only was he a personable and enthusiastic fellow, but he was making his picture outside the Hollywood studio system, which Jim and I had been doing for well over a decade by then.

"I've got a print of the picture that I snuck out of the lab," Tom told me. "But the lab has the negative under wraps, and has exercised its lien."

Tom asked us to look at what he had. It was only partly cut, and was primarily rushes. It was a long way from being released. But it had potential.

"Jim and I are impressed," I told Tom. "It's very long, but there's a picture there."

The story line revolved around a half–Native American, karate expert, and former Green Beret named Billy Jack who confronts a band of motorcycle-riding thugs. He singlehandedly puts a halt to their raping and pillaging of the citizens of a small mountain town, including the customary number of girls attired in bikinis and stylish boots. It was a role fit for John Wayne, but Laughlin pulled it off exceptionally well.

Tom wanted to do some additional shooting, and after some tough negotiating with his original investors, I brought out our checkbook. We put up $300,000 to finish the picture and buy out the investors.

When *Born Losers* was released in 1967, it became a major hit, not only in the U.S. but worldwide. In one theater in Mexico City, the picture ran for more than a year. It didn't receive much critical acclaim, but like so many AIP pictures, it was a success where it counted—at the box office.

Featuring teenage girls being raped and tormented by rampaging sadistic motorcyclists (with nicknames such as Gangrene and Crabs), this exploitation picture [*Born Losers*]—a mixture of vigilantism, paranoia, liberalism, and feminist consciousness—must be the most *amateurish* bad movie that ever wound up on *Variety*'s list of the highest grossing films of all time.

—Pauline Kael

As the theater turnstiles spun in response to the release of *Born Losers*, Laughlin was already writing a script for its sequel, *Billy Jack*. We felt we had a winner in Tom, and we liked the new screenplay enough to work out a deal with him. The picture went into production, with Tom as both its director and star.

Almost from the beginning, however, problems surfaced. After the first ten days of shooting, Jim and I took a look at the dailies—but there wasn't much to see. There were thousands of feet of wild horses... horses galloping east, horses galloping west, horses galloping north and south. He had used up nearly all of the $300,000 we had given him, and had nothing much to show for it but scenes that looked like the Kentucky Derby run amok. It was a disaster.

Jim and I sat down to discuss how to handle what we viewed as a crisis. "Do you think it's time to back out of the picture?" Jim asked.

"You've seen the dailies!" I exclaimed. "I'm not sure there's a picture there yet! And I'm worried about whether the project can be rescued and how much it will cost if we go ahead with it!"

Laughlin insisted that he was following his own creative instincts, and the movie, although he needed to do some reshaping of it, would eventually make us happy. However, after two full days of discussion, Jim and I decided to cut our losses. By that point, we were thoroughly skeptical about whether the picture was ever going to come together in a sensible way and at a reasonable cost. So AIP backed out of the project.

Laughlin was distraught. Nevertheless, he still maintained a strong belief in the picture. He took the footage he had shot for *Billy Jack*—all those thousands of feet of horses—to Fox, which ultimately bought out our interest in the picture. Because AIP's *Born Losers* had done so well at the box office with the same Billy Jack character, Fox was willing to take a chance on the new movie. We were relieved to wash our hands of it.

Almost immediately, however, Fox wanted changes in the movie, too. Again, Laughlin refused to accommodate their requests. He insisted on holding onto all creative control. He began bickering with the studio's production chiefs. After a standoff that lasted several weeks, Fox backed out of the picture, too.

The movie eventually ended up at Warner Bros., and when it was released in 1971, Tom had the last laugh. *Billy Jack* became even more successful than *Born Losers*. The Billy Jack character became something of a charismatic, cult hero that the public found irresistible.

Despite our falling-out with Laughlin over *Billy Jack*, Jim and I still stayed in contact with Tom, and we certainly maintained mutual respect for one another. In particular, Tom liked the way we had distributed *Born Losers*, and so he approached us with the idea for his next Billy Jack film, *The Trial of Billy Jack*. After two weeks of negotiation, we agreed to put up the money to develop a script for the new picture, with an option for AIP to distribute it. But once again, things didn't run smoothly. After the screenplay was written and the movie was shot, Laughlin told us that he had made other plans for distributing the picture. He felt he could do just as well using an informal distribution network that he had pieced together, relying largely on his Native American supporters.

"This is getting ridiculous," I told Jim. "Tom has become impossible to work with. We paid for the script and want to make the picture. I don't think we have any alternative but to sue him." Laughlin had neglected the fact that AIP had a contract with him. We moved ahead with legal action on the grounds that we held an option to distribute his new movie.

At about this same time, Jim and I made another decision: We had never taken *Born Losers* out of release, and it was playing in a small number of theaters. But we decided to reissue it on a much larger scale, with new ads stating, "The original Billy Jack is back."

The ad campaign worked. The greater Detroit area was typical: *Born Losers* played for two weeks in eighty theaters, and grossed $683,000. But even though the rerelease of the picture was making money for everyone—including Laughlin who still had a piece of the movie—he was livid. Tom filed a $5 million suit of his own, insisting that we were encroaching upon his property. He also claimed that in those ads for *Born Losers*, we were trying to pass the film off as a Billy Jack movie—which, of course, we were! After all, it really was the film that first introduced the world to the Billy Jack character.

Over the next few weeks, I met with Tom several times in the elegant party room at the Bistro in Beverly Hills, where he would arrive wearing his Billy Jack garb—the ranger outfit and the broad-billed hat. He came up with a number of schemes to settle both of the lawsuits to everyone's satisfaction. At one point, he even offered to buy AIP, proposing that no money be exchanged in the deal, but claiming that once it was announced that he owned AIP, the company stock would double, thus affording us a big price for our own stock. We never could figure out exactly how that would work.

Whatever Tom proposed, he would always insist, "I'm just looking out for and protecting the Native Americans." He really believed he was half Indian by this time, and was defending the rights of all Indians. To Tom, I must have represented the cigar-smoking white man who took advantage of Native Americans.

When Laughlin's lawsuit finally came before a judge for a preliminary ruling, the court agreed with us that *Born Losers* was a Billy Jack movie. But the judge also mandated that in each of the ads for *Born Losers*, we had to mention twice that the picture was a reissue. While agreeing to comply with the court action, I advised the judge, "Since local theaters often create their own ads—or even cut out parts of the ads that they receive from the distributor—it will be a monumental task to monitor what each of them is doing." Nevertheless, we tried.

My son, Louis, who was working for AIP by then while attending law school, began tracking those local ads, accumulating tear sheets from every newspaper in the cities where *Born Losers* was playing, and asking the local exhibitors to comply with the court order. Meanwhile, Laughlin's own production company was doing the same, and returning to court whenever a violation was uncovered.

Eventually, both lawsuits reached a final settlement on the courthouse steps. Laughlin agreed to withdraw his suit and pay us $2 million for breach of contract when he pulled the distribution of *The Trial of Billy Jack* away from AIP. That money came from his share of the revenues from the reissue of *Born Losers*, which kept him from coming out ahead in the legal squabbling.

Even with the courtroom entanglements, Laughlin and I still remained friendly, although it meant dealing with his strange moods from time to time, in which he continued to proclaim that he was representing the sacred rights of Native Americans. *The Trial of Billy Jack* ultimately grossed $35 million in the U.S. alone—an astonishing amount of money in the early seventies. Another Billy Jack sequel seemed inevitable, and although it took Laughlin several years to get it made, he asked me to have a look at it when it was finished.

I drove to Tom's Brentwood home, where he screened the new picture for me. It was called *Billy Jack Goes to Washington*, and was a remake of the Jimmy Stewart–Frank Capra movie, *Mr. Smith Goes to Washington*, with Laughlin portraying the congressman that had been played by Jimmy Stewart. In the picture, Tom traded in Billy Jack's ranger attire for a tie and jacket more befitting a member of Congress. Unfortunately, however, the Billy Jack character seemed out of place wearing "civilian" clothes, particularly since Tom had gained about forty pounds since the earlier pictures.

The new film just didn't recapture the charming and disarming character Tom had played in *Billy Jack*; one critic said he simply looked "dumpy." Tom released *Billy Jack Goes to Washington* himself in the theaters, where it did almost no business. Subsequently, every major company turned the picture down, and we decided not to distribute it, either.

Although Tom has tried to obtain financing for other film projects since then, he simply hasn't been successful. As of this writing, his most recent major venture was running as a Democratic candidate for President in 1992. Apparently, he took the *Billy Jack Goes to Washington* theme to heart.

The original *Billy Jack* wasn't the only hugely successful picture of that era that got away from AIP. We've made a few mistakes over the years, one of which came in 1968, when Peter Fonda and Dennis Hopper revved up their imaginations and their motorcycles, and brought AIP the idea for *Easy Rider*.

Initially, Dennis had been a little hesitant to get involved with another motorcycle picture, having already starred in *The Glory Stompers* for AIP. "I thought Peter Fonda and I might end up like Roy Rogers and Gabby Hayes—the singing bike riders," he told me. He wanted to make art films instead, not movies for drive-in theaters.

But before long, Peter convinced him of the picture's potential, and they asked Jim and me if we were interested. We liked the concept, although we were concerned about the "down" ending of two bike riders being blasted from their motorcycles by Southern rednecks. But still, we wanted to make it an AIP project. We had some suggestions for Peter and Dennis to consider as they wrote the script. We even advanced them some money while the contracts were being drawn up.

However, in a subsequent meeting at our office, Dennis told me that he wanted to do more than star in *Easy Rider*. "This is our idea and we want it done right," he said. "I want to produce and direct it, too."

"Dennis," I said. "Jim and I think Roger Corman would be the best man to oversee and perhaps direct the project. This could be a big movie, and I'd feel much more comfortable with a director with a track record."

Dennis was unhappy. But we had budgeted $340,000 for the movie, which, for AIP in those days, was a lot of money. "The only way we'll agree is if we have the right to remove you from the director's chair if you fall behind schedule," I finally told him. "You know how AIP works, Dennis. We have to keep things moving. We have to stay on schedule."

At the time, we didn't know that when Dennis was starring in *The Glory Stompers*, he had stepped in and taken over the directing chores when the original director of that movie was unable to continue. He also had directed some footage that he and Peter Fonda had shot in the desert and on Sunset Boulevard for *The Trip*. Unfortunately, I was still thinking of him as a novice at directing.

Dennis left my office that day weighing his options. By the end of the week, he and Peter were negotiating with producer Bert Schneider to make *Easy Rider*—directed by Dennis Hopper. They finalized the deal with Schneider and Columbia, and the picture escaped from our grip. At the time the deal slipped away, the AIP contracts were being drawn up by our lawyers. *Easy Rider* became one of the most successful and influential movies of the 1960s, grossing more than $60 million. Dennis did a remarkable job as director, even winning the prize at the Cannes Film Festival for best film by a new director.

AIP made or released other antiestablishment pictures during the late sixties—for instance, Cher's starring role in *Chastity*, a film that Sonny Bono produced and wrote; despite her youth, we recognized that Cher had talent and charm, more than a decade before she starred in pictures like *Silkwood* and *Mask*.

One of my most memorable experiences of these revolutionary times took place in Cannes, where Hilda and I found ourselves caught up in the antiwar, anti-Gaullist demonstrations of the French youth. Cannes, of course, had become a very special place for me. To most people, the film festival was an opportunity for moviemakers to screen their pictures and compete for prizes—and for French starlets to provide "photo opportunities" on the beach wearing as little as the law would allow. For AIP, however, it was also a marketplace where distributors from around the world would congregate, and where we could sell the foreign rights to many of our movies and set up coproductions on other projects. Jim Nicholson never came to Cannes; he found the festival and the activities surrounding it too hectic for his tastes. But I had a different attitude. Although I stayed at the Hotel du Cap, the most elegant hotel in the area, I made frequent trips to the Carlton Hotel to meet with producers, distributors, and critics from all over the world; it was literally a Tower of Babel, and there was no better way to learn about what had happened in the movie business during the previous year, and what trends might lay ahead.

We also used to host two big lunches every year that became legendary around Cannes. One was at the Carlton Hotel for our distributors throughout the world, in which our foreign department (Jules Stein, Danny Skouras, Rocco Viglietta) would review our international transactions in the previous year, and discuss and preview our new pictures. The other was for leading cinema journalists, held at the Eden Roc Pavilion of the Hotel du Cap; it was the only lunch or dinner at the Cannes Festival in which the sponsor (in this case, AIP) never spoke any business or publicized any pictures—it was designed solely for the enjoyment of those who attended, and was well appreciated for that reason.

The Cannes festival in 1968, however, was unlike any other. It coincided with massive student demonstrations that began at the Sorbonne but quickly spread throughout France. They didn't have any effect upon the festival itself—until the French "New Wave" directors (including Godard, Truffaut, Lelouch, and Malle) spoke out. They demanded that the festival shut down as a sign of support of both the students and striking French workers.

One by one, directors began pulling their films out of the festival. Many of the judges went home.

Nevertheless, Cannes itself certainly wasn't under siege. There was a small demonstration, but it really didn't interfere with any of the sales meetings I had arranged. I was making deals, and was unaffected by what was going on in the rest of the country.

Before long, France's transportation network started to shut down, too. As planes were grounded and trains screeched to a halt, panic spread among many of the people remaining in Cannes. At one point, Danny Skouras frantically called me. "Sam, we gotta get out. If we don't leave now, we're going to be stranded here. I've even heard reports that the students are going to riot in Cannes!"

I wasn't impressed. "That's ridiculous. How bad can things be. Nothing has changed here at the du Cap. Look, I've got more business to take care of "

Danny was staying with his assistant at the Carlton Hotel, and claimed that from their vantage point, Cannes was about to explode. They showed up at the du Cap with their wives and their rented Volkswagen jammed with luggage, some of it tied to the roof and the sides. "Sam, this is it! We're driving to the Italian border. You and Hilda have *got* to leave. It's just too dangerous here."

When they couldn't convince me, they started working on Hilda. But she was even less interested.

"I haven't been shopping at Saint Tropez yet," she said calmly. "I can't leave without doing that!"

Every year, we'd hire the same driver, a Frenchman named Roger, to take us in his Cadillac between our hotel and Cannes, and to bring people to the hotel for meetings. When Danny learned of our plans, he figured we had gone absolutely berserk. "Come to your senses! The revolutionaries will take one look at that fancy Cadillac, and they'll stone you!"

Of course, that never happened. Hilda did her shopping at Saint Tropez and remained remarkably composed during this time; I used to joke that she was like a latter-day Madame Defarge, knitting calmly while the country disintegrated around her. Incidentally, no one stoned the Cadillac.

Meanwhile, I wrapped up the last of my business meetings, and when no one was left to confer with, Roger drove Hilda and me to the French border and we flew home. Most people said there would never be another Cannes festival; the following year, it was bigger than ever.

During that era, we made other types of films besides those with antiestablishment themes, but with mixed results. Robert Thom wrote a screenplay called *Angel, Angel, Down We Go*, which, initially, I didn't think was right for AIP. I had even turned the picture down before eventually changing my mind; frankly, I wish I had held fast to my original instincts.

Instead, we made *Angel, Angel, Down We Go* in 1969, which starred Jennifer Jones as an ex-actress who, along with her bisexual husband, plans a party for their overweight daughter, played by Holly Near. One of the musicians at the party falls for Jones's daughter, then for Jones herself, and finally for Jones's husband. Apparently, the musician has devised a plot to destroy Holly Near's parents and their lifestyle that he resented. Jones eventually dies in a skydiving accident, and bewildered by all that has taken place, Near's character finally goes mad. The movie was not a candidate for the "Uplifting Picture of the Year" award.

After I had originally turned the project down, Thom took the script to Sam Katzman, a maker of many successful "B" pictures (*Rock Around the Clock, Twist Around the Clock*) for Columbia and a number of Elvis's later movies. But even though Thom had piqued Katzman's interest, convincing him that the script had potential, Columbia wasn't biting. Somehow, in one of those weak moments that you regret for years, I finally agreed to coproduce the picture; Katzman put up half of the money, we provided the rest.

When *Angel, Angel, Down We Go* was completed but before its release, I screened it for my wife. "I love it, Sam," she exclaimed. "It's the best picture you've ever made. I think it will be a hit!" Hilda's stamp of approval, however, was more a cause of concern than anything else. Of AIP's five-hundred-plus pictures, Hilda has probably seen no more than two-hundred of them, since the biker, the antiestablishment, and most action pictures were not her style. And while she's a charming lady, she may not be the best judge of what AIP's audiences may like. *Angel, Angel, Down We Go* performed dismally at the box office, despite her rave review. Not surprisingly, I've joked with Hilda for years that her admiration of a picture is the kiss of death! When she likes a movie, it just may be doomed!

The problem with *Angel, Angel, Down We Go* was that the characters just weren't sympathetic. Life is tough and the front page is even tougher; people don't want to walk out of a theater feeling worse than when they came in. With *Angel, Angel, Down We Go*, that is exactly what happened.

Fortunately, at the end of the sixties, AIP produced many more successful than unsuccessful pictures. The film *3 in the Attic* was one of them—the story of a young college student (played by Christopher Jones) who is courting three beautiful coeds at the same time. When each of the girls discovers that the others exist, the three of them conspire their revenge against Jones. They capture and imprison him in an attic, and make love to him with such frequency that his sexual desire burns out. Finally desperate to be left alone, he goes on a hunger strike and eventually is hospitalized.

The fantasy of being a sexual prisoner of a trio of beautiful women must have been too much for young male moviegoers to resist, for *3 in the Attic* quickly emerged as one of AIP's highest-grossing movies to date.

Although I'm proud that AIP accumulated a remarkable track record for making many more commercially successful pictures than box office disasters, in 1969 we wrote the book on how *not* to put a picture together. We had a lot of hope for a movie called *De Sade*—but they were hopes that fizzled. We coproduced the picture with Arthur Brauner and his German film company, and the movie was filmed in Berlin, where we had access to the Charlottenburg Palace for filming both interiors and exteriors. Keir Dullea, who had acted so well in

David and Lisa in 1962, and again in Kubrick's *2001: A Space Odyssey* in 1968, was cast in the lead, with John Huston and Lilli Palmer as his costars.

De Sade should have worked. After all, as one of my colleagues said, "It's got everything a successful picture needs—sexual perversions, orgies, and every other type of bizarre sexual deviation." Nevertheless, I sometimes wondered whether a biography about de Sade was really a subject for a motion picture company like ours, which had concentrated so much on teenage audiences.

In an article in October 1969, *Variety* predicted that *De Sade* would "bridge the generation gap. It will attract both the turned-on hip and the dirty old men." However, even though the movie dealt with sexual subjects, it certainly was not pornographic and, by today's standards, not particularly daring. In truth, the picture was a headache from the start, and didn't do much at the box office either.

Cy Endfield, an American director who had worked in England since the early fifties, was hired to direct *De Sade*. He had made several movies that were well received, including *Zulu*, and Jim and I agreed that he was an acceptable choice to direct our picture.

Not long after the shooting began, however, we started getting reports of serious problems on the set. Deke Heyward, who was overseeing the production for us, sent us an urgent memo that said, "Endfield had been hospitalized. But even when he's on the set, he's having difficulty filming the sex scenes." In a picture like *De Sade*, the sex scenes were just about everything. Admittedly, it was a tough order since these love scenes had to be sexy but not pornographic. But in this case, I realized that we had a crisis on our hands.

The next day, I flew to Berlin myself. In the dead of winter, it wasn't a trip I was eager to make. But winter or no winter, I felt it was necessary. When I arrived in Germany, Endfield was in the hospital. Although he had already shot much of *De Sade* by then, he had skipped over all the sexy scenes, which of course was a good part of the picture.

A representative of our insurance carrier, who had been dispatched to the set, quickly sized up the situation. "Sam, I don't think Endfield is sick at all," he said. "I think that, for some reason, he doesn't want to shoot the sex scenes. Your director seems to have some personal difficulties, and I don't think my insurance company is liable. If I were you, I'd get someone else in here to shoot the sex scenes."

We were faced with a serious situation, which was only made worse by Keir Dullea's reaction. When Keir heard that I was contemplating hiring a new director, he was upset and cornered me on the set. He and his new wife were sharing a house with Endfield and the director's spouse, and apparently the couples had become good friends. "Read my contract, Sam," Keir said. "I have director approval, and I'm not going to okay anyone else to direct the rest of this movie."

I had never given director approval to any actor, but apparently this time it got by our lawyers. Nevertheless, I fired some other ammunition. "Look, Keir, your friend is either sick or malingering. And if this picture doesn't get finished, your career may suffer. This is the best part you've had in a long time. But if the movie collapses because you don't want to do it with another director, no one will ever see you in this wonderful role!"

Keir became very anxious. He felt that his role was an actor's dream, and didn't want to see it fizzle out. So at a small dinner party thrown by my German coproducer, I decided to approach John Huston about taking over the directing chores. "How could we do any better than getting the guy who directed *The Maltese Falcon* and *The African Queen*?" I asked Deke.

Before I ever approached Huston with my proposal, I was confronted with the most wonderful spread of caviar and vodka imported from the U.S.S.R. By the time I finally got past the buffet table, I had eaten about two pounds of the best caviar I've ever tasted. It was the only time I've ever been content with the amount of caviar I had consumed.

Huston, however, turned out to be reluctant to direct the final scenes. "I just can't do it, Sam," he said. "I can't do that to another director, particularly having just worked for him as an actor."

I was concerned, wondering where I was going to find a director on such short notice, especially one who could do daring scenes tastefully. Before long, however, Roger Corman popped into my mind. I called Roger, who was in Los Angeles planning his own next film, and made him the offer to finish *De Sade*. "I don't think so, Sam," he said near the beginning of our conversation. But then maybe he heard the insistence in my voice. By the end of the thirty-minute phone call, he finally agreed. All that was left was to sell the idea to Keir.

The next day, with Roger already on a plane to Germany, I told Keir, "The only director I know who can finish this picture quickly is Roger

Corman. He can handle it. He can tie the loose ends together faster than anyone."

Keir became hysterical. "Roger Corman! That exploitation director!"

"You have Roger all wrong," I argued. "He's very educated, very intelligent. At least talk to him."

When Roger arrived in Berlin, he met with Dullea for an hour. Keir was impressed, gave Roger the thumbs up, and the picture went back into production. Roger shot for ten days, the movie was wrapped up, and all of us flew home, still clinging to great hopes for *De Sade*.

As *De Sade* was being edited, however, my anxiety resurfaced. The picture just didn't have the spirit and the passion it needed. Roger tends to be a hands-off-the-actor type of director, and he did an admirable job under difficult circumstances. But *De Sade* needed someone with a licentious soul.

Despite my uneasiness, Jim Nicholson insisted on moving ahead with a real Hollywood-style premiere—the first in AIP's history—staged at the Rivoli Theater on Broadway (United Artists' flagship house), and complete with red carpet, klieg lights, live radio coverage, and a post-screening party. The stars of the movie were expected to be there, along with New York celebrities ranging from Andy Warhol to Louis Nizer. I had such an ominous feeling about the evening that I wanted to stay in L.A. "Frankly," I told Hilda, "I'm embarrassed by the picture."

Jim, however, pressed me to attend the New York premiere. "This is a big moment for us, Sam. I wouldn't feel right if you weren't there."

It turned out to be a night to forget. Hilda and I arrived early, dressed in black and full of gloom. The screening was supposed to begin at 7:30, but it took forever to get everyone seated. Members of the audience who arrived on time were becoming increasingly restless while the large Warhol entourage chatted with the press outside. "Let's start the show," the crowd began yelling. My stress level was soaring off the meter.

The public relations specialist we had hired to stage the event wasn't having much success trying to speed up the process. "The audience is losing its patience," I pleaded with him. "We have to start."

Finally, at 8:15, just before a mutiny began inside the theater, the film projector mercifully began to roll. The theater was packed, and I tried to relax a little. But I never got the chance. In one of the first scenes, Dullea's De Sade character rides up on horseback, and the horse neighs at the camera; instinctively, the audience neighed right back!

I began to feel ill. From that point on, whenever the horses neighed, so did the audience—when they weren't laughing in inappropriate places. I walked to the rear of the theater and stood there, trying to regain my equilibrium and composure—and perhaps staking out a strategic position for a quick getaway if the audience turned rabid! In fact, the crowd did become increasingly raucous, continuing to laugh at scenes that weren't supposed to be funny and talking back to the screen. It was a real nightmare. I figured it was only a matter of time until they crucified the producers.

At the party afterward, I felt devastated. Jim, however, didn't seem to be doing too badly, although he couldn't have been feeling very good, either, considering the audience reaction. Most of the party guests were polite, telling me, "Congratulations on a wonderful picture." I was convinced they were biting their lips, just waiting to attack the picture in conversations with their friends or in their newspaper reviews the next day. Some people were obviously fumbling for something nice to say. One woman remarked, "Well, um, it's not Oscar material, but you'll make a lot of money!" Another stammered, "The horse's tail sure was braided nicely!" That was the best thing she could think of to say!

De Sade was a poor grosser. We've had films that have done worse. But none has ever been as difficult and as embarrassing as this one.

14

In general, I think that Hollywood doth protest too much about violence in its films. Nearly everyone in the film industry complains about violence in general—however, when it comes to their own movies, they always find a way to justify it. Nevertheless, sometimes the antiviolence denunciations have come from the most unlikely sources. Like Shelley Winters, for example.

Shelley starred in an AIP picture called *Bloody Mama*, a 1970 movie about the escapades of the Barker clan, a well-known family of Depression-era gangsters from the Midwest. Shelley played the rugged Ma Barker, who leads her backwoods sons in violent sprees of robbery, kidnapping, rape, and murder. Eventually, the cops corner the Barker gang and kill them in a gruesome shootout that you wouldn't want to watch just before eating.

The family that *slays* together stays together.—Ma Barker

The meanest brood of hoodlums ever spawned. Only a mother could love THEM. Only they could love a mother like...Bloody Mama.

You gotta believe...you gotta have faith...but first you gotta get rid of the witnesses!

—Advertising copy for *Bloody Mama*

As Shelley had done with *Wild in the Streets*, she wanted to rewrite her role in *Bloody Mama*—in fact, she insisted on rewriting other actors' roles, too. While trying to beef up her own part, she also hoped to change the plot itself more to her liking.

Many stars, particularly in working with the studios, had become accustomed to routinely making changes in their own characters, without any other adjustments in the rest of the script; as a result, their own parts sometimes would fall out of the synch with the rest of the picture, turning an otherwise good story into a confusing and disjointed one. As a rule at AIP, however, we never allowed actors to take that much control, refusing to accommodate their egos. For accomplished actors like Shelley Winters and Vincent Price, we were willing to listen to suggestions for changes in dialogue when they felt that a different word or an altered phrase might relieve some awkwardness they detected. But such changes were more the exception than the rule.

For *Bloody Mama*, we were expecting Shelley to try to rewrite parts of the script. Jim and I girded our loins and firmly repelled her efforts. "I know you mean well, Shelley," I told her. "But we feel we have a strong picture on our hands, and we want to keep it that way."

When *Bloody Mama* was released, we loved the movie and so did Shelley. She headlined a full-fledged publicity tour, appearing on TV and radio shows across the country plugging the film.

At about the same time, however, a group in Hollywood called the Alliance Against Violence in Motion Pictures began making strong antiviolence pronouncements. The organization bought a series of two-page ads in the trade papers, urging their moviemaking colleagues to curtail the violence in their pictures. Ironically, near the top of the ads, there was Shelley's name, affiliated with this antiviolence movement.

Within minutes after I had seen the first ad, I called Shelley. "Shelley, what the hell are you doing? Why is your name in that ad? You said you were proud of *Bloody Mama*!"

"I am, Sam."

"Then why are you leading this blood feast against violence? Do you think *Bloody Mama* is too violent?"

"Sam, *Bloody Mama* isn't a violent picture. It's *against* violence! Don't you see it that way?"

Shelley had assumed the position of so many actors, directors, writers, and motion picture companies who make a movie that might offend segments of the public. To counteract any criticism, they often proclaim that their picture is really *against* what the movie is depicting, whether it is sex or violence. It's a self-defense, self-preservation mechanism.

Personally, I don't believe that an overdose of violence in movies serves anyone's best interest. In fact, it can repel audiences and keep them away from theaters. In AIP's movies, if violence didn't have much of a purpose, we'd cut it.

At the same time, I've always believed that some violence is justified in motion pictures. You can't attract audiences by making movies about accountants inserting notations into their profit-and-loss ledgers (some of my best friends are accountants, but their day-to-day lives aren't the things that great movies are made of). Films need action, and that often translates into a modicum of violence. In fact, some subjects just couldn't be portrayed in motion pictures at all without a certain amount of violence.

Yet some Hollywood producers and directors continue to pontificate endlessly on their antiviolence platforms, while their own movies are still splattered with blood and gore. Like Shelley, they tell me, "No, we're not for violence at all, Sam; we're showing violence because we're *against* it!"

The logic is convoluted, but it's rampant in Hollywood.

There's a lot of hypocrisy in this town when it comes to violence. Some people criticize it when it appears in so-called "non-artful" movies. At the same time, however, these same people praise the violence in the "artful" films such as *Taxi Driver* where the violence is integral to the picture.

As for *Bloody Mama*, Shelley got an unexpected, firsthand taste of violence during the shooting itself. In one scene, she was supposed to punch Don Stroud. Well, she connected with him a little harder than he liked, and, perhaps instinctively, he swung back. He hit her squarely on the nose, she staggered backward and tumbled to the ground.

Shelley was stunned. Her nose was bleeding. She was moaning in pain. But more than that, she was infuriated and embarrassed. Roger sent her to the hospital to have X rays taken. As it turned out, she hadn't broken anything, but she had to apply ice for the rest of the day.

Once Shelley was back on the set, she asked Roger, "Aren't we going to shoot that scene again?"

By then, Roger was already in the middle of another scene. "We'll look at the rushes tomorrow," he said. "If it's not good, we'll shoot it again." But they never did reshoot it. I guess Roger liked the realism of seeing Shelley take a right hand to the nose.

Despite all the talk of the brutal nature of *Bloody Mama*, there were certainly many scenes that weren't violent at all. In one of them, Shelley had to give baths to her sons in the picture—including Stroud and Robert De Niro. "I'm never too good at playing sexy scenes," she said, "since the color film always captures me blushing. But I'll give it a try."

The only way she could do it, though, was to pretend the boys were kids. "It was hard for me to bathe Don Stroud, who is six-foot-three, but Bobby De Niro was much easier," she said after the scene was in the can. "Bobby and I are very close and have had a long friendship. He hunched over and pretended he was a baby; he can make himself little if he wants to. Both of them kidded me because I really washed them all over."

Before and during the shooting, we saw just how seriously Bobby De Niro took his acting. The picture was shot in Arkansas, and he went down there two weeks before everyone else, just to listen to people's accents and live with the folks there. His character was supposed to be a junkie, so he dropped his weight down to about one-hundred-twenty-five pounds by eating only fruit juice and water, which caused scabs to form all over his body. Bobby would go to any length to make his character realistic, as he did years later when he *gained* fifty pounds for his role as a prizefighter in *Raging Bull*.

In 1971, AIP began developing *Boxcar Bertha*, a film that some critics saw as a sequel to *Bloody Mama* when it was released the following year. Others compared it to *Bonnie and Clyde*, with Barbara Hershey and David Carradine playing Warren Beatty and Faye Dunaway-type characters who became involved in a series of train robberies.

Initially, we had hoped that Roger Corman would direct *Boxcar Bertha*. But although Roger agreed to oversee the project, he decided he didn't want to direct it. By this stage in his career, he saw himself more as a producer than a director, and Martin Scorsese was proposed as director for the picture.

At the time, Scorsese was twenty-nine years old. A product of New

York University, and five years out of film school, Marty had edited films like *Woodstock* and worked on some short subjects and one feature, *Who's That Knocking?* But *Boxcar Bertha* would be his first major commercial picture. It was before *Mean Streets*, *Alice Doesn't Live Here Anymore*, and *Taxi Driver*, and to us, he was still a largely unproven commodity. But we were impressed enough to give him a chance.

Boxcar Bertha was filmed in the hillbilly regions of Arkansas, and I made a point of looking at the rushes as they were shipped back to L.A. During the first two days, Scorsese had shot a lot of moving train wheels—and not much else. As I said to Jim, "They're very well shot, but how many train wheels can you show in a movie, even one about train robberies? And how many theaters want to play a train documentary?"

Before long, something else intervened that drew our attention away from train wheels.

The production manager had hired dozens of local people in Arkansas to work as extras and laborers for $20 a day. At first, these locals were excited about the prospect of appearing in a Hollywood movie. But within a couple days, they were ready to mount the barricades, claiming they were being asked to work much too hard and much too long each day for much too little pay. One night, a dozen of them stormed into a local bar where Scorsese was filming. They pulled out some guns, fired a few rounds into the walls, scared the hell out of everyone, and took Scorsese hostage. It was not my idea of Southern hospitality.

"We're not going to let you go until you pay us more money," one of them told Marty. "We can wait this one out a lot longer than you might like."

Most of these guys were Goliaths. They let the actors and the crew leave, but told Scorsese (a rather short man) that he would have to stay put until the issue was resolved to their satisfaction. They were drunk before they had seized the bar, and they wasted no time in raiding one case of liquor after another, drinking right out of the bottles.

Finally, they let Scorsese use a phone, and he tried calling Roger Corman. When he couldn't reach Roger, he phoned Jim and me. "These people want more money, or we're never going to get this picture finished," he told us.

As his captors were becoming more inebriated, Marty himself was becoming increasingly anxious, probably figuring that if this was what filmmaking was all about, it was time to go to law school.

At first, I resisted giving in to the extras. "I'm not sure we can go any higher than twenty dollars a day. That's it!"

"Fellas," Marty pleaded, "they're helping themselves to the liquor in the bar. They've already fired their guns, and they might do it again!"

Finally, as the desperation in Scorsese's voice increased, we relented. "OK, give them an extra twenty dollars a day," I said. "That'll bring them up to forty dollars. Tell them they're not worth any more than that!"

Despite that unexpected interruption, *Boxcar Bertha* was finished in just twenty-four days. Scorsese later said that *Mean Streets* wouldn't have been as high quality a picture if he hadn't had the experience of *Boxcar Bertha* under his directorial belt. Still, even though many critics praised Scorsese's talents, they were offended by the violence in *Boxcar Bertha*—a steady stream of bloodletting that ranged from a plane crash to a crucifixion.

In spite of such criticism, I never regretted making pictures like *Boxcar Bertha*. I couldn't say the same, however, about a movie called *Bunny O'Hare*. It was a film we made and released in 1971, perhaps seduced by the appeal of working with a genuine star, Bette Davis, even though I should have known better. Over the years, I had grown to appreciate working with unknown actors, with their relative lack of ego. By the seventies, when we began working with some better-known actors, we found that big names often have big heads, and when they create problems, they're usually big ones. That was the case with *Bunny O'Hare*.

In retrospect, *Bunny O'Hare* was not only the wrong vehicle for AIP, but it was wrong for Bette Davis, too. After all, here was a woman who was a true Hollywood legend, who had dazzled audiences in films like *Jezebel*, and had won two Academy Awards. Yet by the early seventies, the challenging parts and the ecstatic reviews were behind her. The big drawing cards of the times were Paul Newman, Dustin Hoffman, Ali McGraw, and Barbra Streisand, not Bette Davis. The hit movies were *Klute*, *Summer of '42*, and *Carnal Knowledge*, not pictures with starring roles for actresses past their prime.

So at fifty-nine, Bette Davis and her handpicked director, Gerd Oswald, approached us with the *Bunny O'Hare* project, with a script that called for her to sit on the back of a Triumph 250 motorcycle piloted by Ernest Borgnine, both dressed as aging hippies who robbed banks throughout the Southwest. We agreed to make the movie, paying her $100,000 to star in it; in the early days of AIP, we could have made at least an entire picture for that. But almost from the start, I knew it was a doomed project.

I hadn't been on the set much during the early days of shooting *Bunny O'Hare* but I had heard that director Oswald was having trouble keeping Davis in line. The two of them had initially conceived of the idea for the picture and brought it to us. Rather than following the script, however, Davis insisted on one change after another, and Oswald invariably went meekly along. At her age, this was also a physically difficult picture for her to do, and that didn't help her mood either.

Of course, Davis had been preceded by her reputation. Her lengthy career at Warner Bros. was extremely turbulent, and she was known for her whims and ill temper on the set. By the time of *Bunny O'Hare*, she was more difficult than ever, and most of the other actors and the crew became exasperated trying to work with her.

I was concerned about Oswald, too. I conceived *Bunny O'Hare* as a comedy, a spoof really; both Oswald and Davis wanted it to be a different kind of picture, providing a social commentary on modern America. Ultimately, the movie lacked the humor that could have brought people into the theaters.

For 18 years, American International Pictures has been setting trends, keeping theaters supplied and sustaining a chaotic and undirected industry with an otherwise long absent brand of confident showmanship, innovative production, distribution and sales. When AIP falters, the metastases of current film industry ills is complete. In *Bunny O'Hare*...the golden touch has vanished...

An audience has a right to expect that Miss Davis will supply for their price of admission a degree of flamboyant grotesquery that might be relished. She seems merely dejected, tired, wan, more aged due to cruel photography.

—Los Angeles Times

The shooting of *Bunny O'Hare* reached a crisis during the last scene. The script called for Davis to sit on a motorcycle, look toward the camera and utter, "Screw you!", before turning and puttering off into the sunset.

Well, she wasn't happy about that. "The line should be 'Fuck you!'" she hissed. "No one's going to believe my character would ever say anything else."

In those days, the word "fuck" created instantaneous problems for any motion picture.

"Miss Davis," I pleaded, "you know as well as I do that if we allow you to say that word, the picture is automatically going to get an 'X' rating. That's going to hurt us terribly in the theaters, and it will kill our chances of eventually selling it to T.V."

I tried to reason with her, but she wouldn't budge. To her, AIP represented "the studio," which was synonymous with "the enemy."

Finally, I offered a compromise. "Let's shoot the scene twice," I pleaded, trying not to blurt out who I really wanted to shoot. "You can say the line both ways. Then later, we can make the decision about which one to use."

Davis's eyes narrowed, her hands clenched, and she shook her head from side to side. She had no intention of compromising.

We eventually filmed the scene with the four-letter word she had wanted. But it never made it to the screen that way. During the editing of the movie, we brought in an actress who could do a pretty good Bette Davis impression to record the words "screw you." It was dubbed over Davis's own voice, and that's the way the final scene appeared in the theaters.

We had prevailed, at least for the moment. But eventually, we heard from Bette Davis again. When she saw the finished picture, she filed suit, claiming that we had tampered with the original concept and had somehow breached our contract by overruling her "artistic" demands.

Bette Davis took a look at *Bunny O'Hare*, her latest film made with Ernest Borgnine for American International, and called it a "tastelessly and inartistically assembled slapstick production." Her personal review is contained in a $3,300,000 breach of contract and fraudulent misrepresentation suit filed against AIP on Friday in N.Y. Supreme Court.

The suit, filed for [the] actress by Gottlieb Schiff Fabricant &

Sternklar, N.Y.C., alleges that AIP induced her into making a humorous social commentary film, but after production transformed [the] pic into something different. Also, AIP is charged with materially altering in [the] final footage the script which she had approved and accepted before shooting.

—*Daily Variety*

Bette Davis never pursued the lawsuit and so it was ultimately dismissed. Thereafter, she said she would refuse to work for AIP again—which was just fine with me. In fact, we never asked her to make another picture with us.

In 1988, Larry Cohen (with whom I made a number of movies, including *Black Caesar*, *Hell Up in Harlem*, and *Q*) came to me with a horror picture in which Bette Davis was set to star. "She has worked with me on the script," Larry said. "I think it's a project that might interest you."

He couldn't have been more wrong. "No, thanks, Larry," I told him. "Judging by my past experience, you'll have nothing but problems with her."

Larry, however, showed no hesitation. "Sam, I've been very careful. She worked on the script with me. This is a picture she believes in. I think it's going to work out fine."

Ultimately, Larry made the picture, *Wicked Stepmother*, without me—and he made most of it without Bette Davis, too! Only one week into the shooting, Davis walked off the set and never returned. She told Cohen that she had to fly to New York to get her teeth fixed—and she refused to come back. The script had to be completely reworked without any additional appearances by Davis. Fortunately, Larry is very resourceful, and he managed to sell the picture to MGM and make a profit, no thanks to Davis.

While I was delighted to have severed our ties with Bette Davis, I was just as pleased that AIP's long-term relationship with Vincent Price extended well into the 1970s. Vincent continued making horror pictures for us, many in England, such as *The Abominable Dr. Phibes* and its sequel, *Dr. Phibes Rises Again*. Both Phibes movies were original, stylish horror pictures, leaning heavily on humor, although the ads for the first picture in particular had some people wondering just what kind of movie it was.

In *The Abominable Dr. Phibes*, Vincent plays a character who is seriously disfigured in a car accident. The ad for the movie depicted Vincent, with his metallically-reconstructed face, warmly embracing a beautiful young woman. At that same time, *Love Story* was a big hit across America, where it was being promoted with the slogan, "Love means never having to say you're sorry." Jim created a parody on that line and placed it in the ad and the trailer for *Dr. Phibes*: "Love means never having to say you're ugly."

We previewed *The Abominable Dr. Phibes* widely, which was not our usual course. And everyone in Hollywood loved the movie and the ad. But when the picture opened in 1971 for a trial run it died at the box office. We were puzzled as to why audiences were treating the movie as though it were the black plague—until we took a closer look at our ad campaign. The public just didn't know what to make of the ad and the trailer. Was this a horror movie? Or was it a comedy? In Hollywood, the line was an inside joke; everywhere else, people were confused.

We reshaped the ad, put a serious horror-style tagline on the campaign, and sent the picture out again. This time, it attracted the usual horror fans, and with word of mouth, it also drew a more stylish, campy audience—and convinced us to make what became a profitable sequel.

That experience reinforced just how important ad campaigns can be. In 1971, we picked up the distribution rights to a Danish movie called *Christa*, made by an American producer in the English language. The story revolved about an uninhibited airline stewardess who had turned her promiscuous lifestyle into an art form. The title of *Christa*, however, didn't tell the viewer much about the plot line, so we decided to make a change.

Initially, we were going to call it *Danish Fly Girls*, but someone in the AIP offices pointed out, "If you have 'Danish' in the title, people are going to think it has something to do with pastries!" So we settled instead on *Swedish Fly Girls*, which certainly sounded much more intriguing than *Christa*.

Swedish Fly Girls made a respectable showing in theaters, and with a mild "R" rating, it became a gigantic hit playing the hotel circuit. There was a little bit of nudity in it—enough to win over a lot of tired businessmen who would dial it up on their hotel TVs late at night. It played for years on closed-circuit TV that way, and became a big grosser in hotel chains. Maybe it was the title that attracted viewers. You never know what's going to make America happy.

In 1970, Roger Corman produced and directed *Gas-s-s-s!...or It May Become Necessary to Destroy the World in Order to Save It.* The plot of *Gas-s-s-s!* revolves around the accidental release of experimental nerve gas at a defense plant in Alaska, which ages and kills everyone over the age of twenty-five in just days. The young survivors, in trying to start a new life on a commune, find that their peers begin making the same mistakes as their elders did. It had an interesting cast, including Cindy Williams, Ben Vereen, and Talia Shire—all unknowns at the time. But that was about the most interesting thing about it.

Poor Roger. He filmed all over the Southwest, rewriting the script as he moved through Texas and New Mexico. He encountered rain and sleet in Dallas, where he was trying to film a re-creation of the Kennedy assassination as a blizzard moved through the city. If he weren't such a conscientious director, he might have thrown up his hands, pulled in his umbrella, and gone home right there.

When Roger left for Europe to shoot *Von Richthofen and Brown* for United Artists, he turned over the rough cut to us. Jim and I viewed it, and realized it needed substantial work. We so informed Roger, who didn't disagree.

Roger's handpicked editors eliminated lines, entire scenes, and even one of the leading characters in the film. They also cut out a final shot that Roger adored, in which he positioned the leading man, his lady, and three-hundred extras on a mesa. The camera panned back while the words of God were heard in a voice-over. For some reason, the voice of God had an accent. Roger thought it was one of the most spectacular shots of his film career. The editors thought it belonged on the cutting room floor, which was right where they left it.

We had tried, but the editors just couldn't save the picture. When *Gas-s-s-s!* was released, it was promoted with ads that proclaimed, "Invite a few friends over to watch the end of the world." The picture didn't make any money.

After producing and directing so many pictures, Roger finally decided not to direct again after *Gas-s-s-s!*, only returning to the directoral ranks again in 1990 for a new Frankenstein movie. He had been producing about four pictures a year, and directing most of them on location, but about the time of *Gas-s-s-s!*, he got married to a terrific woman named Julie and decided to settle down. He also formed his own distribution company, New World, and began producing pictures for it. The last movie we worked on together was *Boxcar Bertha*, which Roger produced and Martin Scorsese directed.

Roger and I had a great relationship, probably unmatched in this business, particularly considering the number of pictures we made together. It was an informal and cooperative relationship, and although we have not worked on a picture in many years, our personal friendship has continued. Roger is a unique man who marches to a different drummer.

As we moved through the early 1970s, AIP's growth accelerated dramatically. Our pictures were getting bigger and more costly. We moved to more functional offices on Wilshire Boulevard in Beverly Hills, and for greater efficiency had twenty-eight offices out in the field.

Meanwhile, as our company made more costly movies, we attracted greater prestige, credibility, and even more honors, including the Motion Picture Pioneer's Award. When we received the Pioneer's Award, a letter arrived from the governor of California, who himself later moved on to even bigger challenges:

Dear Sam and Jim:
It is pleasant to know that the industry to which I owe so much has chosen to honor two of the men to whom it owes so much.

The state of which I am administrator joins the motion picture community in the pride of your accomplishments. Sam and Jim, the Governor of California congratulates you and wishes you many more years of success, progress and pioneering accomplishment.

Ronald Reagan

Jim and I also decided to take AIP public with 20 percent of the company stock, first offered as an over-the-counter listing, and then moving onto the Pacific Coast Stock Exchange. Jim and his first wife, Sylvia, had divorced in 1966, and in their divorce settlement, she received half of Jim's 345 shares of AIP stock. Jim and I were uneasy about having that much stock in her hands, and Sylvia agreed to sell it.

By going public, we also brought in some capital to help finance our pictures, while still allowing AIP to maintain its independence.

Amid this whirlwind of change, however, Jim began to feel a little awkward. In the aftermath of his divorce decree, Jim and I were no longer equal shareholders at AIP, which made him feel as though he and I were no longer equal partners. Our titles and responsibilities stayed the same, and the company functioned just as it always had. I certainly didn't feel things were any different. But Jim was a sensitive man, and I think he sensed that something had changed.

Jim also appeared uncomfortable with my decision to hire Larry Gordon from Aaron Spelling's company to head up AIP's own production department. Larry was extremely competent and hardworking; he also was feisty and sometimes seemed like Don Quixote, tilting at windmills—or at me (although there was never any rancor between us). Before Larry joined our staff, all the major decisions about our pictures were made exclusively by Jim and me. But as the company grew, we no longer had the time to handle every transaction, although we still maintained overall control, including the right to approve all projects for production. Jim certainly recognized that we needed someone to head up our production department, but even so, he found it hard to delegate responsibility, even to someone as capable as Larry.

Also, in 1966, Jim had married Susan Hart, a young actress who had appeared in several AIP pictures, including *Pajama Party*, *Dr. Goldfoot and the Bikini Machine*, and *The Ghost in the Invisible Bikini*. He genuinely loved and wanted to spend time with Susan and his new son. AIP was growing fast and required a lot of care and feeding. In the early days, we had been able to personally produce many of our pictures; but the expansion of the company forced us to act primarily as executive producers. In his middle fifties, Jim decided he wanted more out of life than long workdays and the administrative responsibilities of running a film company.

So in January 1972, Jim told me he was leaving AIP, with plans to become an independent producer. "I figure I'll produce a couple pictures a year, and have more leisure time," he said. "I've worked since I was a kid. It's time to slow down a bit."

I tried to talk Jim into staying. "Why don't you make the pictures you want to produce here at AIP?" I told him. But he felt it was time for a change of scenery.

So Jim formed his own company, Academy Pictures Corporation, and made a production deal with Twentieth Century-Fox to use Fox's financing for his pictures. AIP purchased all of Jim's shares of common stock to give him some capital for his own company.

In the trades, Fox president Gordon Stulberg stated that by bringing Nicholson on board, the studio might gain some insights into making what he called "exploitation" pictures. Stulberg described Fox as "the first major in town that can get a very good look at this very special area.... We hope to learn from Jim how to turn that area of exhibition into a source of profitable income for Twentieth."

Even after Jim left American International, he and I still met frequently. We remained general partners in a trust over a large number of pictures that we had produced. We would also get together just to talk over what each of us was doing. I had given Jim two projects to take with him that had been in development at AIP, one of which became his first feature, *The Legend of Hell House*. In the Nicholson-Arkoff tradition, it was a very reasonably priced picture.

However, before that movie was ever released—and before he could begin production on the second ex-AIP project, *Dirty Mary Crazy Larry*—Jim's life took a cruel twist. One evening in mid-1972, he became ill at a restaurant on La Cienega Boulevard, suffering what appeared to be a seizure. After doctors ran a series of tests, followed by exploratory brain surgery, they discovered a brain tumor. Jim began undergoing cobalt treatments, but they couldn't arrest the growing cancer. He died on December 10, 1972, at the UCLA Medical Center. He was fifty-six years old.

Jim's death was an immense personal and professional loss for me. We had been as close as brothers for two decades, and although we worked together for long hours, day after day, we never really had an argument. We were equal partners with enormous respect for one another, and we treasured each other's friendship. Susan Hart asked me to give the eulogy at Jim's funeral, which was held at Manchester Chapel at Inglewood Park Cemetery. Besides Susan, he was survived by their son and three daughters by his first marriage.

15

In Hollywood, moviemaking trends come and go with the speed of a quick fadeout. Sometimes, American International Pictures set the trends that the majors followed. At other times, we recognized a fad that we seized upon and rode to success.

In 1972, *Slaughter* became our first entry into black action filmmaking, following on the heels of MGM's giant hit, *Shaft*. We shot *Slaughter* in Mexico City where we could keep our costs to $750,000. Jim Brown starred as a tough government agent and ex-Green Beret out to avenge the gangland murder of his parents, and finds himself on the trail of a crime syndicate and its chief mobster, played by Rip Torn. Like most of these pictures, *Slaughter* was not stingy with violence, with Brown pulverizing a good portion of Central America before the final curtain descends.

Jim Brown plays Slaughter as if he hated doing it, which is to his credit.

—Roger Greenspun, *New York Times*

Slaughter grossed enough to prompt us to produce a sequel, *Slaughter's Big Rip-off*, in 1973. That was followed by a torrent of other pictures of the same genre, including *Black Caesar*, starring Fred Williamson as a Harlem crimelord; *Coffy*, starring Pam Grier as a nurse turned gun-toting avenger; and *Truck Turner*, with Isaac Hayes (who won an Oscar for writing the music for *Shaft*) cast as a superhero who captures bail runners amid a flurry of chases and shootouts.

Although black moviegoers were the primary audience for these pictures, millions of other people saw them, too. "We're getting a cross section of minority groups—including Latinos and Asians—into the theaters," the exhibitors reported. "There are some young whites, too, who seem to enjoy the adventure and the action of these pictures."

Because of the times—a period in which public schools in cities like Boston were being desegregated, and some black militants were resorting to violence—all of us making these black action pictures felt we were treading in a delicate area. Nevertheless, as sensitive as we tried to be, the black films in general, including our own, came under repeated attack. The leader of one black organization, while pleased that the new film genre was providing work for many black actors, called me and complained, "These films don't depict black families. All you're showing is cops and criminals."

I pointed out to him one of the harsh realities of filmmaking. "Audiences just don't go to see pictures about families, whether the families are black or white. Unfortunately, moviegoers aren't drawn to films that show normal family life, unless they are romantic or comedic in nature. That's the situation we're faced with. We need some action on the screen to get people into the theaters."

A lot of splinter groups continued to have an idealized vision of the types of movies we should have been making, but few of these pictures would have been commercial. The bottom line is that the bottom line counts.

Even so, not all of AIP's black action pictures fit the "blaxploitation," guns-and-violence stereotype. We made a black horror comedy called *Blacula*, which starred veteran Shakespearean actor William Marshall as an African prince who tries to persuade Count Dracula to abolish the slave trade, only to fall under the curse of the count. It was written by Joan Torres and Raymond Koenig, and holds a rather unique distinction in the AIP annals: It was one of the few scripts that ever showed up in our office in such good shape that it was virtually ready to shoot. Most screenplays have just a kernel of an idea, and a lot of rethinking and rewriting is necessary. But an agent put *Blacula* on my desk, I read it in one sitting, walked down to Larry Gordon's office, and announced, "Let's make it." It was a campy script with an engaging sense of humor. We made some minor changes to adapt it to the actors and the locations we selected. But it was a remarkably clean script.

Blacula became the first of a series of black horror pictures, including several more from AIP (*Scream Blacula Scream, Sugar Hill*). Paul Maslansky, years before his successful series of *Police Academy* movies, directed one of those horror features. After a decade in Europe as an independent, and AIP's release of his pictures *Death Line* (which we retitled *Raw Meat*) and *Castle of the Living Dead*, he returned to the U.S., looking for work. He showed up in my office, asking for a shot at directing.

I think I surprised Paul with my response. "I want a black comedy horror picture made. See if you can find a script that meets that description. If you can, you can direct it."

Paul uncovered an inexpensive screenplay with a strange name—*Mama Voodoo* or something like that—and he brought it into our office. I knew it would never become our big picture of the year. But I gave him the go-ahead, with a budget of $350,000. It eventually turned into a very successful movie called *Sugar Hill*. Since then, Paul has produced pictures all over Europe, such as *The Russia House* with Sean Connery and Michelle Pfeiffer; I don't know any American producer who can make movies in Europe any better.

Over the years, our black action pictures were consistently successful where it counted, which was at the box office. *Coffy*, which was made for $500,000, grossed more than $2 million in domestic rentals. *Foxy Brown* earned $2.46 million in the U.S. *Truck Turner* grossed $2.23 million domestically.

The pictures that did the best were usually followed by sequels, although that frequently meant doing some creative juggling of plot lines. In 1973, for instance, we made *Black Caesar*, a modern-day version of *Little Caesar* that was positioned to capitalize on the enormous success of the *The Godfather*, which also was released that year. In *Black Caesar*, Fred Williamson played a Godfather-style mobster named Tommy Gibbs ("the cat with the .45 caliber claws"). At the end of the movie, Gibbs is wounded by a policeman, and struggles from midtown Manhattan to Harlem to die. That should have been the end of Gibbs—but when we saw that *Black Caesar* had earned domestic rentals of $2 million, we weren't going to let a minor detail like Gibbs's death get in the way of a sequel!

Through the magic of screenwriting, Gibbs was resurrected in *Hell Up In Harlem*, which (like *Black Caesar*) was written and directed by Larry Cohen. Here's how he handled the sticky dilemma: At the beginning of *Hell Up In Harlem*, Larry again showed a scene of Tommy Gibbs being shot on the streets of Manhattan, but this time, through physical strength and a powerful will to live, he somehow fights his way back to life (one of the white characters comments, "You would need a cannon" to kill Gibbs). Gibbs was once again ready for action, returned from the dead. For ninety-six minutes in *Hell Up In Harlem*, he resumed a lifestyle of crime and chaos, dealing with his enemies with weapons ranging from machine guns to beach umbrella poles.

As popular and prevalent as these black action pictures became, they didn't curtail the ongoing criticism and demands from various black splinter groups over the years. These were not large organizations, and they couldn't boast of much of a constituency. But they were vocal and got our attention.

One of the organizations demanded that AIP channel some of the profits from these movies into black banks. "We also want the right to read and approve every script," one of their representatives told us. "We want to make sure that you aren't putting anything offensive on the screen."

The request, I felt, was absolutely ridiculous. "We've never submitted our scripts to *anyone* for their approval, and I see no reason to start now," I told the organization's leaders. "The minute we give up ground like that, we're opening the door to even more intrusions from outsiders."

Some of our actors like Pam Grier went to bat for us. She had started with AIP as the phone operator on our switchboard, biding her time and ultimately getting the chance to act. She eventually starred in six AIP movies—including *Foxy Brown*, *Bucktown*, *Sheba Baby*, and *Scream Blacula Scream*. And she repeatedly told the press that she took those roles because they showed black women in positions of power. According to Pam, our pictures depicted black women in a positive light.

Nevertheless, the tensions never really subsided, and at one point they actually escalated into violence just days after we had discharged a black publicist from our staff. Like other employees—both white and black—whom we had let go from time to time, this fellow just wasn't doing the job. But apparently he had contacted a couple of the black splinter groups, claiming that he had been discriminated against in his firing. These organizations demanded that we rehire him.

We tried to point out that AIP was aggressively bringing more blacks into the company, particularly as crew members on our pictures. At a time when there weren't many blacks in the Hollywood unions—and when some unions had blatantly closed their membership rolls to minorities—we pushed open the doors for a number of people, helping them get into craft unions like the Directors Guild and Screen Editors Guild. "Remember that most of these films have all-black casts," we told our critics. "Some are directed by black directors and written by black screenwriters."

Still, that apparently wasn't enough for some of the activists. Richard Zimbert, AIP's executive vice president and chief counsel, found that out the hard way. Richard's car was parked in the parking structure of our Wilshire Boulevard offices one evening when we heard—and felt—a huge explosion. By the time we reached the lot, his car was engulfed in flames. It had been firebombed.

Richard's automobile was a total loss. Some of our most outspoken critics asserted that they were in no way involved with the terrorism. No one ever claimed responsibility for the bombing, and the police never found out who did it.

Of all the pictures we made aimed primarily at black audiences, I'm most proud of *Cooley High* and *Cornbread, Earl & Me*. *Cornbread, Earl & Me* was a genuine attempt to reflect what life was like in the black ghetto, with all its pain and frustrations in light of the prejudices of white America. The story revolved around a high school basketball star named Cornbread (played by Keith Wilkes) who lived a crime-free life and won a college scholarship that was to be his "escape" from the ghetto. However, those dreams were shattered when he was gunned down by police officers who mistook him for a rapist. His heartbroken mother worked hard to clear her son's name, although she ran into many obstacles along the way, including a racist police sergeant who repeatedly tried to interfere with the investigation.

[I]t's not every day that we get films that persist in extolling truth and decency even while making a bloody display of the unfairness of life. And judging by the warm-weather fare of the recent past, it isn't likely that this spring and summer will offer too many films that—like *Cornbread*—can appeal to youngsters on a wholesome ethical plane while telling a story that bears some resemblance to life, and death, on real city streets.
—Lawrence Van Gelder, *New York Times*

Cooley High also was a stretch for AIP, much different than the conventional black action pictures for which we were becoming known. It was a property brought to us by Steve Krantz, a producer who made a number of successful pictures for us, including *Heavy Traffic* and *The Nine Lives of Fritz the Cat*. We hired black filmmaker Michael Schultz to direct the picture—the first of his many directorial efforts which eventually included *Car Wash*, *Sgt. Pepper's Lonely Hearts Club Band*, and *Carbon Copy*. The picture was penned by black screenwriter Eric Monte, loosely based on his own experiences growing up in Chicago; Monte also created the TV series, *Good Times*.

Cooley High is the story of a group of kids at a vocational high school in Chicago. One of them (played by Glynn Turman) loves poetry and wins a college scholarship, despite having just about the worst grades of any student west of the Mississippi, and hopes to make a career as a Hollywood screenwriter; most of his classmates, however, are more interested in drinking, cutting classes, and joyriding. Turman and his basketball-playing buddy (Lawrence Hilton-Jacobs) share a host of real-life adolescent experiences, from cutting classes to drinking wine to enjoying their first loves.

[*Cooley High*] shows what the black American can be when creative talents are given an opportunity free of the strong sex-and-violence requirements of exploitation pictures. A bittersweet, nostalgic coming-of-age drama inspired by its writer Eric Monte's own experiences.
—Kevin Thomas, *Los Angeles Times*

> Though [*Cooley High*] parallels *American Graffiti*...[it] is in its own right a superior film. Impressively written by Eric Monte and directed with an almost unwavering sense of pace by Michael Schultz...*Cooley High* is good history, good entertainment and good art.
> —Lawrence Van Gelder, *New York Times*

At about the same time AIP was enjoying success with the black action pictures, we tapped into another genre—martial arts movies—that was quite successful for us in the early seventies. Many of these movies were filmed in the Far East, with directors (Chien Lung, Heang Feng) and stars (Wang Yu, Chang Yi, Angela Mao) whose names meant nothing to American audiences. They all featured innumerable karate fights—so many of them that the plot lines themselves were almost an afterthought.

We produced and/or distributed more than a dozen of these "kung fu" pictures—*Screaming Tiger*, *Deep Thrust—the Hand of Death*, *Shanghai Killers*, and *Bamboo Gods and Iron Men* among others. Some of them tried to break the monotony of the karate fights by instilling some comedic scenes, but most of the jokes got lost in the translation. Perhaps we needed Woody Allen to liven up the comedic dialogue, applying the same approach he had used in *What's Up, Tiger Lily?*

Deep Thrust was a takeoff on *Deep Throat*, which in 1972 had become the most famous pornographic film of all time. But if someone who paid to see *Deep Thrust* was expecting to see Asia's answer to Linda Lovelace, they were seriously disappointed. Yes, there was an attractive female kung fu expert in the picture, but she didn't do anything kinkier than propel a well-aimed right foot into the midsection of her opponents. In one scene, a martial arts combatant jams his fingers *through* the belly of one of his enemies; as one of my employees quipped, "That's about the only penetration the audience is going to see in this movie."

Golden Needles emerged as one of our most successful martial arts pictures, although we were hoping it would fare even better at the box office. It was produced by Fred Weintraub and Paul Heller, who had an enormous hit in 1973 with Bruce Lee's *Enter the Dragon*. At the time I had lunch with Weintraub and Heller, they had only an idea for *Golden Needles*—no script and, in fact, not even a one-sentence synopsis in writing. But they intended to bring back *Enter the Dragon* director Robert Clouse for the new picture, and they described a plot line that intrigued me—combining a martial arts theme with a *Maltese Falcon*-type search for a Sung Dynasty gold statuette that promises either healing powers or death. Joe Don Baker was eventually hired for the lead, and I thought the picture might work. True, I knew that the popularity of kung fu was not going to last forever, but we might sneak *Golden Needles* in before the trend was knocked out of the ring for good.

The picture was budgeted at under $1 million, with a month long shooting schedule in Hong Kong. The script called for a ship to be destroyed and sunk, and we located an old one for that purpose. Unfortunately, before it could even be delivered to us, it unexpectedly sunk! (This reaffirmed my belief that using ships in movies is an invitation to disaster; today, I would never put as much as a canoe in any picture.)

With the ship at the bottom of the ocean, Clouse had to do some scrambling. At the last minute, the script had to be frantically rewritten. The picture never became a blockbuster, but because we sold it to network television hungry to cash in on the kung fu craze, we made a substantial profit on the picture.

In 1977, AIP used Chuck Norris, a karate expert-turned-actor, to help exploit still another popular trend—citizens-band radios—in the picture *Breaker! Breaker!* I was approached by a young producer-director named Don Hulette, who had shot portions of an action film and needed some money to finish it. I looked at his footage, and thought it was interesting but not earth-shaking. It did have a hook, however. In the picture, Norris portrays a truck driver who is extricated from a sticky situation when CB communications alert other truckers to come to his rescue.

At the time, I wasn't even aware that Norris had won international attention as a karate champion. I was much more interested in the CB radios, which were a hot trend that I figured we could exploit. I put up $100,000 so Hulette could finish the movie, gave it the title *Breaker! Breaker!*, and when it was released, we had a hit on our hands, primarily because of Norris's own fame, even though it was his first picture.

Freddie Fields, the producer/agent who made pictures like *Looking for Mr. Goodbar* and *American Gigolo*, was making a CB radio movie of his own at the same time, with a much larger budget and a more distinguished cast. Fields called me, trying to talk me into delaying the release of *Breaker! Breaker!* so his movie could be issued first. "We'll help create the market that your picture can capitalize on," he said.

I didn't buy his argument, however, and we released our picture on schedule. Norris's name value was much more than I had imagined, and the movie did extremely well. By the time Fields's film was issued, the CB craze was already on a downward slide. Although his picture cost much more to make, ours outgrossed his many times over.

As I had suspected, the martial arts craze and, even more so, the CB fad were short-lived. Even the moviegoers who flocked to see what the genres offered began to realize that the karate films in particular were all starting to look alike. Frankly, I began to feel exactly the same way. After a dozen martial arts films, I had seen enough kicks, jabs, thrusts, punches, pokes, jabs, chops, jumps, and leaps to last me a lifetime. It was time to put down our black belt and move on to something else.

16

Throughout the 1970s, AIP's steady growth continued. We were producing and/or distributing about twenty to twenty-five pictures a year, and as both the workload and our staff increased in size, I was forced to entrust more of the day-to-day oversight of many of our pictures to others in the company. Nevertheless, AIP continued to run smoothly, even though our expansion became the butt of occasional, good-natured jokes.

In 1975, for instance, at a dinner at the Beverly Hilton Hotel, director-writer Hal Kanter told the crowd that he had conducted a personal survey so he would be well-prepared for the remarks he would make about me that night. "I discovered that nineteen out of twenty people had never heard of Sam Arkoff," Hal quipped. "What's impressive is that I conducted the survey in the offices of AIP!"

When I took the podium, and gazed out upon the packed ballroom I commented, "Leon Blender, AIP's sales-distribution executive vice president, tells me that we had three pictures back in 1955 that never drew this big an attendance anywhere!" The line got a laugh, but it wasn't stretching the truth by very much.

In the seventies, as AIP had done since the early days, I continued to give opportunities to young actors and directors who I felt showed promise. Ivan Reitman was one of them. Long before Ivan directed *Ghostbusters*, *Stripes*, *Legal Eagles*, and *Twins*, I met him in Cannes. He had called me at my hotel, introduced himself over the phone, and seemed almost desperate to meet me. "I've made a picture called *Cannibal Girls*," he said, "and I'm having trouble finding a distributor for it. I'd sure like you to look at it."

Reitman was a talented young Canadian who had made *Cannibal Girls* for less than $100,000, which was quite a feat for 1973. It starred two young comedians, Eugene Levy and Andrea Martin, who later made names for themselves on *SCTV* and *Saturday Night Live*. In Ivan's satirical picture, Levy and Martin investigate the legend of a group of female cannibals who live in the small town where the pair arrives for a weekend of romance.

I thought the picture was funny, and, on the spot, said, "Sure, we'll take it. I'd like to distribute it in the Western Hemisphere (except Canada, of course)." Ivan and I shook hands, and his career got an enormous boost.

Reitman brought me David Cronenberg, another aspiring Canadian director anxious to make his first picture. David wanted to call it *Shivers*; we suggested *It Came From Within*, a more horrific title. It was a well-made picture, and David's directorial debut, followed later by movies like *Scanners*, *The Dead Zone* and *The Fly*. Cronenberg has a very distinctive style and a genuine feel for the macabre.

John Milius was another filmmaking newcomer who achieved an important breakthrough at AIP. Milius had worked for us for a couple years immediately after he had graduated from U.S.C. film school, doing a variety of odd jobs while launching his screenwriting career for us. In 1969, he, Willard Huyck and James Gordon White collaborated on a screenplay, *The Devil's 8*, a *Dirty Dozen*-type picture that Burt Topper directed for AIP. Before long, Milius had struck paydirt with the major studios, too, establishing himself as the writer of star roles such as *Jeremiah Johnson* for Robert Redford and *The Life and Times of Judge Roy Bean* for Paul Newman. For the latter screenplay, he was paid a whopping $300,000. Nevertheless, John wasn't content with solely screenwriting. As he approached his thirtieth birthday, he wanted a shot at directing, too.

Larry Gordon and I had been talking about making a picture about John Dillinger. We knew about Milius's desire to direct, and so as we planned *Dillinger*, Larry said, "Let's see if we can get John to write the script; if we like it, we'll let him direct."

Larry approached Milius, asking if he'd be interested in writing the script for *Dillinger* for us.

"You don't have enough money to pay what I ask for a screenplay," John told him, showing no modesty.

"Well," Larry added, "if the script is good, you can direct the picture."

That was all Milius needed to hear. He was finally being offered a chance to direct.

When Larry told Milius's agent that we would pay only a fraction of Milius's going price for the screenplay, as well as for directing, the agent refused to accept the offer. Even after he talked to Milius, the agent couldn't believe that John wanted the deal. But Milius couldn't wait to get started.

Warren Oates was cast as John Dillinger, with a supporting cast that included Ben Johnson, Michelle Phillips, Cloris Leachman, and Harry Dean Stanton. Richard Dreyfuss had a small part as Baby Face Nelson. *Dillinger* was shot in the heart of Oklahoma in typical AIP fashion, cutting corners whenever we could. The crew, in fact, had bought a lot full of old automobiles that Warren Oates and the others drove in the picture. When the filming was done, part of the set was turned into a used car lot, selling the vehicles for a profit to the townspeople. Those locals paid extra to get their hands on an automobile that had been filled with bullet holes during the filming of a Hollywood motion picture.

On *Dillinger*, we assigned Buzz Feitshans to represent us on the set. Buzz's father, Fred, had been an editor for us for years, and when Buzz became an apprentice editor, we took him into the AIP family. He also served as my projectionist for screenings at my home. Buzz proved himself so ably on *Dillinger* that we ultimately gave him producer credit on the picture. John Milius was just as impressed, and asked Buzz to produce many Milius films. Today, Buzz is still a senior producer in Hollywood.

What is extraordinary [in *Dillinger*] is the finesse of the shoot-outs and glory-dying, a nuance or two beyond even Sam Peckinpah. And there is one scene, of the gang trapped in a roomy mansion raked by FBI gunfire, that is one of the most beautiful action sequences I've ever seen, a symphony of splintering wood, crashing glass and hysterically scampering figures in voluminous, smoky interiors. Whether we owe the splendor of this sequence to Milius or to cinematographer Jules Brenner I don't know, but it's a zinger.

—Peter Schjeldahl, *New York Times*

Dillinger got some additional attention in a 1976 AIP picture called *Dragonfly*, which starred Susan Sarandon and Beau Bridges, and was directed by Gilbert Cates. Bridges played a fellow who had been released from an insane asylum. He thought he had killed his mother, but finds out that she's alive and is the one who had him committed.

In one scene, Bridges goes to a movie theater, where the picture that's playing is so violent that he becomes physically ill. It was an important scene in the plot because it confirmed that this man was probably incapable of a violent act since he couldn't even stand to see violence on the screen.

Gil Cates had to find a piece of film for Bridges to view in the theater. Because he was working with such a low budget, Gil asked me, "Can I go into AIP's archives, and see what I can find?" He pulled out *Dillinger*, selecting a violent scene from that picture as the one that made Bridges sick. For moviegoers who knew AIP pictures well, it turned into a real tongue-in-cheek scene.

Cates is a terrific piece of manpower, not only a good director, but also a two-term president of the Directors Guild, the director of the Academy Awards show, and a big man at the UCLA film school. It's always bothered me that we only found one piece of material, *Dragonfly*, that we both cared for enough to work on together. But there is still time.

Even after Jim Nicholson left AIP, I insisted on sticking to some of the basic principles that helped launch the company back in the fifties. Jim was no longer there to contribute the great titles that he was so adept at creating, but that didn't change the attention we gave to this critical element of a picture's success. So in the seventies, AIP made or released pictures with names like *The Incredible Melting Man*, *The Devil Within Her*, *Tentacles*, and *Empire of the Ants*. They were titles with clarity, that grabbed the audience's attention, piqued their curiosity, and lured them to the box office in large numbers.

Even today, many of my filmmaking colleagues still don't seem to feel as strongly about the value of a good title as I do. For instance, when Steven Spielberg titled one of his recent pictures, *Arachnophobia*, I was surprised. The picture had a budget of more than $20 million, yet very little thinking must have gone into the choice of a title. By the name *Arachnophobia* alone, I'm convinced that most of the American public had no idea what the picture was about, at least not in the vital, early days of release when a title should grab the public from the moment they hear it. Back in the early days of AIP, we made a move called *The Spider* for $100,000. The title couldn't have been any clearer. If we had named it *Arachnophobia*, half of our audience probably would have figured we had made a movie about Greeks!

As AIP's pictures got bigger and our budgets became more "respectable," by necessity I became more daring as a businessman. Although I might have preferred to maneuver with the parachute fully deployed, leaving the free falls to the more adventurous in the industry, risk-taking is part of the moviemaking game. Every time you make a picture, you're taking a chance. Even so, I would tell my staff, "I'm still a pessimist in an optimist's business. Let's try to minimize the company's risk whenever we produce a new movie."

Toward that end, we'd still rely on some of the same distribution strategies that we had used in the early days with our combinations. We'd start out with perhaps one-hundred prints and ship them out to three territories, testing the movie with different audiences. Based on the box office returns, we'd evaluate what we had. When we were disappointed with the results, we'd make some changes.

That's what happened in 1974 when we distributed *Walking Tall*, a picture produced by Charles Pratt and made by Bing Crosby Productions. The film was based on a true story of a Tennessee sheriff named Buford Pusser who succeeded in a one-man crusade against local prostitution, gambling, and bootlegging by employing his own strong-arm tactics. We released the movie in three testing areas—in Tennessee, as well as in cities in the Southwest and in the Northwest.

The picture opened on a Wednesday, and by Friday, we could already see that the grosses were not what we had hoped for, particularly since we felt that *Walking Tall* was a very strong picture. We reviewed the artwork promoting the picture, and decided that the problem might lie right there. It depicted Pusser with a gun in his hand. We felt that we needed something even more eye-opening.

"Rework the art a little," we told our artist. "Take out the gun from the ad and put a baseball bat in the sheriff's hand. That's an image most people don't associate with an enforcer of law and order."

With the support of the revamped advertising, we released *Walking Tall* in three other regions. It was like sending out a different movie. We more than doubled the box office receipts, thanks to a relatively simple change in the advertising campaign; so instead of facing a box office disaster, we had a very successful picture and two successful sequels. A lot of "auteurs" don't like to face the fact that, to some degree, the motion picture industry is a trial-and-error business.

During the seventies, I took AIP into some areas that we had rarely—if ever—tread in before. One of them was X-rated animation features. In 1973, producer Steve Krantz and animator Ralph Bakshi made *Heavy Traffic* for us, the story of a white kid growing up in the Brownsville section of Brooklyn who spends most of his time drawing cartoons in his apartment. He finally escapes to the streets, where most of his energies are spent trying to lose his virginity. The language was graphic; so was the eroticism. But the picture also had a real creative flair, some wonderful humor, and an effective combination of animation and live actors.

The X-rating was ridiculous; after all, this was an animated picture. Certainly, it wasn't made for children, but it was a high-class feature. Even so, the rating didn't seem to hurt us at the box office, where the picture did very well. It was probably the best of the genre of X-rated animated movies.

Bakshi's *Heavy Traffic* is rated X, not because it's pornographic in any way but because it employs the small gestures and words of obscenity to make its rude statement about the quality of what might be dangerously described as the New York Experience...*Heavy Traffic* may well turn out to be the most original American film of the year.

—Vincent Canby, *New York Times*

The following year, we made a sequel to Bakshi's 1972 feature, *Fritz the Cat*. (AIP had taken over the Bakshi film after its initial release when its distributor went out of business.) The sequel was another

The Arkoffs and the Nicholsons at the Venice Airport on their way to the 1966 Venice Film Festival showing of *The Wild Angels,* From left: Susan and James Nicholson, our son, Louis, me and my wife, Hilda, with our daughter, Donna. Over Donna's right shoulder is Fulvio Lucisano, with whom AIP coproduced approximately twenty-five movies in Italy.

Woody Allen got his start with AIP in his classic 1966 redo of an existing Japanese spy film.

Jack Nicholson was involved in two of AIP's landmark hippie/druggie movies. He wrote the screenplay to *The Trip* (1967) and starred with Dean Stockwell in *Psych-Out* (1968).

Cher in her first straight acting role, *Chastity* (1969), written for her by Sonny Bono.

Hot on the heels of their stardom in *The Graduate* and *Midnight Cowboy*, we put together two earlier films that Dustin Hoffman and Jon Voight had made in Europe as unknowns.

Shelley Winters as Ma Barker in *Bloody Mama* (1970), with her brood, (from left) Don Stroud, Robert Walden, Clint Kimbrough, and Robert De Niro (in his first "mainstream" film).

Our two two-headed movies: *The Incredible Two-Headed Transplant* (1971) and *The Thing With Two Heads* (1972).

Unlikely bikers Bette Davis and Ernest Borgnine in *Bunny O'Hare* (1972).

At a Variety Club International convention in London in 1972: actress Susan Hart and husband James Nicholson, Hammer Films' Sir James Carreras and his wife, and Sam and Hilda Arkoff.

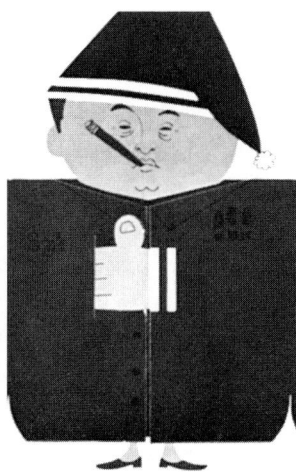

Several of the Arkoff New Year's cards through the years: I call the 1985 one (top right) "an ass on an ass."

Some of our monster movies of the 1970s: A very popular double bill and a scene from *Godzilla vs. the Smog Monster.*

Vincent Price was one of AIP's top stars from *House of Usher* in 1960 through *Dr. Phibes Rises Again* in 1972.

We got noted Shakespearean actor William Marshall to star as Blacula in two films in the early seventies, merging the then-popular "blaxploitation" craze with horror movies.

After Jim's departure from AIP, I produced this 1974 animated sequel to Ralph Bakshi's *Fritz the Cat*.

Hilda and I in London at a Variety Club International gala with Prince Philip in 1974.

Jodie Foster, then just thirteen, starred with Martin Sheen in AIP's *The Little Girl Who Lives Down the Lane* (1976).

Here's Joan Collins (above) long before she started vamping as Alexis Carrington on *Dynasty*, at the mercy of some oversize creatures in *Empire of the Ants* (1977).

George Hamilton and Susan Saint James in *Love at First Bite* (1979), AIP's popular Dracula spoof.

Margot Kidder and James Brolin in our latter day horror hit, *The Amityville Horror* (1979).

Angie Dickinson and Michael Caine in *Dressed to Kill* (1980), one of the last pictures actually made by AIP.

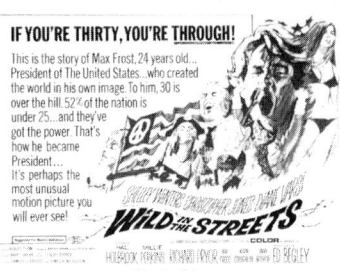

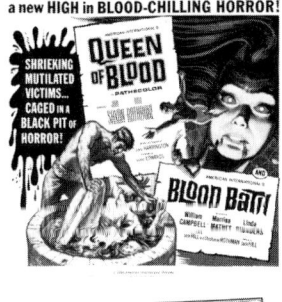

An AIP movie-ad retrospect with some of the company's memorable product through the years.

Cheers from Sam and Hild

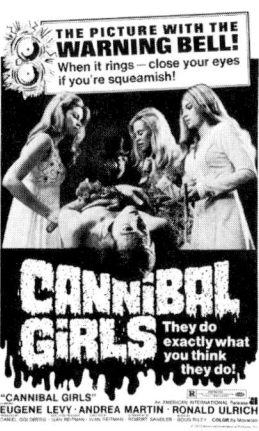

animated picture, this one called *The Nine Lives of Fritz the Cat*. Steve Krantz produced and Robert Taylor directed. But to call it a disappointment would be philanthropic. It just didn't have the energy and the spirit of the original. It received an R-rating, but was not well-received by either critics or moviegoers, even at the Cannes Film Festival where it had been entered in competition. Every picture you release can't be a winner, and this one certainly falls into the second tier of AIP features. In fact, the film would have needed nine lives just to recoup all the money we had hoped to make with the picture, but didn't!

Despite features like *Heavy Traffic*, explicit movies have never really been AIP's forte. When we did distribute foreign films that were on the sexy side, we often did so under the name "Transamerican." I just felt that some of these pictures were a little bolder than those I wanted to have our own name attached to. But after two years of using the Transamerican name, we got a surprise in the mail from Louis Nizer, the eminent attorney, informing me that the Transamerica Corporation had just bought United Artists. Even though the names were not identical, and even though Transamerica had never been in the motion picture business until it bought U.A., Nizer now insisted that we could no longer attach Transamerican to our pictures.

I thought it was a ridiculous claim, and expressed that sentiment rather firmly in a phone conversation with Nizer. "Look, Sam," he said, "next time you're in New York, stop by my office. Maybe we can work this out."

Nizer knew I was an attorney, and at that meeting in his office two weeks later, he seemed to be trying to impress me. He had a parade of young male and female lawyers drifting into and out of his office, entering and exiting from multiple doors, carrying files, contracts, casebooks, and documents that allegedly supported his claim that AIP needed to divest itself of the Transamerican name.

"Sam, we've done all the research and the preliminary legal work," Nizer said, sitting behind his desk on an elevated platform intended to make him look a bit taller and more intimidating than he really was. "I'd sure hate for this to end up in court. But my client wants to do whatever it takes to protect its name."

I was unmoved. Nizer's putting on a good show, I thought to myself, but he's not going to change my mind.

"Go ahead and sue!" I said. "Our name is as important to us as yours is to you!"

Of course, I was hoping Nizer would say something like, "We'll give you $2 million not to use the name anymore." In fact, I would have settled for $1 million! But no such luck. Instead, the meeting ended in a stalemate and a polite handshake.

In the ensuing days and weeks, I waited for Nizer to make the next move—but he never did. I presume he advised his client that a lawsuit wouldn't get anyone anywhere, and the whole matter was dropped.

Still, there were plenty of other controversies and problems that needed my attention. Even though AIP was doing a lot of things right in the seventies and had earned the respect of most exhibitors, I recognized that some theater-owners still viewed us as the "little guy on the block" whom they could target for abuse. One evening, with my patience running on empty, I gave hell to a roomful of exhibitors during my keynote address at the convention of the National Association of Theatre Owners of Texas. I tried to keep the tone light and maintain some degree of humor. But at the same time, I made my point forcefully, accusing them of not providing an accurate count at the box office, thus keeping AIP and other film companies from getting back a fair return on our investment.

"If some of you exhibitors would stop crying and start paying distributors what they are honestly entitled to for their pictures, everyone would profit," I told them. "It is shameful that it is still necessary for distributors to spend huge sums each year policing some of you whom we do business with just to get a fair count at the box office.

"We are happy you are so prosperous and that your concession stands are so profitable, but the time has come for you to pay your fair share of the cost of producing and distributing motion pictures. Otherwise, I warn you, there suddenly won't be—can't be—enough pictures to keep your theaters open."

I received some polite applause at the end of the speech. As expected, the exhibitors who came up to me afterward *all* insisted it was "the other guy" who wasn't giving AIP accurate numbers. Some of them even thanked me for raising the issue. "A lot of your colleagues with the same complaint give their story anonymously to the trades," one of the exhibitors said. "I appreciate you being so up-front with us."

During this same time, I was also becoming increasingly concerned about the skyrocketing amounts of money spent by the studios on their pictures, in part because these bigger budgets forced AIP to increase our own budgets to keep pace, even though we never came close to their "sky's-the-limit" spending. I saw the runaway spending as something of a Titanic mentality. And as usual, I didn't keep my ideas to myself.

In 1976, at a press conference in Los Angeles, I warned that the film industry's inflated budgets had placed it on a suicidal course. "If we can't get these film budgets under control in the next few years, we're ultimately going to see a financial debacle in Hollywood," I said. "The major studios are spending ten to fifteen million on picture after picture. This can't go on forever. There just isn't an endless source for those kinds of dollars."

Before long, however, the industry was boosted—at least for the time being—by ancillaries like home video and cable TV that provided new money from different media. Both the studios and the independents continued to make ever bigger budget pictures throughout the eighties, ignoring the signs of distress in the industry.

Stars who demand exorbitant salaries, of course, are a major reason for the escalating cost of moviemaking. But while the studios were all but offering their prized actors blank checks, AIP was holding the line. In many instances, our pictures in the 1970s featured ambitious young actors who got their first real exposure through our films—before their asking price reached colossal proportions. Margot Kidder starred in Brian De Palma's *Sisters*, a 1973 AIP horror picture. In 1975, Nick Nolte and Don Johnson starred in *Return to Macon County*, the first lead roles of their careers. The picture was a sequel to *Macon County Line*, a big success for AIP in 1974, produced, written by, and starring Max Baer Jr. Baer didn't want to become involved in the follow-up picture, so we found another project for him (*The McCullochs*), and looked for a couple of fresh faces to star in *Return to Macon County*. My son, Louis, who was the picture's executive in charge of production, cast Nolte and Johnson in the movie, giving Nolte the leading role based on his intense and magnetic look, since his credits, even at age thirty-five, were minimal.

In other AIP pictures, Jodie Foster starred in *The Little Girl Who*

Lives Down the Lane, released in 1977 on the heels of *Taxi Driver*. Melanie Griffith, Keith Carradine, and Desi Arnaz Jr. teamed up in our 1977 movie, *Joyride*. Joan Collins, four years before she turned into the wicked lady on *Dynasty*, starred in *Empire of the Ants*, another 1977 picture.

If the planet earth could keep finding oil like American International gets film plots from the literary lode of H. G. Wells, the energy crisis would be over. The latest Wells-inspired exploitationer is *Empire of the Ants*, an above-average Bert I. Gordon effort about ants that grow big after munching on radioactive waste.

—Variety

In *Empire of the Ants*, Joan Collins is attacked and devoured by an army of crazed ants—a scenario that intrigued David Letterman not long ago. When I was scheduled as a guest on Letterman's late-night show, he asked me to bring some footage of Collins's awesome battle with the man-eating (or in this case, woman-eating) ants to show on the air. Unfortunately, however, the Screen Actors Guild had instituted a ruling—which I never did understand—that in older pictures like this, the actor or actress would need to grant permission before TV could reprise a scene from the film. And when I asked Joan, she refused to give us the go-ahead. "It's just not dignified," she explained.

What could I say, "Joan, you've not always done things that were dignified"? Nevertheless, she refused to change her mind. Letterman and I had to get by without scenes of the crazed giant insects feasting on the sultry star.

At times, although I generally found it offensive to pay for big-name stars, AIP would stretch our budget a little to corral an actor with name value, although we still always seemed to get them for less money than what they were used to making. John Huston, Henry Fonda and Shelley Winters headlined our 1977 picture *Tentacles*, which was our response to *Jaws* and all the other movies that brought terror to the depths of the oceans. And for *Hennessy*, a 1975 thriller, we had a strong cast of Rod Steiger, Lee Remick—and Queen Elizabeth II as an unpaid "extra"!

In *Hennessy*, Steiger plays a man plotting to assassinate the Queen in revenge for the accidental shooting deaths of his family members in a street battle between the IRA and the British army in Belfast; his plan is to detonate himself as a human bomb as the Queen speaks before Parliament. Originally, the movie was a project of British Lion, which invited us to join the production; we would distribute in the Western Hemisphere, they would take the Eastern Hemisphere. I was initially anxious, more on behalf of British Lion than us because of the sensitive nature of the subject matter.

"Are you sure you really want to make a movie about an assassination attempt on the Queen?" I asked Barry Spikings of British Lion. He insisted there was nothing to worry about. After all, there had been a successful book and movie, *Day of the Jackal*, about an assassination attempt on DeGaulle; Spikings didn't figure there would be any problem with the Queen. So we committed ourselves to the project.

Before long, however, the board of directors of British Lion developed a bad case of weak knees. They decided that a movie about a plot to blow up the Queen might be a public relations disaster in England. I had tried to tell them the same thing weeks earlier. They ultimately spelled out their change of heart in a terse note to me that said, "We're bowing out."

Since we had already cast the movie, AIP decided to move ahead without British Lion, completing the picture on our own. As production continued, we were lucky enough to locate some newsreel footage of the Queen speaking before Parliament, in which she apparently reacted to a noise or commotion in the chambers, turning her head quickly with a quizzical look on her face. "If we splice this news footage into the picture," I told our production crew, "it wil look as though she is reacting to Steiger as he makes his way toward her. And that's exactly what we want."

The concluding sequence is fascinating for the shrewd way in which the fictional footage has been intercut with the newsreel footage, which it perfectly matches. Unless you pay close attention, it does

seem as if Elizabeth II looks up from the prepared text of her speech to glower benignly at the interruption caused by the two-footed bomb.
—Vincent Canby, *New York Times*

When the movie was completed, we routinely sent it to the British film review board for its stamp of approval—but never heard a word. Finally, I called, and was connected to a board member, who didn't bear particularly cheery news. "We are quite troubled by this picture," he told me. "It looks as though the Queen is acting in your picture. And we just find that unacceptable."

I pulled a letter out of my files, which we had written to Buckingham Palace, explaining that we were making the movie, and asking them to contact us if they had any objections. A copy of the script had been sent to the palace as well. In fact, we never heard back from the Queen or her staff.

To try to resolve the issue for good, I retained a barrister in London who arranged for me to meet with one of the Queen's aides—a Lord, as I recall. I flew to London, and on the day of the meeting, my British counsel apparently got nervous about standing up to the Royal Family, and backed out. So I was ushered into Buckingham Palace alone, where I was greeted and offered tea by at least a dozen attendants. Finally, I was escorted into my meeting with the aide.

"I must confess," he said, "that we do fear that the public will believe that the Queen has agreed to be in your picture, which is about an assassination attempt on her own life. I'm sure you can understand how uncomfortable this would be for Her Majesty."

I was becoming pretty uncomfortable myself. We talked and politely disagreed for more than an hour. Finally, I proposed a compromise. "We'll put a disclaimer at the beginning of the movie, stating that neither the Queen nor anyone in the Royal Family participated in any way in the making of this picture. We'll also note that we've used newsreel footage, and that the story is purely fiction."

Happily, he found my suggestion totally acceptable. We had another round of tea to celebrate the resolution of the crisis.

Hennessy was now cleared by the Queen's staff, but that didn't end our problems. EMI, which was the distributor of AIP's movies in England for many years, suddenly was overcome by a need to protect

Her Majesty. Bernard Delfont, an immigrant to the U.K. who headed EMI (and who had just been made a Lord in his own right), went directly to the press without first consulting me, and announced that his company was "a defender of the Palace. We will not distribute *Hennessy*." Delfont called the other major circuit in England, the Rank Organization, and convinced them it would be a mistake to distribute the picture. Rank joined EMI in what I perceived as a boycott.

"It looks like we're going to be playing drugstores," I told reporters. Eventually, we fared a little better than that, but not by much, playing in the Paramount Theater in the West End, and then finally in a few other movie houses affiliated with one of the minor chains. To make me feel at home, one of them put the word "Drugstore" up on its marquee, took a picture of it and sent it to me! Thank God the movie did reasonably well in the rest of the world.

The problems were different but no less hectic the following year when AIP jumped into production of *A Matter of Time*, a picture budgeted at $5 million. The project was brought to AIP by Jack Skirball, an independent producer, and the movie had a wonderful, strong cast—Liza Minnelli, Ingrid Bergman, and Charles Boyer. I had met Liza, who wanted to give her father Vincente another picture to direct, which would also be the first time father and daughter had worked together. Over the years Vincente Minnelli had become one of Hollywood's most respected directors. But by the time he directed *A Matter of Time* in 1976, he was past his prime, and as a result, I think the picture suffered. It turned out to be his last movie.

A Matter of Time was the story of a girl (played by Liza) from the Italian provinces who works as a chambermaid in a Rome hotel, and is befriended by an elderly contessa (Bergman). It was a coproduction with an Italian film company headed by Giulio Sbarigia, and we each put up half the money. The picture was shot in Rome and Venice, where the production costs would be less.

Vincente hadn't worked on a film in six years—since *On a Clear Day You Can See Forever*. A couple of my friends in Hollywood warned me, "He hasn't done a picture in a number of years. Be careful what you're getting yourself into. When he was making the big musicals, MGM surrounded him with the best cameramen and the best set designers. All of them knew what the pictures needed without even asking him. He probably won't have that kind of support in Italy."

With that advice in mind, I was initially hesitant to hire Vincente for *A Matter of Time*. But I found him, at age sixty-six, to be a charming man who I felt might be able to pull this picture together. I thought it was worth the risk.

Almost immediately after the shooting began in Rome, the production fell behind schedule. When I was on the set, Vincente would talk endlessly about the sets and the costumes, but he just couldn't seem to pull the picture together. As a result, the production began to flounder. I tried to talk to him a few times—"Vincente, I think you need to take stronger control of the picture; these actors need more guidance from you."

Our original shooting schedule was fourteen weeks—long by AIP standards. But it dragged on for many additional weeks, with corresponding increases in the picture's cost (most of which, fortunately, were borne by our Italian partner in the coproduction since our investment was contractually fixed). Once the shooting was mercifully completed, Vincente had more problems in the editing room. When I looked at the first edit of the movie, it was difficult to follow and much too long. I had several meetings with Vincente, but his final cut wasn't much of an improvement. I began to look for another way to salvage the project.

At one point, Liza sent her then-husband, Jack Haley Jr., to discuss the future of the picture with me. Haley had earned a reputation as a magician in the editing room, particularly in assembling *That's Entertainment!* By the end of our meeting, I told him, "Why don't you see what you can do with the picture. Maybe you can save it." Haley went to work on the picture, although we never publicly announced his involvement in the movie. However, despite Haley's best efforts, even he couldn't rescue it.

Poor Liza. Poor Vincente. Poor us.

Because *A Matter of Time* has moments of real visual beauty, and because what the characters say to each other is mostly dumb, it may be a film to attend while wearing your earplugs.

—Vincent Canby, *New York Times*

Fortunately, for every *A Matter of Time*, there have been a dozen or more pictures that I can look back on with pride and fondness. One of the best was *Love at First Bite*, which many people in Hollywood considered a surprise hit. After all, spoofs in the horror genre usually don't work, but this one certainly did. Back in the 1960s, AIP had tried the satirical approach with some of our Poe pictures, and had gotten away with it. But many horror movies are spoofs or put-ons anyway. Satirizing them is redundant.

Love at First Bite was a zany lampooning of the Dracula myth. The picture was originated by the late screenwriter Robert Kaufman and George Hamilton, who made a deal with Melvin Simon, a shopping center developer who was dabbling in films. I agreed to assume half of the cost of the $3 million production in return for the distribution rights and a share of the ownership. I thought we had an agreement.

Kaufman went to work on the script. He had written several pictures for AIP, including *Ski Party*, *Dr. Goldfoot and the Bikini Machine*, and *Dr. Goldfoot and the Bikini Bombs*. When I read the finished screenplay for this new picture, I thought Bob had done an excellent job, creating enough gags to, well, leave the audience screaming. The story revolved around a blasé New York City that doesn't seem to care about the presence of Dracula (played by George Hamilton). Dracula had moved into the Plaza Hotel after being driven out of his Translvanian castle by the Romanian Communist government, making room for a training facility for the country's gymnastics team. Trying to survive on the mean streets of New York, Dracula has experiences that he never had to deal with back home, like becoming drunk on the blood of a wino on skid row.

Milt Goldstein, an executive with Simon's company, and I were having problems. We had an oral agreement but by the time the contracts were drawn up and ready to sign, he wanted to change the terms of the agreement, taking away part of our ownership and distribution rights. I told him, "The deal's off unless we return to the original terms." We were at a stalemate, with neither side willing to give in.

Meanwhile, Stan Dragoti, a former advertising executive who later directed *Mr. Mom*, was hired to direct the picture, and Goldstein took the movie into production. As the picture was nearing completion, Goldstein tried to interest the majors in the movie; but upon looking at the film after the first cut, the studios unanimously found nothing worth pursuing.

Goldstein was becoming frustrated, and finally told Kaufman, "I'm tired of negotiating. I'm going to sell the picture directly to television." For Kaufman, who considered this his picture, Goldstein's decision might as well have been to set fire to the negative. I was at the Regency Hotel in New York when Kaufman called me. He was furious and on the brink of hysteria. "Sam, this picture deserves theatrical release," he said. "You have to take a look at it. Something's got to be done before Goldstein markets it as a movie-for-TV."

I phoned Goldstein and asked for a print of the picture so I could screen it. "Forget it, Sam," he said. "You're not going to see the picture unless you agree to take the picture on my terms."

I refused. "I made a different deal with you before you *changed* the terms."

I got back in touch with Kaufman, who still wanted me to look at the picture. Unfortunately, however, the film was being edited at MGM. "Bob, I don't quite know how we can work this out," I told him. "It would be something of a Mission Impossible to sneak me onto the MGM lot to screen the movie. I'm not exactly inconspicuous."

Kaufman reluctantly agreed. "That mug of yours—let alone your bulk—is too recognizable," he finally said. "Who else can you send in to preview it for you?"

We finally agreed on Jere Henshaw, AIP's head of production. "Jere's a bit bulky, too," I said, "but he isn't as portly as me."

Three days later, Bob drove toward the guard gate of the MGM Studios. Jere was in the backseat of the car, curled up on the floor, with a blanket covering him. He was like a teenager trying to sneak into a drive-in theater without paying.

Bob nervously stopped his car at the gate, and smiled meekly. The guard took a quick glance inside the vehicle. Apparently, his suspicions weren't raised by the "blanket rolls" in the backseat. He waved the car through.

The Henshaw-Kaufman caper wasn't the stuff that John le Carré might use for a sequel to *The Spy Who Came in From the Cold*, but it got Jere onto the lot. We later joked, "Barnum & Bailey probably could sneak its entire herd of elephants onto the MGM lot without raising any eyebrows at the front gate."

Henshaw and Kaufman previewed the movie together that afternoon. Later that day, when Jere reported back to me, he was very enthusiastic. "It has a lot of potential, Sam. In fact, it's very funny in parts. But it needs to be recut. If it's edited properly, it could be a hit. A big hit."

I got Goldstein on the phone, and told him that I was ready to deal with him without seeing the picture. We finally came to an agreement that we both could live with, not far from the original deal. *Love at First Bite* was recut by Henshaw and was released by AIP in April 1979 to spirited reviews and enthusiastic audiences. It became one of the biggest hits in AIP's history. I don't think any horror spoof has ever worked better.

Mr. Hamilton's knack for comedy has been a well-kept secret until now, but he's certainly funny in *Love at First Bite*, a coarse, delightful little movie with a bang-up cast and no pretensions at all.
—Janet Maslin, *New York Times*

Kaufman was a talented writer, and *Love at First Bite* was the height of his success. Subsequently, he signed a deal with me to write more screenplays, and wrote three of them after I had merged AIP with Filmways. But when I subsequently left the company, he couldn't get along with Filmways' executives. (Coincidentally, neither could I.)

Bob was so facile with ideas; he could sell anyone on just about anything. He had scripts all over town, but many of them never went into production. In an industry that savors young writers, some executives began to ignore Bob. He passed away in 1991 at age sixty. His wife told me he died of a broken heart.

17

Sometimes, the most frightening movie "monsters" aren't three stories tall, breathing fire, and leveling buildings with a single swipe of their paws. In the most successful picture in AIP's history, the "monster" was, in fact, a house.

AIP made *The Amityville Horror* in 1979, starring Margot Kidder, James Brolin, and Rod Steiger. However, the real star was the eerie, macabre home itself that terrorized the family who lived in it.

The Amityville Horror was the ultimate haunted house story, based on a presumably true incident about the Lutz family, who moved into a home in Amityville, Long Island—a home with an actual terrifying history of a mass murder that took place there. Living in the house, the Lutzes endured an onslaught of unexplainable, frightening experiences, from goop oozing from the toilets and walls, to a priest being struck blind as he prayed for the family's well-being. If the American Dream is to own your own home, this was the American Nightmare.

Although houses had been featured as the "monsters" in other AIP pictures—mostly notably, *House of Usher*—this story seemed a little different. I've always been skeptical about the purported legitimacy of "haunted" house stories, but there were "supernatural" occurrences in the actual Amityville home that really couldn't be explained and that softened my skepticism, at least in this case. Apparently, millions of people reacted the same way. After the release of the book and then the movie, crowds came to Amityville, and congregated around the house like it was a major tourist attraction. The movie was a hit; the house itself was almost as big a sensation.

As important as *The Amityville Horror* was in the history of AIP, we might not have ever made the picture were it not for a bookstore owner in the San Fernando Valley. In 1977, I was browsing through his shelves, selecting some books to take on an upcoming vacation. "Here's one, Sam, that you've got to read. Everyone says it would make a terrific movie."

Of course, I had heard that line hundreds of times before over the past forty years. I politely smiled as he handed me a copy of a novel by Jay Anson called *The Amityville Horror.* I recognized Anson's name since, in addition to being a novelist, he wrote many of the five-or-ten-minute shorts (e.g., "How Movie X Was Made") that the networks tacked onto the end of their feature movies to stretch out and fill the two-hour time slots. At the time, I wasn't aware that he had written a book—and certainly not one that would become one of the hottest properties in Hollywood.

As I packed for my vacation, I never put *The Amityville Horror* in my suitcase. I took some books that I wanted to read for pleasure, but didn't want anything that might turn it into a working vacation. So I left *Amityville* at home on the dining room table.

Nevertheless, when I returned home, my daughter, Donna, had read the book—and gave it rave reviews. She echoed the sentiments of the bookstore owner. "You have to read this book, Dad," she said. This time, I took the suggestion more seriously.

I read *The Amityville Horror* cover to cover in one sitting. Immediately after I turned the last page, I made contact with Anson and his publishing company, and found out that Anson had turned the book over to his associates, Ronald Saland and Elliot Geisinger, to produce a movie. Ironically, the book had gone virtually unnoticed by the studios, although executives at CBS had recognized its potential. The network, in fact, negotiated with Saland and Geisinger, and bought the rights to the book, planning to turn it into a TV movie with an $800,000 production budget.

I went back to work, but couldn't get the book out of my mind. Finally, I called CBS's vice president in charge of movies-for-TV. *"The*

Amityville Horror should be a bigger picture," I told him. "This is more than a TV movie. Let's sit down and talk about how we can make this a theatrical release."

He agreed. I showed up at CBS for our meeting, carrying my checkbook. My message to the network was clear: "I want to make this picture."

After a week of negotiations, AIP obtained all the rights (except for two network TV screenings bought by CBS for $1.7 million) to *The Amityville Horror,* and we immediately moved into preproduction. The picture had a shooting schedule of seven weeks, which was short by existing Hollywood standards. It was budgeted for $4.6 million, and came in at $4.7 million at a time when the average picture at the majors cost $13 million to $15 million. Ironically, the New York *Daily News* eventually reported that we had spent $25 million on the picture; the newspaper's film critic just couldn't believe that we had made it for relatively small change. Even in those latter years of AIP, however, excessive spending was never part of our standard operating procedure. Good habits are hard to break.

Nevertheless, there were nonstop headaches during the shooting of the picture. Some of the people behind the cameras—from producers Saland and Geisinger (who had also produced Anson's short network trailers) to the Lutzes themselves—created a hornet's nest of problems, frequently getting in the way and contributing very little to the project itself. (I often thought that if I could conjure up the demons of Amityville, I'd turn them loose at the homes of those individuals who had tormented us throughout the making of the picture!) Fortunately, Jere Henshaw, our head of production, not only did a terrific job in his production responsibilities, but also skillfully kept the producers and the Lutzes out of our hair as much as possible. Eventually, the movie was finished, and proved to be worth the rocky road.

We opened *The Amityville Horror* in July 1979 in 810 theaters. And it was an instant hit. It eventually earned a staggering $65 million in domestic theatrical revenues alone, becoming the most successful independently produced picture to that time. Ultimately, in 1990, *Teenage Mutant Ninja Turtles* finally beat the record. *Ninja Turtles* grossed about twice as much as *The Amityville Horror,* but even so, if you compare our 1979 dollars with their 1990 dollars—and adjust for inflation—our grosses were just as big.

Ironically, we released *The Amityville Horror* at about the same time I had merged AIP with Filmways, a move designed to channel more capital into the company to finance bigger-budget movies. Admittedly, hindsight is always twenty-twenty. But the success of *The Amityville Horror* could have almost singlehandedly achieved the same goal, without all the difficulties and the heartache that the merger eventually brought with it.

When the possibility of a merger first surfaced, it hadn't been something I had actively sought. Filmways was a conglomerate consisting of a number of dissimilar companies (from a book publisher to a television production outfit to an insurance firm) woven together and promoted by a Wall Street firm. It was headed by Richard Bloch, who had made his fortune in Arizona real estate, and really didn't know much about the entertainment business. Bloch, however, had joined the board of directors of the original Filmways when it was solely a TV production firm founded by producer Martin Ransohoff. When Ransohoff, a capable producer and executive, left Filmways, Bloch was promoted to chairman.

Filmways first approached me with the merger offer in 1978, nearly a year before it eventually took place. After weeks of negotiation, we were close to making a deal—but I got cold feet and broke off the talks. "I'm an independent, and I just don't want to merge with anyone," I told my staff at AIP. "It goes against everything that Jim Nicholson and I stood for. I'm going to listen to my gut." I thought AIP would still be capable of making movies successfully for much less money than the majors.

But not everyone agreed. Many in the industry believed that, in the years ahead, there just wouldn't be much room in Hollywood for an independent. Production budgets were skyrocketing. So were the costs of prints and advertising. Thus, although we had an outstanding year in fiscal 1979–1980—even outgrossing the Disney Studios in domestic theatrical revenues (AIP had five percent of the North American grosses, compared to Disney's four percent)—the future was less certain. One of my financial staff members put it bluntly: "To stay competitive, AIP is going to need access to greater amounts of capital."

So the talks with Filmways were reopened. And this time, the deal went through, although I was anxious up to the very end and had a lot of sleepless nights. On a Saturday in July, just two days before the merger was scheduled to be finalized, I convened an emergency meeting of AIP's board of directors. I had heard that some of Filmways' subsidiaries—including its publishing and insurance interests—weren't faring as well as their financial figures had shown. And I was becoming more nervous with each tick of the clock. For a guy who flew by the seat of my pants through most of my moviemaking career, this decision was driving me crazy.

By Monday morning, we got an opinion back from our brokerage company. The bottom line: "Everything with Filmways seems to be okay." I took a deep breath and signed on the dotted line, formalizing the merger. Filmways had acquired AIP. The decision (and ultimately the mistake) were entirely mine.

In the immediate aftermath of the new corporate situation, not much changed. I kept the title of president and chief executive of AIP, and my contract gave me a significant amount of autonomy. We kept the rights of ownership and distribution to a substantial number of our pictures. AIP also stayed in our offices on Wilshire Boulevard, about five miles from Filmways' corporate headquarters in Century City. It had been agreed that I'd still have the independence to make the pictures I wanted, free from any heavy-handed corporate oversight. And that's the way it was, at least for the first few weeks.

In the meantime, in late July and August of 1979, the Museum of Modern Art (MOMA) in New York staged a tribute to American International Pictures on our twenty-fifth anniversary, with a retrospective featuring thirty-nine of AIP's movies, ranging from our first, *The Fast and the Furious,* to the newest, *The Amityville Horror.* The museum screened the best known AIP works, including *Wild in the Streets, House of Usher, Beach Party,* and *Cooley High,* as well as what the museum called our "lesser-known but interesting and often abrasive works" such as *Black Caesar* and *Girls in Prison.*

On opening night of the MOMA retrospective, I told the gathered audience, "In the early days of AIP, if anyone had told me that our pictures would be shown in the Museum of Modern Art, I would have been startled. That was the furthest thing from my mind. We did not deliberately make art. We were making economical pictures for our youthful market, but at the same time, I guess we were also unconsciously doing something unique and evolutionary."

Not only are [American International's] films rich in their depiction of our culture, but indeed they have played a not insignificant part in it. If *Beach Party, The Trip,* and *The Wild Angels,* among others, helped establish filmmaking trends by anticipating public interest, they also addressed something familiar in their audiences. Looking back, we are not surprised. The young filmmakers attracted to AIP were already moving to the beat of a changing America....

Filmmakers at AIP had to work quickly and economically. Restricted conditions invited a resourcefulness that produced cinematic invention, and a vision at once arresting, engaging, and entertaining. The films may evidence limited means, but they do so with a heady assurance that is both healthy and attractive. AIP's filmmakers delight in the making of films, and their enthusiasm is evident. Behind most of their colorful images is an intelligence that is reacting to the complex social forces of American life and expressing that reaction in ways that are sometimes outrageous and often unusual, dramatic, and vivid.

—Adrienne Mancia and Larry Kardish
Department of Film
The Museum of Modern Art

Those were kind words from Mancia, Kardish, and the Museum of Modern Art, who put on a wonderful retrospective. Frankly, I couldn't have said it better.

After the euphoria of the opening of the MOMA retrospective, I got back to work in Los Angeles. But as I began to get to know Richard Bloch better, I became concerned about the future of AIP. Bloch never let his naïveté or inexperience in the entertainment industry interfere with his inflated ambitions. That's a virus quite common in Hollywood.

Bloch wanted to become a movie mogul, the next Louis B. Mayer or Darryl Zanuck. Since he had a relatively small investment in the conglomerate, he wasn't risking personal financial suicide by doing so, even though he was placing his company in jeopardy. To most people, Bloch seemed like a pleasant enough fellow, and he loved rubbing shoulders with actors and directors. In point of fact, he was star struck. He also wanted the ego gratification that comes with wielding power in the motion picture industry. But his fantasy was about as unrealistic as a McGovern for President landslide victory.

"You don't have the history, the clout in this town," I warned Bloch. "You don't have the backing or the strength. It's not going to be that easy for an independent to grow as fast as you want to."

Bloch was unconvinced. "But the exhibitors hate the majors," he argued. "They'll be eager for a company like Filmways to supply them with product."

"They have the same kind of love-hate relationship that brothers and sisters have," I told him. "The exhibitors and the majors are dependent on each other. They *need* each other." Then I added, "The way the picture business is going, we don't have to be a major, as long as we produce pictures with box office appeal. Anyway, I like the way of the independent; it's easier to do things—and it's much cheaper."

I reminded Bloch that throughout AIP's history, neither Jim nor I ever wanted to be a major. "Besides," I said, "if you get too big, you become a financial and banking operation, and moviemaking ceases to be fun. I want to stay close to my pictures."

At my very first Filmways board meeting, I discovered that no one else shared my taste for open-neck shirts. Although that wasn't a critical factor in my deteriorating relationship with Filmways, its corporate executives—who began to look like marionettes—did stare at me with curious expressions, as though I were some sort of alien who hadn't caught the last flying saucer home.

Meanwhile, Bloch moved ahead with his expansion plans at full throttle. Based on the value of Filmways' subsidiaries, he obtained a $60 million credit line from local banks, and set out to acquire film properties. Curiously, because of the large financial stake I had in AIP, I also was the biggest shareholder of Filmways. Even so, I still did not own enough stock to control the corporation. Bloch had the company's directors on his side, most of whom owed their allegiance and their jobs to him. In fact, there was hardly a neutral director in the group. So he and his associates fiddled while Rome began to burn.

Some of Bloch's friends were trying to develop film properties of their own, and when they couldn't interest me in them—when I'd tell them that we just didn't have the money for their high-priced projects—they'd go directly to him. Bloch would come back to me, waving scripts in his hands, questioning my judgment in rejecting so many "good ideas." For me, the whole scenario was turning out to be worse than the most frightening horror movie AIP had ever made.

Bloch wanted to make Roman Polanski's *Pirates,* which I flatly rejected. "It will cost a fortune to build those pirate ships," I told him. "Shooting on the sea is the hardest kind of shooting. Besides, it isn't a good script. Why waste the money?" Bloch finally agreed to drop the project, and the picture was made with someone else's money.

Bloch then became obsessed with the urge to make a film with Sergio Leone—specifically, the picture that eventually became *Once Upon a Time in America.* It was an interesting concept, but the script was larger than most big-city telephone directories. Again, I warned Bloch that it was not for us. When it was eventually financed (by the Ladd Company, not by Bloch), it ran for nearly four hours! A lot of Hollywood marriages don't last that long. Incidentally, *Once Upon a Time in America* never earned back more than the cost of its prints and advertising in U.S. theatrical release.

Before long, Hollywood agents told me that they had begun to recognize Bloch as an "easy mark." One of them said, "Once the majors turn down a big, expensive picture, we'll come to Bloch with it. He's often a receptive audience." I, of course, never liked these big-budget movies, particularly if they were not genre films. In my years at AIP, we had developed our own scripts, and had never considered expensive package deals. But Bloch insisted on operating in a different manner.

I soon realized that Bloch and I would never get along. We began to spar repeatedly about the pictures the company was going to make, and although no one scored a knockout punch, I felt like we were both drawing blood and really getting nowhere. There were other points of contention, too: As a member of Filmways' board of directors, I discovered that the financial reports issued by Filmways and its subsidiaries included inaccurate figures, making the subsidiaries look much more prosperous than they really were. When I discussed this situation with Bloch, he jumped upon problems with some AIP sales contracts that had been drawn up early in 1979, before the merger, by one of our New York employees who was overseeing the syndication of some low-cost TV programs to which we owned the rights. When I learned of the problem contracts, I told Bloch immediately; he in turn claimed that we had overstated our TV assets when the merger was being negotiated. In reality, because of tax write-offs, the TV assets of our pictures were actually far *larger* than the figures set forth in our financial statement.

Tensions rose between Bloch and myself. I could see how Filmways was being run, and I knew I couldn't work in that environment indefinitely. In December 1979, just five months after the merger was finalized, I walked into Bloch's office, advised him of what I thought of him and his ego, and resigned. Under my contract with Filmways, I had the option of going independent after two years; I told him I wanted to accelerate the process. I agreed, however, to stay on the job for another three months to make the transition as orderly as possible. Finally, in March 1980, I relegated Filmways—and painfully, American International Pictures—into my history.

The merger was the biggest mistake of my life—but I figure everyone is entitled to one major mistake, and this was definitely mine. Bloch and Filmways had bought AIP because of what we had accomplished over the last quarter century; then they promptly tried to change us, just like the bride who attempts to transform her new husband. I had a wonderful twenty-six years with AIP, and when the situation turned sour, I didn't see the point in hanging on and fighting for years in court in what might be a losing battle. Certainly that wasn't the way I wanted to spend the next few years of my life.

Bloch brought in Raphael Etkes from MCA/Universal to run AIP. He told *Variety,* "You can clearly assume my intent is to change the company radically in terms of the type of pictures made.... I plan to turn it into a major maker of pictures of quality and stature."

I remained the largest stockholder in Filmways until December 1980, when I sold all my stock to entertainment executives Norman Lear and Jerry Perenchio, who were looking for a motion picture company. They thought they could get along with Bloch; less than a year later, however, they couldn't make the arrangement work, either, and they sold their shares back to Bloch.

Over the next two years, Filmways lost money on nearly every picture it made. The value of its stock plummeted. Thank God I had already sold my stock long before then. By 1981, even with its substantial assets (including the AIP film library), Filmways was faring so poorly that it was on the brink of Chapter 11. It sold its insurance division in a desperate attempt to survive. Ultimately, amid losses of $52.7 million in fiscal 1982, Filmways was swallowed up by

Orion Pictures, which was looking for a company to take over after its deal with Warner Bros. ended. Richard Bloch disappeared from Hollywood, taking his dreams of creating a major studio with him.

I believe that even though the film business became tougher and more hazardous for independents in the 1980s, AIP could have continued and done quite well. Ironically, my final American International "legacy" was three of our most successful pictures—not only *The Amityville Horror,* but also *Love at First Bite* and *Dressed to Kill.* All of them either were already made just prior to the merger, or were finished shortly thereafter. If I had delayed the merger, the large profits from those three pictures could have provided the broad financial base for which I had turned to Filmways.

Dressed to Kill was produced by AIP during 1979. By the time it was released in January 1980, I had already decided to leave Filmways.

Brian De Palma, who directed *Dressed to Kill,* was already a known commodity to us. He had made one of his early pictures, *Sisters,* his first suspense thriller, starring Margot Kidder, for AIP in 1973. *Dressed to Kill* had a much higher budget, particularly by AIP standards—$6 million—and starred Angie Dickinson, Michael Caine, and Nancy Allen.

De Palma and his partner, George Litto, had seriously considered an offer from Ray Stark (producer of pictures like *Funny Girl* and *The Way We Were*) to make the movie with him, but they were hesitant because Stark wanted a multipicture deal. So they began talking with AIP.

"A $6 million budget sounds fair," I told Litto. "But you and Brian will have to guarantee one-half of any excess over $6 million. If you bring the picture in for more, you'll be responsible for half of that extra money."

Litto and De Palma said yes. Through the filming, De Palma struggled to stay within budget. Ultimately, the picture cost $6.5 million. De Palma and Litto put up $250,000 to cover their share of the overrun. But they more than made it back. The picture was both a financial and artistic success.

During my time at Filmways, I had tried to impress upon Bloch that the biggest problem in the motion picture business was films that were not brought in on budget. Hundreds of millions of dollars were (and still are) wasted each year in budget overages, and for a variety of reasons: Sometimes, the budgets were unrealistic to begin with, nothing more than wishful thinking considering the record of the particular producer, director and/or star. When they started to lose control of the budget, the film company was often reluctant to take strong measures to rein in the spending because of the personalities involved.

Bloch refused to take any measures to control his own budgets, rejecting methods like the one we had used with *Dressed to Kill*. "The majors don't put these kinds of clauses into their contracts," he told me, "so I'm not going to, either." Perhaps he was simply nervous about developing a reputation among producers, directors, and actors as being "difficult." Whatever the reasons, almost all of the pictures produced by Filmways in its relatively short history went substantially over budget, some by as much as 100 percent, which had much to do with Filmway's ultimate failure.

Under the wary eye of AIP, however, *Dressed to Kill* was a picture I was proud of, a truly brilliant film, full of unexpected plot twists and more thrills and heart-stopping moments than the roller coaster at Coney Island.

De Palma.... deliberately set out to work in the Hitchcock tradition, and directed this Hitchcockian thriller that's stylish, intriguing, and very violent.... He places his emphasis on the same things that obsessed Hitchcock: precise camera movements, meticulously selected visual details, characters seen as types rather than personalities, and violence as a sudden interruption of the most mundane situations.

—Roger Ebert

As I had expected, *Dressed to Kill* was savagely attacked by feminist groups, outraged by its "violence against women." More than a year following the picture's release—and after I had left Filmways—the feminists were still fuming. A group called Women in Film invited me to participate in a panel discussion designed to tackle the subject. They were ready to sacrifice me to the lions. But as an old high school and college debater, I showed up and had a good time arguing with them.

I was amazed at just how humorless most of the audience was, and how committed the women were to the male conspiracy theory in

Hollywood. Moderator Carol Roper noted that sixty-two horror pictures were in production that year, with most of them depicting the rape, mutilation, and murder of women. She and other panelists claimed that violence was as rampant as the plague in motion pictures. For more than two hours, I listened to their overkill of psychobabble, in which they proclaimed that movies depicting victimized and powerless women were made by the "threatened" males who produce and direct the pictures. "The man who hates women doesn't move beyond his hate by making movies of it," one of them said.

I listened as politely as possible, but ultimately had to come to the defense of Hollywood. "First of all, I question some of your statistics. But that aside, I'm not unsympathetic to the possible ill effects of violent movies. Nevertheless, violence and violent emotions are critical components of drama. If you're going to make films that don't deal with violence, you will turn out only *Rebeccas of Sunnybrook Farm.*"

I tried to explain that women have always been "persecuted" in the arts, long before there was a motion picture camera. "Look at literature as far back as you want to go," I said. "It's always been the damsel in distress, while the husky men have always been able to slay the dragon. At the same time, we never made a picture at AIP that portrayed the rape and mutilation of women. Our Poe pictures, for instance, were period pieces in which we showed various instruments of torture, but only men were subjected to the torture."

Just as important, I noted that by definition, horror pictures have violence and murders in them. "And if you made an actual count, you'd discover that more men are murdered in these pictures than women. But who's counting?!"

I also argued that when millions of people go to see a picture like *Friday the 13th*—which was not an AIP movie, but came from one of the majors—they aren't being exploited. "They know what they're going to see. They are not unsophisticated. They see the trailers, they talk to their friends. If a film is too tough for them, they won't buy a ticket."

More recently, the meetings of organizations like Women in Film have assumed a different tone. I attended one session during which Pauline Kael received an award. And during her acceptance speech, she said, "I don't think you women really want to remake the motion picture business; you just want the same jobs that the men now have, and you want to do the same things the men do." I tend to agree with her, that in positions of power, women would engage in the same excesses—whether it's violence or big-budget movies—as men.

There was one other AIP release—*Mad Max*—that reached American theaters shortly before my departure from Filmways and was a big success. It was an Australian production that featured Mel Gibson in his first starring role, and was shaped by producer Byron Kennedy and a young doctor named George Miller who decided he would rather direct movies than practice medicine.

Kennedy and Miller made *Mad Max* on a relatively low budget, and the action-adventure picture became an instant hit in Australia. Our contact at Roadshow, AIP's distributor there, told me about the movie, suggesting, "If I were you, I'd try to grab the U.S. and Canadian distribution rights before someone else does. This could be a big film for you."

Even before we had seen *Mad Max,* we acquired the U.S. and Canadian rights. When I finally screened the picture, I was struck by its quality and its originality...an action picture at its best. But I was also concerned by the opening scenes in which native Australians are speaking in a thick dialect and local jargon that would be virtually unacceptable for American audiences. "I know our exhibitors pretty well," I told my staff. "They'd listen to this soundtrack, and say, 'These are a bunch of limeys talking.' The actors might be Australian, but the exhibitors would consider anything that isn't 'American English' to be 'limey.' After the first reel, they'd decide not to book the picture."

We contacted Kennedy and Miller, and told them, "We really need to do some looping. It's a great picture, but American audiences are going to object to those dialects."

We paid for Kennedy and Miller to fly to the U.S., and we set them up at Titra, the dubbing studio in New York where, for years, we had performed voice surgery on our Italian imports. Mel Gibson—who was born in America, and never developed an accent after moving to Australia in his youth—remained Down Under, and didn't participate in the looping. But we got just the voices we needed in New York.

Miller, a film buff making his first feature, shows he knows what cinema is all about. This is the most audience-involving film since

Halloween (in fact, Miller's work is reminiscent of John Carpenter's and also of the Canadian David Cronenberg).

—*Variety*

Those early months after leaving Filmways were a tough time for me. I knew I had made a terrible mistake in agreeing to the merger, but I accepted it and moved ahead in other directions. I guess I could have retired, which a lot of friends were encouraging me to do. But I was only sixty-one years old, which is much too young to go calmly into the darkness.

In planning my professional future, I decided I didn't want to get back into distribution. At AIP, we had both produced and distributed motion pictures, and although I enjoyed it, distribution is a tough end of the business. After twenty-six years, I felt I had done it and didn't want to start another domestic theatrical distribution company (although I did continue to license pictures for domestic TV, foreign rights, and other areas).

I still wanted to be involved in producing pictures. It's such an exhilarating activity—from the selection of projects to negotiations of all kinds, from the production itself to the merchandising. I love the excitement and the action.

When news of my split with Filmways became known, I had a number of offers from major companies, financiers, and others. Ray Stark was one of those who called me. I had had an exciting battle with him over *Dressed to Kill,* the Brian De Palma picture, which Ray thought he had and I wound up with after a spirited battle involving agencies, lawyers, and others. "We'll be partners," Ray said, "and we'll jointly produce movies." But I finally decided to turn down the offer. I wanted to be able to make the films I wanted to make, without a studio chief peering over my shoulder and making decisions for me. I guess I was just too much of an independent.

In 1981, I went back to making and otherwise dealing in pictures under a new AIP logo, Arkoff International Pictures, and have been involved in a substantial number of productions and acquisitions since then. In 1981, for instance, I teamed with Joe Roth to executive produce and finance a picture called *The Final Terror,* starring the young Rachel Ward and Daryl Hannah in their first leading roles. (Roth is now the head of Twentieth Century-Fox, but more importantly, is married to my daughter, Donna.)

In 1982, I joined forces with Larry Cohen in making *Q: The Winged Serpent*. Larry is the successful writer, director, and producer who made several pictures (*Black Caesar, Hell Up In Harlem, The Private Files of J. Edgar Hoover*) quite economically for AIP in the 1970s. The Hoover picture, in fact, was the first screen portrayal highly critical of the FBI chief.

Cohen had begun shooting *Q* on his own, but early in the production schedule, he came to me for some additional financing. For my investment, I acquired ownership and the foreign distribution to the picture, which made AIP quite a bit of money.

Q was the story of a giant creature who nests at the top of New York's Chrysler Building, periodically dive-bombing toward the streets of Manhattan to harass shocked pedestrians. The winged beast became the biggest thing to hit a New York high-rise since King Kong turned the Empire State Building into his personal playground.

During the shooting, Larry had a crew on the roof of the Chrysler Building, aiming their cameras at the street below, where actors dressed in police uniforms were pointing their rifles skyward, as if firing at the winged bird. Larry planned to add the bird to the scene later with special effects. However, the sight of what looked like a small army of New York's finest with their weapons pointed at one of the city's most famous buildings attracted an enormous crowd of passersby. It also brought the press sprinting toward the area.

Normally, press coverage is welcome. But Larry was working with a nonunion crew, and New York is a city where you seriously risk life and limb by shooting nonunion. I could already feel our bones crunching under the attack of a union goon squad.

"Hell, Larry," I said, "we might have gotten ourselves into a very tight spot here, particularly if we get the kind of press coverage it looks like we're going to. All the unions are going to be on our necks."

The next morning, the *Daily News* made our worst dreams come true. It ran a front-page picture of the "police raid" on the Chrysler Building. "Maybe it's time to get unlisted phone numbers," I nervously joked with Larry.

Fortunately, no one asked if we were shooting with a union crew, and Larry certainly didn't offer the information. Within a couple days, we had packed up our equipment and were heading back to L.A., ducking for cover all the way home.

I took a print of *Q* with me to the Cannes Film Festival that year. I was still doing business there and sponsoring my annual luncheon at the du Cap for the English-language press, where the turnout was as impressive as always. Roger Ebert often tells the story that while I was chatting with him and a few other friends during the luncheon, Rex Reed breezed into the room, grabbed me by the arm, and couldn't contain his enthusiasm.

"Sam," he said, "I just saw *Q*! What a surprise! That wonderful Method performance by Michael Moriarity, right in the middle of all that dreck!"

"Why, thank you," I told him. "The dreck was my idea!"

My other projects have included executive producing *Up the Creek,* a movie financed and distributed by Orion Pictures, and produced by my son, Louis, and myself. The picture was a Beach Party-type comedy about white water racing. Orion proposed a budget of $7 million for it, while I offered to make it my way for roughly half that, even though we planned to shoot on location in Oregon. For the filming, we needed lots of Teamsters to truck the rafts from downriver back to the starting points. There were many union Teamsters in Oregon eager to work on the picture—and since they lived nearby, they could go home each night and save us the cost of hotel rooms and evening meals. But Orion insisted upon hiring a caravan of Teamsters and their trucks from Los Angeles, and having them drive up to Oregon, where we would have to pay for their bed and board seven days a week. It was a prohibitive and unnecessary cost, and an example of the studio waste so prevalent in the 1980s.

During this time, I also served as a consultant in producing and packaging a number of pictures made in Canada; since my wife is originally from Canada, and since AIP had produced more than one-hundred pictures throughout the world over the years, these Canadian ventures (and other co-ventures with other foreign countries) seemed like a natural extension of what I had already been doing.

My eldest grandson, Dan Pinder, is twenty as this book is written, and in my current motion picture projects, is quite helpful in defining the present movie tastes of his contemporaries. My other grandchildren—Zack, Julia, Aerin (and more to come)—are younger and of Disney age, and will probably be of more value in this regard later on.

In 1992, Arkoff International Pictures had six projects in the works with three studios. This has been a new experience for me, since after so many years of being an independent in the production and/or distribution of more than five-hundred pictures, I am now producing, financing, and distributing with major companies. However, since I am no longer involved in domestic distribution myself, and since the majority of independent distribution companies have either vanished or are limping along, I decided that this is the best way to go at this time. To cushion the "shock," most of AIP's projects are coproductions with my son, Louis, and Willie Kutner, who are younger men and (according to them) better able to speak the language of the younger executives of the major companies. They take the majors in stride; to me, it's like visiting Alice in Wonderland.

I sometimes joke that, in a sense, I've joined the "enemy"—that is, I'm part (albeit on the periphery) of the studio system that I sniped at and avoided for almost forty years. Who says you can't teach an old dog new tricks?

18

It has been a long time since 1954, when the first carloads of teenagers parked their Chevy convertibles at drive-in theaters from California to New Jersey, adjusted the speakers to the highest volume settings, and watched John Ireland race his sports car to Mexico in *The Fast and the Furious,* American International Pictures' first movie.

Jim Nicholson and I nurtured AIP into a significant force in the film industry, working so closely together that Hollywood considered us a single entity. By the time Jim had left AIP in 1972 and I merged the company with Filmways seven years later, tens of millions of people around the world had been entertained by our pictures.

Although I am still involved in making movies, Hollywood is a far different town than it was almost four decades ago when Jim and I took the bold step of creating a small distribution company that grew into AIP. Admittedly, the motion picture industry will continue because the public wants to see movies, whether in theaters or in their homes. I'm not one of those Chicken Littles who panics at each new innovation—from TV to home video—convinced that the sky is falling on America's movie houses. At the same time, however, the film industry is evolving, and some of the changes may not bode well, particularly for those who have become accustomed to the bonanza of extravagant budgets of the 1980s. The costs of making and merchandising pictures can't continue to spiral.

Today's movie budgets are enough to shock my electrocardiogram readings right off the charts. Even "cheap" pictures are more expensive than I ever could have imagined. As I've written earlier, I warned colleagues in the late 1970s that they just couldn't continue spending $10 to $15 million on picture after picture. So they didn't. Instead, they began spending much, much more, relying on the ancillaries (like cable TV, home video) to support their extravagant outlays.

In the old AIP, in a typical year in the early seventies, we might produce that entire year's schedule of approximately twenty pictures for about $20 million. Today, $20 million would be a modest sum for the majors to spend on *one* picture. In recent years, *The Bonfire of the Vanities* had a production budget of more than $40 million; *Godfather III* cost $55 million; *Days of Thunder* carried a price tag of $60 million; and *Terminator 2: Judgment Day* cashed in at about $90 million, making it the most expensive picture in history. While the actual dollar cost of *Hook* may not have exceeded that of *Terminator 2*, the rich, complicated deals given to *Hook*'s participants (director, actors) made it a movie that had to net huge amounts of money before its backers ever saw any return.

Some observers believe that with budgets like that, the studios could be setting themselves up for a calamity. No one can predict with any certainty what will attract an audience and what won't. All you can do is take calculated risks and minimize your exposure. But when pictures have budgets approaching $100 million, you're *not* minimizing your exposure.

At AIP, Jim Nicholson and I made quick decisions, at least when quick decisions were merited and the risks could be kept under control. Of course, we knew we would have to take some chances because we wanted to produce a certain number of pictures a year. But we never took foolish risks. This is a gambling business, but like the Las Vegas casinos, we tried to take only calculated chances.

As a film producer, one of my primary responsibilities has always been to keep costs under control. You can bet that when Pope Sextus hired Michelangelo to paint the Sistine Chapel ceiling, he told the artist, "Here is exactly how much you can spend. Not a single lira more. Keep that in mind as you work. These are the ground rules, and if you can't follow them, find someone else to support your artistic endeavors."

The studios should be telling producers and directors the same thing. I can't imagine another industry anywhere that would not only allow employees (in this case, producers, directors, and actors) to go excessively over budget, but would actually defend and protect them when they do.

Of course, the arts aren't what they used to be. They've changed dramatically over the centuries. In medieval times, a patron (often the king or the Pope) provided the money to support the sole artist who would do the writing, the painting, or the sculpturing. The patron would maintain some control over the work of art—perhaps he'd want his own picture painted, or he'd decline to publish something that might be harmful to him. Even so, there was a clear line of demarcation between the patron and the artist, with each party in the arrangement knowing what he was providing and what was expected of him. And if his paintings or his writings were not well-received, only he (and his family) would suffer.

Today, the sole artists—writers, painters, sculptors, musicians—often still work in somewhat the same manner. But filmmaking is different. Take a look at the motion picture industry today, and you'll see that the stakes (e.g., the budgets) are enormous. Unlike an artist such as Van Gogh, who may have never sold a painting during his lifetime, motion picture companies are involved in such an expensive enterprise that they must get an immediate return—or there may not be a tomorrow for them. The production of a single film has become like fighting a war or at least erecting a building—it requires a community effort. When you make a movie, many dozens and even hundreds of people are involved. There is still a patron, of course, who is the source of the revenues. But the people who are supposed to look out for the interests of the modern-day patron often abandon those responsibilities. Movie directors want to be treated as sole "auteurs," even though working with $20–$50 million film budgets is not the same as an artist working alone in his attic. Too often, however, some of the studio executives who are minding the bank accounts have given in and lost control. That's what has been happening throughout the industry today—although there's evidence that many companies are aware of the problem and are finally giving more than lip service to possible solutions, promising to turn over a new leaf and turn down risky projects.

Even so, many present-day producers, directors, and/or stars wouldn't dream of making a picture on a short schedule or a limited budget like we did at AIP, although they have much better equipment, including faster film and more mobile cameras and lights. They seem to have forgotten that many of the most popular films of the past—such as *It Happened One Night*, which transformed Columbia into a major company—were shot in just four to five weeks.

Yet while I can live with some of the longer production schedules nowadays, many producers and directors still exceed the lengthier shooting schedules that they themselves have previously approved in writing. That can throw a budget into chaos unless someone is there to ensure that the picture is brought in on schedule and at the projected price. Unfortunately, in some cases, production executives do not want to appear "anticreative," and they may fear jeopardizing their jobs or their chances of promotion if a producer, actor, or particularly director complains to the press about intrusions into the creative process. Some of the people who run the studio production departments are thinking things like, "Well, I don't want to upset the 'artist.'" Consequently, they're willing to let matters go unchecked, week after week, sometimes month after month, with accompanying budget overruns of millions—sometimes tens of millions—of dollars.

While the concept of the "auteur" may be legitimate, particularly in Europe where smaller specialty pictures still get made, the film director of a substantial movie in the States is not the sole artist. He or she may want to take complete credit for a picture—and protest any changes that are made without his or her approval—but there are writers, cinematographers, editors, and many others who play critical roles in the making of pictures, too. It's hardly a one-man act. Still, American directors continue to be allowed to assume a great amount of control over a project—while asking for even more control—with few checks and balances from the studio production departments. As a result, film debacles like *Heaven's Gate* occur with too much frequency, even if not to that degree.

In lectures at film schools and at recent AIP retrospectives in cities from London to New York, from Honolulu to Munich, I have said, "The studios need to start recognizing that *they're* the ones with the ultimate responsibility, and that they can no longer give in to unreasonable demands made by directors, producers, or stars. With AIP, at least until we went public years after the launching of the company, Jim and I were personally liable on the notes at the bank. It was our checkbook that was on the line. And to use the vernacular, "when you're pissing your own money, you don't piss it away quite as quickly."

Let me emphasize, however, that even though I have always stressed the necessity of bringing a movie in on budget, I've never measured a picture by cost alone. Throughout AIP's history, we always insisted on making commercial pictures of technical quality. A lot of people in the industry, both then and now, continue to claim that they cannot make quality pictures without spending lots of money. But the most expensive movies are not necessarily the best ones. A picture should cost what it has to cost—and no more.

There is another troubling trend in Hollywood. Although Americans had bought more than one billion theater tickets a year for more than a decade, sales dropped to about 950 million in 1991. We don't yet know whether that was due to competition from other media (e.g., home video, pay TV) or to a passing economic recession. But I believe that the number of theater-goers are more likely to go down than up in the future; the question is whether new or improved ancillaries can make up the difference.

At the same time, some studio chiefs still often make pictures primarily for themselves, for one another, or for the critics—and not for those ticket-buyers. And when that happens, you can predict with some certainty that those movies are going to be financial disasters. On the other hand, when you give audiences something that they want, they'll put up with $7 admission prices and $3 candy bars, and line up in the middle of a blizzard for a picture that truly entertains them. Just as important, if they like the picture, they'll come back again and tell their friends—and even their parents. Although many motion picture people are fond of saying, "If it's a good picture, the public will come," the fact is that if there is no public desire to see a given movie, the initial audiences will be too small to create positive word of mouth, and the picture will be yanked by exhibitors before long.

The old Hollywood cliché is probably true that no one ever started out to make a bad picture. But a lot of movies have gone into production with no vision of who might eventually pay to watch them. Too often, studio executives authorize the production of a picture, and then take it to their sales and promotion departments, and say, "Sell it!" The sales executives may look at the movie and, as they scramble to somehow create a sales campaign that will work, mumble under their breath, "Sell it to whom?!" At AIP, we knew *why* and *for whom* we were making every picture. But when there's too large a gap between the creative and the sales sides of picturemaking, it can add up to a lot of red ink.

Could the AIP of old make it today? Not if it were run like some of the independent film companies of recent history. In earlier times, independents failed because of a lack of money; during the 1980s, they failed because of too *much* available money. More dollars were put into independent production and distribution companies in the eighties than at any time in history, with Wall Street and private financing pouring over $1.5 billion into firms that immediately tried to emulate the majors—and were ultimately killed by their own prosperity. These independents overspent when it wasn't necessary to do so, and thus set into motion the forces of their own self-destruction. They established too many highly-staffed, in-house units, from distribution to advertising to publicity. Weintraub...Cannon...De Laurentiis...New World...Lorimar...Vista...New Century...Atlantic. Like Filmways, they all made the mistake of thinking they could become a major. They were making pictures that cost too much money. They were spending a lot of money that didn't show up on the screen, with huge budgets for prints, advertising, and promotion. And where are they now?

All of these ill-fated independents believed the ancillary rights (from home video and cable TV) would compensate for any shortfalls at the box office. At the time, that was not an uncommon belief in Hollywood. The studios, too, began looking toward the ancillaries as a savior. As production costs rose, home video and pay TV were seen as vehicles to bail out the industry, and in fact, they did become a critical new source of income. Even if a picture was a flop at the box office, it often fared well in the video marketplace; consumers were willing to spend $2.50 to watch a picture in their living rooms that, six months earlier, they hesitated to spend $7 on at the theater.

When VCRs first proliferated, producers came out of the woodwork, making pictures with advances from home video companies and assuming that the ancilliaries would an insatiable source of dollars. But they were wrong. The public may be receptive to some inexpensive films that demonstrate real originality. But the costs of prints and advertising have grown so enormously that they often exceed the cost of the movie itself, building up additional costs to recoup.

Certainly, it's harder for independents to get started today. But I still believe that an enterprising company sensitive to economics as well as creativity can make a go of it. New Line is one of the few companies left in the field of independent domestic theatrical distribution. Since New Line's inception, founder Bob Shea has run a tightly-knit, economical, no-nonsense organization, and the company has avoided falling prey to the temptations and pitfalls that many other independents and the mini-majors have slid into. May this tribe increase in number.

In addition to the independent distributors and the major distributors—both of whom provide money or credit with which movies are made—a new breed has emerged in the last ten years known as the independent production companies. These companies raise their own money for their productions and distribute their pictures domestically through the American majors, but they handle their own foreign sales. They appear to be a solid new entry into the production of pictures, but the jury is still out on how important they will become. Several of these independent production companies, such as Morgan Creek, have fared well, but others are on the precipice.

Perhaps a decade from now, the makeup of production and distribution companies will have changed radically. The American motion picture studios, which have dominated the worldwide distribution of important pictures, may lose much of that position in the years ahead to foreign companies, a process that seems to have already started.

But more than ever before, both the independents and the majors have to aggressively control their costs. And that means controlling salaries, which in today's star-struck environment is extremely difficult. The biggest stars and directors make millions of dollars per picture, even though their names alone can't guarantee a movie's success. Nevertheless, studios so often approve the making of a picture with the stipulation, "We'll go ahead with the movie if you can get so-and-so for the lead."

In essence, everyone is covering his or her own backside. After all, a studio production chief can say, "Sure the picture was a bomb, but you can't blame me. I got actors, writers, and directors with great box-office track records. I did everything I could." For that same reason, the studios make too many sequels and also hesitate to tackle a property that is too original. It's the whole concept of "insurance," of making certain that no one sticks his or her neck out too far.

Of course, in the process of scrambling to get "name" stars, no one realizes that with very few exceptions, audiences don't really go to the movies to see particular stars; the public cares about *characters* it can identify with, not necessarily actors whose names they recognize. *E.T.* didn't have any big star in its cast. Nor did *The Karate Kid, Ghost, Teenage Mutant Ninja Turtles,* or *Home Alone.* Yet people cared, they identified, they gave a damn. Audiences want to be moved to some kind of emotion, whether its laughter or tears, joy or terror. And you don't need a big-name actor or actress to do that.

Simple pictures like *E.T.* have warmth and originality that captivate audiences. And they turn out to be much more appealing than many pictures with bigger budgets, bigger stars, and glorious, expensive, and perhaps unnecessary special effects that often get in the way of the basic story itself. These pictures frequently get bogged down by their own immense size.

I call this "the doctrine of stuffing bananas with bananas"—taking an actor from Column A (the most expensive list of actors), an actress from the same stratosphere, a top writer, and a big-name director, too. The producers have stuffed banana after banana, and as the whole project gets bigger, more costly, and more ponderous, they're left with a banana split that never gets off the ground at the box office. The public really doesn't care how big and how costly a picture is, but it knows what it wants to see.

Not long ago, an aggressive independent called Miramax—primarily an art and specialty distributor—released *sex, lies and videotape,* a picture produced for under $2 million. It was a well-made movie, indistinguishable from major company productions that cost ten times as much, or more. *sex lies and videotape* had a first-time director and two unknown leading actors—and the movie did very well. And it turned that director and those actors into stars.

In short, stars don't make movies. Movies make stars. I was always quite content with having talented unknowns in starring roles—and, in fact, I still am. Not only will hungry actors work for a lot less money, but they waste less production time over concerns about their own egos and power.

With young actors, you usually also don't have to deal with the "barnacles" attached to the starships, which sometimes create more problems. Nobody questions the value of most of the "barnacles"—the agents, personal managers, lawyers, business managers, and estate planners (I draw the line at astrologers!). But unfortunately, there are prima donnas in the group who make sensible business dealings very difficult. They're usually working hard to get the best deals for their clients, which is certainly OK, but sometimes they're fighting and competing with one another over the tiniest details of every last clause. Today, it usually takes longer to make a deal than to make a movie! Unfortunately, like Dr. Frankenstein, when we create stars, we frequently create our own monsters, too.

The stars and some directors, however, still wield enormous power in Hollywood, and their salaries exceed the boundaries of common sense. Not only do they receive enormous paychecks up front, but many get percentages of the picture's gross profits or revenues as well—a system that had its origins in the beginning of the television era when one-third of the nation's theaters closed. At that time, the studios pleaded poverty, claiming they could no longer pay high salaries to actors. So the agents argued, "Give us a percentage of the picture and you won't have to pay us as much salary." When the movie business recovered, however, the stars got even bigger salaries—and they kept their profit percentage points, too.

In some respects, I expect that the years ahead will be particularly stressful in Hollywood, with the budgetary pressures and the competitiveness in Hollywood only intensifying in the future. It has always been a tough business to break into, simply because everyone's attracted to the arts—or should I say to the fame and money associated with the arts. Not everyone wants to be a plumber or an accountant, but everybody, it seems, wants to make movies, particularly today. The roaring eighties are over, however, and the debris of many independents and larger companies have littered the bankruptcy courts. Still, the motion picture industry will continue, although the cast may change.

Whether in the best of times or the worst of times, I believe there will always be independents in the movie business. New independent companies will find niches to fill that the majors don't wish to enter. Young actors, writers, and directors who have something new and original to offer will discover avenues for displaying their talents, too. After all, since theatrical pictures can't be made on an assembly line, where thousands of replicas are produced from a single mold, this will continue to be a business that values originality. Yes, it's a tough industry, and there are no guarantees of success. But the audience's overall demand for entertainment will not go the way of the horse and buggy. There will always be room for people with talent and initiative.

Perhaps none of our AIP pictures were "classics" in the tradition of *Gone With the Wind* or *Citizen Kane,* but I've never believed that any of us really make movies for posterity. There's a difference between today's motion pictures and the art of Rembrandt, da Vinci, and Michelangelo, which have lived and flourished for centuries. Probably not a single picture produced by anyone will be anything but a historical memento in a few hundred years. Technical progress is moving so fast that the pictures of the twentieth century may be shown in museums and they might be studied in colleges. But they'll be relics of an earlier era.

Even so, I love movies, and I think I've made some good ones and nourished some talent over the years. I'm very proud of what Jim Nicholson and I accomplished. We started with almost no money. We weren't subsidized by popes, princes, or governments. We built a company in order to build a future for ourselves. And we gave a lot of people a lot of enjoyable Saturday nights in the process.

As I've written earlier, I guess I could have retired many times in the past decade or so. Many of my retired friends urged me to do so. They said I had enough money, I had worked hard and long for many years, and now I should take it easy. One weekend, my wife and I visited some of them in Palm Springs, and when I realized that they spend their time playing golf and tennis (which I don't do) and shopping with their wives (which I won't do), and generally sinking into a vegetative condition, I said "no." I need a crises or two a day to get my blood flowing, and you don't find those crises on tennis courts or in shopping malls.

Some say that this industry is a young man's game, but I have never believed that. The test for me is whether I still enjoy the game—and I do. So why retire?

Also, my loving wife, Hilda, told me a long time ago, "I'm very fond of you, but there's no place for you at home in the daytime hours, Sam; I'm just not prepared to have you come home for lunch every afternoon." Our housekeeper has expressed the same sentiments in Spanish. With that in mind, I have this image of myself wandering aimlessly through the parks of Los Angeles waiting for 7:30 so I can go home for dinner.

So I'll continue to fly by the seat of my pants, making movies as long as there are audiences willing to watch them and as long as there are crises to resolve. I wouldn't have it any other way.

American International Pictures Filmography

Compiled by Alvin H. Marill

(Date is year of U.S. release; name of director is in italics)

THE FAST AND THE FURIOUS (1954). *Edward Sampson* and *John Ireland*. John Ireland, Dorothy Malone.

FIVE GUNS WEST (1955). *Roger Corman*. John Lund, Dorothy Malone, Touch (Mike) Connors, Paul Birch.

OPERATION MALAYA (1955). *David MacDonald*. Narrators: John Humphrey, Winford Vaughn Thomas, John Slatter, Chips Rafferty.

OUTLAW TREASURE (1955). *Oliver Drake*. John Forbes, Adele Jergens, Glenn Langan.

APACHE WOMAN (1955). *Roger Corman*. Lloyd Bridges, Joan Taylor, Lance Fuller, Paul Birch.

THE BEAST WITH 1,000,000 EYES! (1955). *David Kramarsky*. Paul Birch, Lorna Thayer, Dick Sargent.

DAY THE WORLD ENDED (1955). *Roger Corman*. Richard Denning, Lori Nelson, Adele Jergens, Touch (Mike) Connors, Paul Birch.

THE PHANTOM FROM 10,000 LEAGUES (1955). *Dan Milner*. Kent Taylor, Cathy Downs, Michael Whelan.

FEMALE JUNGLE (1956). *Bruno Ve Sota*. Lawrence Tierney, John Carradine, Jayne Mansfield, Kathleen Crowley.

THE OKLAHOMA WOMAN (1956). *Roger Corman*. Richard Denning, Peggy Castle, Cathy Downs, Touch (Mike) Connors.

GUNSLINGER (1956). *Roger Corman*. John Ireland, Beverly Garland, Allison Hayes, Bruno Ve Sota, Jonathan Haze, Richard Miller.

GIRLS IN PRISON (1956). *Edward L. Cahn*. Richard Denning, Joan Taylor, Adele Jergens, Lance Fuller.

HOT ROD GIRL (1956). *Leslie Martinson*. Lori Nelson, John Smith, Chuck Connors, Frank L. Gorshin.

IT CONQUERED THE WORLD (1956). *Roger Corman.* Peter Graves, Beverly Garland, Lee Van Cleef, Sally Fraser.

THE SHE CREATURE (1956). *Edward L. Cahn.* Chester Morris, Marla English, Tom Conway, Cathy Downs, Lance Fuller.

RUNAWAY DAUGHTERS (1956). *Edward L. Cahn.* Marla English, Anna Sten, Gloria Castillo, Lance Fuller, Adele Jergens, Frank L. Gorshin.

SHAKE, RATTLE AND ROCK (1956). *Edward L. Cahn.* Fats Domino, Joe Turner, Lisa Gaye, Touch (Mike) Connors, Margaret Dumont.

FLESH AND THE SPUR (1957). *Edward L. Cahn.* John Agar, Marla English, Touch (Mike) Connors.

NAKED PARADISE (1957). *Roger Corman.* Richard Denning, Beverly Garland, Lisa Montell. (Later reissued as THUNDER OVER HAWAII)

VOODOO WOMAN (1957). *Edward L. Cahn.* Marla English, Tom Conway, Touch (Mike) Connors, Lance Fuller.

THE UNDEAD (1957). *Roger Corman.* Pamela Duncan, Richard Garland, Allison Hayes, Mel Welles, Bruno Ve Sota.

DRAGSTRIP GIRL (1957). *Edward L. Cahn.* Fay Spain, Steve Terrell, John Ashley, Frank Gorshin.

ROCK ALL NIGHT (1957). *Roger Corman.* Abby Dalton, Dick Miller, The Platters, Bruno Ve Sota, Ed Nelson, Barboura Morris, Jonathan Haze.

I WAS A TEENAGE WEREWOLF (1957). *Gene Fowler Jr.* Michael Landon, Yvonne Lime, Whit Bissell.

INVASION OF THE SAUCER-MEN (1957). *Edward L. Cahn.* Steve Terrell, Gloria Castillo, Frank Gorshin.

ROCK AROUND THE WORLD (aka THE TOMMY STEELE STORY) (1957). *Gerald Bryant.* Tommy Steele, Nancy Whiskey, The Steelemen.

REFORM SCHOOL GIRL (1957). *Edward Bernds.* Gloria Castillo, Ross Ford, Edward (Edd) Byrnes, Jan Englund.

THE AMAZING COLOSSAL MAN (1957). *Bert I. Gordon.* Glenn Langan, Cathy Downs, William Hudson.

THE CAT GIRL (1957). *Alfred Shaughnessy.* Barbara Shelley, Robert Ayres, Kay Callard, Paddy Webster.

SORORITY GIRL (1957). *Roger Corman.* Susan Cabot, Dick Miller, Barboura (Morris) O'Neill, June Kenney.

MOTORCYCLE GANG (1957). *Edward L. Cahn.* Steve Terrell, Anne Neyland, John Ashley.

I WAS A TEENAGE FRANKENSTEIN (1957). *Herbert L. Strock.* Whit Bissell, Robert Burton, Phyllis Coates, Gary Conway.

BLOOD OF DRACULA (1957). *Herbert L. Strock.* Sandra Harrison, Louise Lewis, Gail Ganley, Jerry Blaine.

THE VAMPIRE (1957). *Fernando Mendez.* Abel Salazar, Carmen Montejo, German Robles, Jose Luis Jimenez.

THE VAMPIRE'S COFFIN (1957). *Fernando Mendez.* German Robles, Abel Salazar, Ariadne Welter, Yeire Beirute.

JET ATTACK (1958). *Edward L. Cahn.* John Agar, Audrey Totter, Gregory Walcott, James Dobson, Victor Sen Yung.

SUICIDE BATTALION (1958). *Edward L. Cahn.* Michael Connors, John Ashley, Russ Bender, Jewell Lain, Bing Russell.

VIKING WOMEN AND THE SEA SERPENT (1958). *Roger Corman.* Abby Dalton, Susan Cabot, Brad Jackson, June Kenney.

THE ASTOUNDING SHE-MONSTER (1958). *Ronnie Ashcroft.* Robert Clarke, Kenne Duncan, Marilyn Harvey, Jeanne Tatum.

DRAGSTRIP RIOT (1958). *David Bradley.* Yvonne Lime, Gary Clarke, Connie Stevens, Fay Wray.

THE COOL AND THE CRAZY (1958). *William Whitney.* Scott Marlowe, Gigi Perreau, Dick Bakalyan, Dick Jones.

THE BONNIE PARKER STORY (1958). *William Witney.* Dorothy Provine, Jack Hogan, Richard Bakalyan, Joseph Turkel.

MACHINE GUN KELLY (1958). *Roger Corman.* Charles Bronson, Susan Cabot, Morey Amsterdam, Jack Lambert, Barboura Morris.

ATTACK OF THE PUPPET PEOPLE (1958). *Bert I. Gordon.* John Agar, John Hoyt, June Kenney.

WAR OF THE COLOSSAL BEAST (1958). *Bert I. Gordon.* Sally Fraser, Dean Parkin, Roger Pace, Russ Bender.

HELL SQUAD (1958). *Burt Topper.* Wally Campo, Brandon Carroll, Frederic Gavlin, Greg Stuart.

TANK BATTALION (1958). *Sherman A. Rose.* Don Kelly, Marjorie Hellen, Edward G. Robinson Jr., Frank Gorshin.

HIGH SCHOOL HELLCATS (1958). *Edward Bernds.* Yvonne Lime, Brett Halsey, Jana Lund, Suzanne Sydney.

HOT ROD GANG (1958). *Lew Landers.* John Ashley, Jody Fair, Gene Vincent, Russ Bender, Maureen Arthur.

THE SCREAMING SKULL (1958). *Alex Nicol.* John Hudson, Peggy Webber, Alex Nichol, Russ Conway, Toni Johnson.

TERROR FROM THE YEAR 5000 (1958). *Robert J. Gurney Jr.* Ward Costello, Joyce Holden, John Stratton, Salome Jens.

THE SPIDER (1958). *Bert I. Gordon.* Edward Kemmer, June Kenney, Gene Persson, Sally Fraser, Gene Roth.

THE BRAIN EATERS (1958). *Bruno Ve Sota.* Ed Nelson, Alan Frost, Joanna Lee, Jody Fair, Jack Hill, Leonard Nimoy.

HOW TO MAKE A MONSTER (1958). *Herbert L. Strock.* Robert H. Harris, Gary Conway, Gary Clarke, John Ashley.

TEENAGE CAVEMAN (1958). *Roger Corman.* Robert Vaughn, Darrah Marshall, Leslie Bradley, Frank De Kova.

NIGHT OF THE BLOOD BEAST (1958). *Bernard L. Kowalski.* Michael Emmet, Angela Greene, John Baer, Ed Nelson.

SHE GODS OF SHARK REEF (1958). *Roger Corman.* Don Durant, Bill Cord, Lisa Montell, Jeanne Gerson.

WHITE HUNTRESS (1958). *George Breakston.* Susan Stephan, John Bently, Robert Urquhart.

NAKED AFRICA (1958). *Cedric Worth.* Nature documentary narrated by Quentin Reynolds.

SUBMARINE SEAHAWK (1959). *Spencer Bennet.* John Bentley, Brett Halsey, Wayne Heffley, Steve Mitchell.

PARATROOP COMMAND (1959). *William Whitney.* Richard Bakalyan, Ken Lynch, Jack Hogan, Jimmy Murphy.

OPERATION DAMES (1959). *Louis Clyde Stoumen.* Eve Meyer, Chuck Henderson, Don Devlin, Ed Craig, Cindy Girard.

TANK COMMANDOS (1959). *Burt Topper.* Wally Campo, Robert Barron, Maggie Lawrence, Donato Farretta, Jack Sowards.

HORRORS OF THE BLACK MUSEUM (1959). *Arthur Crabtree.* Michael Gough, June Cunningham, Shirley Ann Field.

THE HEADLESS GHOST (1959). *Peter Graham Scott.* Richard Lyon, Liliane Sottane, David Rose, Clive Revill.

DADDY-O (1959). *Lou Place.* Dick Contino, Sandra Giles, Bruno Ve Sota, Gloria Victor, Ron McNeil.

ROAD RACERS (1959). *Arthur Swerdloff.* Joel Lawrence, Sally Fraser, Marian Collier, Skip Ward, Alan Dinehart, Jr.

DIARY OF A HIGH SCHOOL BRIDE (1959). *Burt Topper.* Anita Sands, Ronald Foster, Chris Robinson, Wendy Wilde.

GHOST OF DRAGSTRIP HOLLOW (1959). *William Hole Jr.* Jody Fair, Martin Braddock, Russ Bender, Leon Tyler.

SIGN OF THE GLADIATOR (1959). *Vittorio Musy Glori.* Anita Ekberg, Georges Marchal, Folco Lulli, Chelo Alonso, Jacques Sernas.

GOLIATH AND THE BARBARIANS (1959). *Carlo Campogalliani.* Steve Reeves, Chelo Alonso, Bruce Cabot, Luciano Marin.

A BUCKET OF BLOOD (1959). *Roger Corman.* Dick Miller, Barboura Morris, Antony Carbone, Ed Nelson.

THE GIANT LEECHES (1959). *Bernard L. Kowalski.* Ken Clark, Yvette Vickers, Bruno Ve Sota, Jan Shepard.

THE CURSE OF THE AZTEC MUMMY (1959). *Rafael Portello.* Ramon Gay, Rosita Arenas, Crox Alvarado, Lobo Negro.

THE CURSE OF THE CRYING WOMAN (1959). *Rafael Baleson.* Rosita Arenas, Abel Salazar, Rita Macedo, Domingo Soler.

ROBOT VS. THE AZTEC MUMMY (1959). *Rafael Portello.* Ramon Gay, Rosita Arenas, Crox Alvarado, Luis Acevas Castaneda.

THE ANGRY RED PLANET (1960). *Ib Melchior.* Gerald Mohr, Nora Hayden, Les Tremayne, Jack Kruschen.

CIRCUS OF HORRORS (1960). *Sidney Hayers.* Anton Diffring, Erika Remberg, Jane Hylton, Donald Pleasence.

THE JAILBREAKERS (1960). *Alexander Grasshoff.* Robert Hutton, Mary Castle, Michael O'Connell, Anton Van Stralen.

HOUSE OF USHER (1960). *Roger Corman.* Vincent Price, Mark Damon, Myrna Fahey, Harry Ellerby.

WHY MUST I DIE? (1960). *Roy Del Ruth.* Terry Moore, Debra Paget, Bert Freed, Juli Reding, Lionel Ames.

BEYOND THE TIME BARRIER (1960). *Edgar G. Ulmer.* Robert Clarke, Darlene Tompkins, Arianne Arden, Vladimir Sokoloff.

THE AMAZING TRANSPARENT MAN (1960). *Edgar G. Ulmer.* Marguerite Chapman, Douglas Kennedy, James Griffith.

JOURNEY TO THE LOST CITY (1960). *Fritz Lang.* Debra Paget, Paul Christian (Hubschmid), Walter Reyer, Luciana Paluzzi.

BEWARE OF CHILDREN (aka NO KIDDING) (1960). *Gerald Thomas.* Leslie Phillips, Geraldine McEwan, Julia Lockwood, Noel Purcell.

ASSIGMENT—OUTER SPACE (1960). *Antonio Margheriti.* Rik Von Nutter, Gaby Farinon, David Montressor, Archie Savage.

THE WORLD OF THE VAMPIRES (1960). *Alfonso Corona Blake.* Mauricio Garces, Silvia Fournier, Erna Martha Bauman, Guillermo Murray.

THE CURSE OF NOSTRADAMUS (1960). *Frederick Curiel* and *Stim Segar.* German Robles, Julio Aleman, Domingo Soler.

THE CURSE OF THE DOLL PEOPLE (1960). *Benito Alazarki.* Elvira Quintana, Ramon Gay, Robert G. Rivera, Jorge Mondragon.

THE INVISIBLE CREATURE (aka THE HOUSE ON MARSH ROAD) (1960). *Montgomery Tully.* Tony Wright, Patricia Dainton, Sandra Dorne.

SAMSON VS. THE VAMPIRE WOMEN (1961). *Alfonso Corona Blake.* Santo, Lorena Valazquez, Jaime Fernandez, Orfelia Montesco.

THE PHANTOM PLANET (1961). *William Marshall.* Dean Fredericks, Coleen Gray, Dolores Faith, Anthony Dexter.

FLIGHT OF THE LOST BALLOON (1961). *Nathan Juran.* Mala Powers, Marshall Thompson, James Lanphier, Douglas Kennedy.

PORTRAIT OF A SINNER (1961). *Robert Siodmak.* Nadja Tiller, Tony Britton, William Bendix, Natasha Parry.

GOLIATH AND THE DRAGON (1961). *Vittorio Cottafavi.* Mark Forest, Broderick Crawford, Eleanora Ruffo, Gaby Andre.

KONGA (1961). *John Lemont.* Michael Gough, Margo Johns, Jess Conrad, Claire Gordon, Jack Watson.

THE HAND (1961). *Henry Cass.* Derek Bond, Reed De Rouen, Bryan Coleman, Walter Randall, Tony Hilton.

ALAKAZAM THE GREAT (1961). *Teiji Yabushita* (Japanese version), *Lee Kresel* (U.S. version). Feature-length cartoon. Voices: Frankie Avalon, Jonathan Winters, Dodie Stevens, Arnold Stang.

THE PIT AND THE PENDULUM (1961). *Roger Corman.* Vincent Price, Barbara Steele, John Kerr, Luana Anders, Antony Carbone.

HOUSE OF FRIGHT (1961). *Terence Fisher.* Paul Massie, Dawn Addams, Christopher Lee, David Kossoff.

BLACK SUNDAY (1961). *Mario Bava.* Barbara Steele, John Richardson, Ivo Garrani, Andrea Checchi.

MASTER OF THE WORLD (1961). *William Whitney.* Vincent Price, Charles Bronson, Henry Hull, Mary Webster, Wally Campo.

OPERATION CAMEL (1961). *Sven Methling Jr.* Nora Hayden, Paul Hagen, Ebbe Langberg.

GUNS OF THE BLACK WITCH (1961). *Domenico Paolella* (Italian version), *Lee Kresel* (U.S. version). Don Megowan, Silvana Pampanini, Emma Danieli, Livio Lorenzon.

LOST BATTALION (1961). *Eddie Romero.* Leopoldo Salcedo, Diane Jergens, Johnny Monteiro, Joe Dennis.

JOURNEY TO THE SEVENTH PLANET (1961). *Sidney Pink.* John Agar, Greta Thyssen, Ann Smyrner, Mimi Heinrich.

TWIST ALL NIGHT (1961). *William Hole Jr.* Louis Prima, June Wilkinson, Sam Butera and the Witnesses.

THE PREMATURE BURIAL (1962). *Roger Corman.* Ray Milland, Hazel Court, Richard Ney, Heather Angel, Alan Napier.

TALES OF TERROR (1962). *Roger Corman.* Vincent Price, Peter Lorre, Basil Rathbone, Debra Paget, Maggie Pierce, Wally Campo.

INVASION OF THE STAR CREATURES (1962). *Bruno Ve Sota.* Robert Ball, Frankie Ray, Gloria Victor, Dolores Reed.

THE BRAIN THAT WOULDN'T DIE (1962). *Joseph Green.* Virginia Leith, Herb Evers, Adele Lamont, Bruce Brighton.

PANIC IN YEAR ZERO (1962). *Ray Milland.* Ray Milland, Frankie Avalon, Jean Hagen, Richard Bakalyan, Joan Freeman.

BURN, WITCH, BURN! (1962). *Sidney Hayers.* Janet Blair, Peter Wyngarde, Margaret Johnson, Kathleen Byron.

MARCO POLO (1962). *Hugo Fregonese.* Rory Calhoun, Yoko Tani, Robert Hundar, Pierre Cressoy, Camillo Pilotto.

WHITE SLAVE SHIP (1962). *Silvio Amadio.* Pier Angeli, Edmund Purdom, Armand Mestral, Ivan Desny.

WARRIORS FIVE (1962). *Leopoldo Savona.* Jack Palance, Giovanna Ralli, Serge Reggiani, Folco Lulli.

NIGHT TIDE (1963). *Curtis Harrington.* Dennis Hopper, Linda Lawson, Luana Anders, Gavin Muir, Marjorie Eaton.

REPTILICUS (1963). *Sidney Pink.* Carl Ottosen, Ann Smyrner, Mimi Heinrich, Marla Behrens.

SAMSON AND THE SEVEN MIRACLES OF THE WORLD (1963). *Riccardo Freda.* Gordon Scott, Yoko Tani, Gabriele Antonini.

THE RAVEN (1963). *Roger Corman.* Vincent Price, Peter Lorre, Boris Karloff, Hazel Court, Olive Sturgess, Jack Nicholson.

OPERATION BIKINI (1963). *Anthony Carras.* Tab Hunter, Frankie Avalon, Scott Brady, Gary Crosby, Jody McCrea, Eva Six.

THE YOUNG RACERS (1963). *Roger Corman.* Mark Damon, William Campbell, Luana Anders, Robert Campbell, Patrick Magee.

FREE, WHITE AND 21 (1963). *Larry Buchanan.* Frederick O'Neal, Annalena Lund, George Edgley, George Russell, John Hicks.

BATTLE BEYOND THE SUN (1963). (Originally NEBO ZOVYOT in USSR, 1959). *Thomas Colchart (Roger Corman) and Francis Ford Coppola).* Edd Perry, Arla Powell, Andy Stuart, Barry Chertok.

BEACH PARTY (1963). *William Asher.* Bob Cummings, Frankie Avalon, Annette Funicello, Harvey Lembeck, Morey Amsterdam, John Ashley.

THE MIND BENDERS (1963). *Basil Dearden.* Dirk Bogarde, Mary Ure, John Clements, Wendy Craig, Michael Bryant, Edward Fox.

THE HAUNTED PALACE (1963). *Roger Corman.* Vincent Price, Debra Paget, Lon Chaney, Jr., Leo Gordon, Elisha Cook.

X—THE MAN WITH THE X-RAY EYES (1963). *Roger Corman.* Ray Milland, Diana Van Der Vlis, Don Rickles, Harold J. Stone, John Hoyt.

ERIK THE CONQUEROR (1963). *Mario Bava.* Cameron Mitchell, Andrea Checci, Fulco Lulli, Giorgio Ardisson.

PRISONER OF THE IRON MASK (1963). *Francesco De Feo* (Italian version). *Lee Kresel* (U.S. version). Michael Lemoine, Wandisa Guida, Jany Clair.

THE TERROR (1963). *Roger Corman.* Boris Karloff, Jack Nicholson, Sandra Knight, Richard Miller, Dorothy Neumann.

DEMENTIA 13 (1963). *Francis Coppola.* William Campbell, Luana Anders, Bart Patton, Mary Mitchell, Patrick Magee.

SAMSON AND THE SLAVE QUEEN (1963). *Umberto Lenzi.* Alan Steel, Pierre Brice, Moira Orfei, Massimo Serato.

GOLIATH AND THE SINS OF BABYLON (1963). *Michele Lupo.* Mark Forest, Eleanora Bianchi, Giuliano Gemma, Livio Lorenzon.

SUMMER HOLIDAY (1963). *Peter Yates.* Cliff Richard, Lauri Peters, Melvyn Hayes, Una Stubbs, Pamela Hart, The Shadows.

THE COMEDY OF TERRORS (1963). *Jacques Tourneur.* Vincent Price, Peter Lorre, Basil Rathbone, Boris Karloff, Joe E. Brown.

CALIFORNIA (1963). *Hamil Petroff.* Jock Mahoney, Faith Domergue, Michael Pate, Susan Seaforth, Rudolpho Hoyos.

SAMSON IN THE WAX MUSEUM (1963). *Alfonso Corona Blake.* Santo, Lorena Valazquez, Jaime Fernandez, Orfelia Montesco

ATTACK OF THE MUSHROOM PEOPLE (1963). *Inoshiro Honda, Eiji Tsuburaya.* Akiro Kubo, Yoshio Tsuchiya, Hiroshi Koizumi, Hiroshi Tachikawa.

THE CRAWLING HAND (1964). *Herbert L. Strock.* Peter Breck, Kent Taylor, Rod Lauren, Sirry Steffen.

MUSCLE BEACH PARTY (1964). *William Asher.* Frankie Avalon, Annette Funicello, Buddy Hackett, Morey Amsterdam, Don Rickles.

ATRAGON (1964). *Inoshiro Honda.* Tadao Takashima, Yoko Fujiyama, Yu Fujiki, Kenji Sawara, Tetsuko Kobayashi.

PYRO (1964). *Julio Coll.* Barry Sullivan, Martha Hyer, Sherry Moreland, Soledad Miranda, Luis Prendes.

GOLIATH AND THE VAMPIRES (1964). *Giacomo Gentilomo* and *Sergio Corbucci.* Gordon Scott, Gianna Maria Canale, Jacques Sernas.

BLACK SABBATH (1964). *Mario Bava.* Boris Karloff, Mark Damon, Jacqueline Pierreaux, Michele Mercier.

EVIL EYE (1964). *Mario Bava.* John Saxon, Leticia Roman, Valentina Cortesa, Dante Di Paolo, Robert Buchanan.

THE LAST MAN ON EARTH (1964). *Ubaldo Ragona* (Italian version), *Sidney Sakolow* (U.S. version). Vincent Price, Franca Bettoia, Emma Danieli, Giacomo Rossi Stuart.

THE UNEARTHLY STRANGER (1964). *John Krish.* John Neville, Garbriella Licudi, Philip Stone, Patrick Newell, Jean Marsh.

BIKINI BEACH (1964). *William Asher.* Frankie Avalon, Annette Funicello, Keenan Wynn, Martha Hyer, Harvey Lembeck, Don Rickles.

THE MASQUE OF THE RED DEATH (1964). *Roger Corman.* Vincent Price, Hazel Court, Jane Asher, Nigel Green, Patrick Magee.

COMMANDO (1964). *Frank Wisbar.* Stewart Granger, Dorian Gray, Maurizio Arena, Ivo Garrani, Fausto Tozzi.

TORPEDO BAY (1964). *Charles Frend* and *Bruno Vailati.* James Mason, Lilli Palmer, Gabriele Ferzetti, Geoffrey Keen.

PAJAMA PARTY (1964). *Don Weis.* Tommy Kirk, Annette Funicello, Jody McCrea, Buster Keaton, Dorothy Lamour, Harvey Lembeck.

THE T.A.M.I. SHOW (1964). *Steve Binder.* The Beach Boys, Chuck Berry, Marvin Gaye, The Rolling Stones, The Supremes.

DIARY OF A BACHELOR (1964). *Sandy Howard.* William Traylor, Dagne Crane, Joe Silver, Denise Lor, Dom DeLuise, Chris Noel.

THE TIME TRAVELERS (1964). *Ib Melchior.* Preston Foster, Philip Carey, Merry Anders, John Hoyt, Dennis Patrick.

VOYAGE TO THE END OF THE UNIVERSE (1964). *Jack Pollack.* Dennis Stephans, Francis Smolen, Dana Meredith, Irene Kova.

THE DAY THE EARTH FROZE (1964). *Aleksandr Ptushko* and *Gregg Sebelious.* Nina Anderson, Jon Powers, Ingrid Elhardt, Peter Sorenson.

GODZILLA VS. THE THING (1964). *Shinichi Sekizawa.* Akira Takarada, Yuriko Hoshi, Hiroshi Koisumi, Emi Ito.

THE WRESTLING WOMEN VS. THE AZTEC MUMMY (1964). *Rene Cardona.* Lorena Velazquez, Armando Silvestre, Elizabeth Campbell, Maria Eugenia San Martin.

UNDER AGE (1964). *Larry Buchanan.* Anne MacAdams, Judy Adler, Roland Royter, George Russell.

HERCULES, PRISONER OF EVIL (1964). *Antonio Margheriti.* Reg Park, Mireille Granelli, Ettore Manni, Maria Teresa Orsini.

NAVAJO RUN (1964). *Johnny Seven.* Johnny Seven, Warren Kemmerling, Virginia Vincent, Ron Soble.

SOME PEOPLE (1964). *Clive Donner.* Kenneth More, Ray Brooks, Annika Wills, David Andrews.

DR. ORLOFF'S MONSTER (1964). *Jesus Franco.* Jose Rubio, Agnes Spaak, Perla Cristal, Pastor Serrador.

CONQUERED CITY (1965). *Joseph Anthony.* David Niven, Lea Massari, Ben Gazzara, Martin Balsam, Michael Craig.

TOMB OF LIGEIA (1965). *Roger Corman.* Vincent Price, Elizabeth Shepherd, John Westbrook, Oliver Johnston, Derek Francis.

THE LOST WORLD OF SINBAD (aka SAMURAI PIRATE) (1965). *Senkichi Taniguchi.* Toshiro Mifune, Makoto Satoh, Jun Fanado.

THE WAR OF THE ZOMBIES (1965). *Giuseppe Vari.* John Drew Barrymore, Susy Andersen, Ettore Manni, Ida Galli, Mino Doro.

BEACH BLANKET BINGO (1965). *William Asher.* Frankie Avalon, Annette Funicello, Deborah Walley, Jody McCrea, Buster Keaton.

WAR-GODS OF THE DEEP (1965). *Jacques Tourneur.* Vincent Price, Tab Hunter, David Tomlinson, Susan Hart, John LeMesurier.

OPERATION SNAFU (aka OPERATION WARHEAD) (1965). *Cyril Frankel.* Alfred Lynch, Sean Connery, Cecil Parker, Stanley Holloway.

GO-GO MANIA (1965). *Frederic Goode.* The Animals, Herman's Hermits, Peter and Gordon, Matt Monro, The Beatles, Billy J. Kramer.

SWINGER'S PARADISE (1965). *Sidney J. Furie.* Cliff Richard, Susan Hampshire, Walter Slezak, The Shadows.

SKI PARTY (1965). *Alan Rafkin.* Frankie Avalon, Deborah Walley, Dwayne Hickman, Yvonne Craig, Aron Kincaid, Robert Q. Lewis.

TOKYO OLYMPIAD (1965). *Kon Ichikawa.* Documentary about the Olympic Games in Tokyo.

TABOOS OF THE WORLD (1965). *Romolo Marcellini.* "Mondo"-style documentary narrated by Vincent Price.

HOW TO STUFF A WILD BIKINI (1965). *William Asher.* Annette Funicello, Dwayne Hickman, Jody McCrea, Mickey Rooney, Buster Keaton.

SERGEANT DEADHEAD (1965). *Norman Taurog.* Frankie Avalon, Deborah Walley, Cesar Romero, Eve Arden, Buster Keaton, Harvey Lembeck.

DR. GOLDFOOT AND THE BIKINI MACHINE (1965). *Norman Taurog.* Vincent Price, Frankie Avalon, Dwayne Hickman, Susan Hart.

DIE, MONSTER, DIE! (1965). *Daniel Haller.* Boris Karloff, Nick Adams, Freda Jackson, Patrick Magee.

PLANET OF THE VAMPIRES (1965). *Mario Bava.* Barry Sullivan, Norma Bengell, Angel Aranda, Fernando Villena.

SPACE MONSTER (1965). *Leonard Katzman.* Russ Bender, Francine York, James Brown, Baynes Barron.

SAMURAI PIRATE (1965). *Senkichi Taniguchi.* Toshiro Mifune, Makoto Sato, Jun Funato, Ichiro Arishima.

EYE CREATURES (1965). *Larry Buchanan.* John Ashley, Cynthia Hull, Warren Hammack, Chet Davis.

VOYAGE TO THE PREHISTORIC PLANET (1966). *John Sebastian (Curtis Harrington).* Basil Rathbone, Faith Domergue, Marc Shannon.

THE BIG T.N.T. SHOW (1966). *Larry Peerce.* Petula Clark, Roger Miller, Joan Baez, Ray Charles, The Byrds, Ike & Tina Turner.

SECRET AGENT FIREBALL (1966). *Mario Donen.* Richard Harrison, Wandisa Guida, Dominique Boschero, Alcide Borik.

SPY IN YOUR EYE (1966). *Vittorio Sala.* Brett Halsey, Pier Angeli, Dana Andrews, Gaston Moschin, Tino Bianchi.

HALLUCINATION GENERATION (1966). *Edward Mann.* George Montgomery, Danny Stone, Renate Kasche, Tom Baker, Marianne Kanter.

BLOOD BATH (1966). *Jack Hill* and *Stephanie Rothman.* William Campbell, Lori Anders, Sandra Knight, Marissa Mathes.

QUEEN OF BLOOD (aka PLANET OF BLOOD) (1966). *Curtis Harrington.* John Saxon, Dennis Hopper, Basil Rathbone, Judi Meredith.

THE GHOST IN THE INVISIBLE BIKINI (1966). *Don Weis.* Tommy Kirk, Deborah Walley, Aron Kincaid, Nancy Sinatra, Boris Karloff.

THE DIRTY GAME (1966). *Christian-Jaque.* Henry Fonda, Robert Ryan, Vittorio Gassman, Annie Girardot, Bourvil, Jacques Sernas.

THE GREAT SPY CHASE (1966). *Georges Lautner.* Lino Ventura, Bernard Blier, Mirielle Darc, Francis Blanche, Jess Hahn.

SANDS OF BEERSHEBA (1966). *Alexander Ramati.* Diane Baker, Tom Bell, David Opatoshu, Theodore Marcuse.

TARZAN AND THE VALLEY OF GOLD (1966). *Robert Day.* Mike Henry, Nancy Kovack, Manuel Padilla Jr., David Opatoshu.

FRANKENSTEIN CONQUERS THE WORLD (1966). *Inoshiro Honda.* Nick Adams, Tadao Takashima, Kumi Mizumo, Yoshio Tsuchiya.

FIREBALL 500 (1966). *William Asher.* Frankie Avalon, Annette Funicello, Fabian, Chill Wills, Harvey Lembeck.

THE WILD ANGELS (1966). *Roger Corman.* Peter Fonda, Nancy Sinatra, Bruce Dern, Diane Ladd, Gayle Hunnicutt, Marc Cavell.

THE GIRL-GETTERS (1966). *Michael Winner.* Oliver Reed, Jane Merrow, Barbara Ferris, Julia Foster, Harry Andrews, David Hemmings.

BANG, BANG, YOU'RE DEAD! (1966). *Don Sharp.* Tony Randall, Senta Berger, Terry-Thomas, Herbert Lom, Klaus Kinski.

WHAT'S UP, TIGER LILY? (1966). *Senkichi Taniguchi* (Japanese version), *Woody Allen* (U.S. version). Narrated by Woody Allen.

DR. GOLDFOOT AND THE GIRL BOMBS (1966). *Mario Bava.* Vincent Price, Fabian, Franco Franchi, Ciccio Ingrassia, Laura Antonelli.

TRUNK TO CAIRO (1966). *Menachem Golan.* Audie Murphy, George Sanders, Marianne Koch, Joseph Yadin.

LA DOLCE VITA (1966) (English language version). *Federico Fellini.* Marcello Mastroianni, Anita Ekberg, Anouk Aimee.

KING AND COUNTRY (1966). *Joseph Losey.* Dirk Bogarde, Tom Courtenay, Leo McKern, Barry Foster.

THE MAN FROM COCODY (1966). *Christian-Jaque.* Jean Marais, Liselotte Pulver, Philippe Clay, Nancy Holloway.

DOOR TO DOOR MANIAC (1966). *Bill Karn.* Johnny Cash, Donald Woods, Kay Forester, Pamela Mason.

NASHVILLE REBEL (1966). *Jay Sheridan.* Waylon Jennings, Gordon Oas-Heim, Mary Frann, Cece Whitney.

IN THE YEAR 2889 (1966). *Larry Buchanan.* Paul Peterson, Quinn O'Hara, Charla Doherty, Neil Fletcher.

ZONTAR, THE THING FROM VENUS (1966). *Larry Buchanan.* John Agar, Susan Bjurman, Anthony Houston, Patricia De Laney.

CURSE OF THE SWAMP CREATURE (1966). *Larry Buchanan.* John Agar, Francine York, Shirley McLine, Bill Thurman.

CREATURE OF DESTRUCTION (1966). *Larry Buchanan.* Les Tremayne, Aron Kincaid, Pat Delaney, Neil Fletcher.

SEXY MAGICO (1966). *Mino Loy, Luigi Scattini.* Black Eva, Nana Pilou, Leila Sohl, Rosetta Esperanza.

MONSTER FROM A PREHISTORIC PLANET (1966). *Haruyasu Noguchi.* Tamio Kawaji, Yoko Yamaoto, Tatsuya Fugi, Koji Wada.

THE RETURN OF THE GIANT MONSTERS (1966). *Noriaki Yuasa.* Kojiro Hongo, Kichijiro Ueda, HIsayuki Abe, Reiko Kasahara.

VOYAGE TO THE PLANET OF PREHISTORIC WOMEN (1966). Filmed in USSR in 1962 as RED PLANET OF STORMS. New footage: *Derek Thomas (Peter Bogdanovich)*. Mamie Van Doren, Mary Mark, Paige Lee.

WAR ITALIAN STYLE (1967). *Luigi Scattini*. Franco Franchi, Ciccio Ingrassia, Buster Keaton, Martha Hyer, Fred Clark.

RIOT ON SUNSET STRIP (1967). *Arthur Dreifuss*. Aldo Ray, Mimsy Farmer, Michael Evans, Tim Rooney.

THUNDER ALLEY (1967). *Richard Rush*. Annette Funicello, Fabian, Diane McBain, Warren Berlinger, Jan Murray.

DEVIL'S ANGELS (1967). *Daniel Haller*. John Cassavetes, Mimsy Farmer, Beverly Adams, Marc Cavell, Wally Campo.

THE MILLION EYES OF SU-MARU (1967). *Lindsay Shonteff*. Frankie Avalon, George Naer, Shirley Eaton, Klaus Kinski.

PSYCHO-CIRCUS (1967). *John Moxey*. Christopher Lee, Leo Genn, Suzy Kendall, Klaus Kinski, Anthony Newlands, Margaret Lee.

HELL'S ANGELS ON WHEELS (1967). *Richard Rush*. Adam Roarke, Jack Nicholson, Sabrina Scharf, Jana Taylor.

THOSE FANTASTIC FLYING FOOLS (aka BLAST OFF) (1967). *Don Sharp*. Burl Ives, Troy Donahue, Daliah Lavi, Terry-Thomas, Gert Frobe.

BORN LOSERS (1967). *T.C. Frank*. Tom Laughlin, Elizabeth James, Jane Russell, Jeremy Slate, William Wellman, Jr.

THE TRIP (1967). *Roger Corman*. Peter Fonda, Susan Strasberg, Dean Stockwell, Dennis Hopper, Salli Sachse, Luana Anders.

IT'S A BIKINI WORLD (1967). *Stephanie Rothman*. Deborah Walley, Tommy Kirk, Bob Pickett, Suzie Kaye, Sid Haig, The Animals.

HOUSE OF 1,000 DOLLS (1967). *Jeremy Summers*. Vincent Price, Martha Hyer, George Nader, Anne Smyrner, Maria Rohm.

THE GLORY STOMPERS (1967). *Anthony Lanza*. Dennis Hopper, Jody McCrea, Chris Noel, Jock Mahoney, Sondra Gale.

THE COBRA (1967). *Mario Sequi*. Dana Andrews, Peter Martell, Anita Ekberg, Elisa Montes, Jesus Puente.

MARYJANE (1968). *Maury Dexter*. Fabian, Diane McBain, Kevin Coughlin, Patty McCormack, Russ Bender, Michael Margotta.

PSYCH-OUT (1968). *Richard Rush*. Susan Strasberg, Dean Stockwell, Jack Nicholson, Bruce Dern, Adam Roarke.

THE WILD RACERS (1968). *Daniel Haller*. Fabian, Mimsy Farmer, Alan Haufrecht, Judy Cornwell, Talia Coppola (Shire).

THE CONQUEROR WORM (1968). *Michael Reeves*. Vincent Price, Ian Ogilvy, Rupert Davies, Hilary Dwyer.

THE MINI-SKIRT MOB (1968). *Maury Dexter*. Jeremy Slate, Diane McBain, Sherry Jackson, Patty McCormack, Ross Hagen.

THE SAVAGE SEVEN (1968). *Richard Rush.* Robert Walker Jr., Adam Roarke, Larry Bishop, Joanna Frank, Duane Eddy, Penny Marshall.

WILD IN THE STREETS (1968). *Barry Shear.* Shelley Winters, Diane Varsi, Christopher Jones, Hal Holbrook, Millie Perkins.

ANGELS FROM HELL (1968). *Bruce Kessler.* Tom Stern, Arlene Martel, Stephen Oliver, Jack Starrett, Ted Markland.

THE GLASS SPHINX (1968). *Luigi Scattini.* Robert Taylor, Anita Ekberg, Gianna Sera, Jack Stuart, Angel Del Pozo.

THE YOUNG, THE EVIL AND THE SAVAGE (1968). *Anthony Dawson.* Michael Rennie, Mark Damon, Eleanora Brown, Sally Smith.

HELGA (1968). *Erich F. Bender* (German version), *Terry Van Tell* (U.S. version). Ruth Gassman, Eberhard Mondry.

THE WILD EYE (1968). *Paolo Cavara.* Philippe Leroy, Delia Boccardo, Gabriele Tinti, Luciana Angelillo.

THE YOUNG ANIMALS (1968). *Maury Dexter.* Tom Nardini, Patty McCormack, Joanna Frank, David Macklin, Russ Bender.

THE DESPERATE ONES (1968). *Alexander Ramati.* Maximilian Schell, Raf Vallone, Irene Papas, Theordore Bikel, Matia Perschy.

CERVANTES (aka THE YOUNG REBEL) (1968). *Vincent Sherman.* Horst Buchholz, Gina Lollobrigida, Jose Ferrer, Louis Jourdan.

THE ROAD HUSTLERS (1968). *Larry E. Jackson.* Jim Davis, Scott Brady, Andy Devine, Bruce Yarnell, Robert Dix.

MAD CHECKMATE (aka IT'S YOUR MOVE) (1968). *Robert Fiz.* Edward G. Robinson, Adolfo Celi, Terry-Thomas, Maria Grazzia Buccella.

KILLERS THREE (1968). *Bruce Kessler.* Robert Walker Jr., Diane Varsi, Dick Clark, Maureen Arthur, Merle Haggard.

THE BRUTE AND THE BEAST (1968). *Lucio Fulci.* Franco Nero, George Hilton, Nino Castelnuovo, Lyn Shayne, John MacDouglas.

3 IN THE ATTIC (aka UP IN THE ATTIC) (1968). *Richard Wilson.* Christopher Jones, Yvette Mimieux, Judy Pace, Maggie Thrett.

ATTACK OF THE MONSTERS (1968). *Inoshiro Honda.* Nobuhiro Najima, Miyuki Akiyama, Yuko Hamada, Christopher Murphy.

HIGH, WILD AND FREE (1968). *Gordon Eastman.* Nature film narrated by Gordon Eastman.

THE DEVIL'S 8 (1969). *Burt Topper.* Christopher George, Ralph Meeker, Fabian, Tom Nardini, Leslie Parrish.

HELL'S BELLES (1969). *R.G. McMullen.* Jeremy Slate, Adam Roarke, Jocelyn Lane, Angelique Pettyjohn.

MICHAEL AND HELGA (1969). *Erich F. Bender.* Ruth Gassman, Felix Franchy, Hildegard Linden, Elfi Reuter.

SUCCUBUS (1969). *Jess Franco.* Janine Reynaud, Jack Taylor, Howard Vernon, Michel Lemoine, Nathalie Nord.

MAFIA (1969). *Damiano Damiani.* Claudia Cardinale, Franco Nero, Lee J. Cobb, Nehemiah Persoff, Serge Reggiani.

DESTROY ALL MONSTERS (1969). *Inoshiro Honda.* Akira Kubo, Jun Tazaki, Yoshio Tsuchiya, Kyoko Ai, Kenji Sawara.

CHASTITY (1969). *Alessio De Paola.* (Screenplay: Sonny Bono). Cher, Barbara London, Stephen Whittaker, Tom Nolan.

GOD FORGIVES, I DON'T! (1969). *Giuseppe Colizzi.* Terence Hill, Bud Spencer, Frank Wolff, Gina Rovere, Jose Manuel Martin.

THE DAY THE HOT LINE GOT HOT (1969). *Etienne Perier.* Robert Taylor, Charles Boyer, George Chakiris, Marie DuBois.

THE OBLONG BOX (1969). *Gordon Hessler.* Vincent Price, Christopher Lee, Hilary Dwyer, Rupert Davies, Sally Geeson.

HELL'S ANGELS '69 (1969). *Lee Madden.* Tom Stern, Jeremy Slate, Conny Van Dyke, Steve Sandor, G.D. Spradlin.

SPIRITS OF THE DEAD (1969). *Roger Vadim, Louis Malle, Federico Fellini.* Jane Fonda, Peter Fonda, Brigitte Bardot, Alain Delon.

DE SADE (1969). *Cy Endfield.* Keir Dullea, Senta Berger, Lilli Palmer, John Huston, Anna Massey, Uta Levka.

ANGEL, ANGEL, DOWN WE GO (aka CULT OF THE DAMNED) (1969). *Robert Thom.* Jennifer Jones, Jordan Christopher, Roddy McDowall.

TWO GENTLEMEN SHARING (1969). *Ted Kotcheff.* Robin Phillips, Judy Geeson, Hal Frederick, Esther Anderson, Hilary Dwyer.

MADIGAN'S MILLIONS (1969). *Stanley Prager.* Dustin Hoffman, Elsa Martinelli, Cesar Romero, Gustavo Rojo. (Filmed in 1967)

FEARLESS FRANK (1969). *Phillip Kaufman.* Jon Voight, Monique Van Vooren, Joan Darling, Severn Darden. (Filmed in 1967)

EXPLOSION (1969). *Jules Bricken.* Don Stroud, Gordon Thomson, Michele Chicione, Robin Ward, Cec Linder, Richard Conte.

THE DUNWICH HORROR (1970). *Daniel Haller.* Sandra Dee, Dean Stockwell, Ed Begley, Sam Jaffe, Talia Coppola (Shire).

THE SAVAGE WILD (1970). *Gordon Eastman.* Gordon Eastman, Maria Eastman, Carl Spore, Arlo Curtis.

THE CYCLE SAVAGES (1970). *Bill Brame.* Bruce Dern, Melody Patterson, Chris Robinson, Scott Brady.

SCREAM AND SCREAM AGAIN (1970). *Gordon Hessler.* Vincent Price, Christopher Lee, Peter Cushing, Judy Huxtable, Uta Levka.

BORA BORA (1970). *Ugo Liberatore.* Haydee Politoff, Corrado Pani, Doris Kunstmann, Rosine Copie.

BLOODY MAMA (1970). *Roger Corman.* Shelley Winters, Don Stroud, Pat Hingle, Diane Varsi, Bruce Dern, Robert De Niro, Alex Nicol.

THE CRIMSON CULT (1970). *Vernon Sewell.* Boris Karloff, Christopher Lee, Rupert Davies, Barbara Steele, Virginia Wetherell.

HORROR HOUSE (1970). *Michael Armstrong*. Frankie Avalon, Jill Haworth, Mark Wynter, Dennis Price, Gina Warwick.

VENUS IN FURS (1970). *Jess Franco*. James Darren, Barbara McNair, Klaus Kinski, Maria Rohm, Dennis Price, Margaret Lee.

WEDDING NIGHT (1970). *Piers Haggard*. Dennis Waterman, Tessa Wyatt, Alexandra Bastedo, Eddie Byrne, Martin Dempsey.

COUNT YORGA, VAMPIRE (1970). *Robert Kelljan*. Robert Quarry, Roger Perry, Michael Murphy, Michael Macready, Donna Anders, Judy Lang.

I AM A GROUPIE (1970). *Derek Ford*. Esme Johns, Billy Boyle, Richard Shaw, Neil Hallett, Charles Finch, Eliza Terry.

THE SWAPPERS (1970). *Derek Ford*. James Donnelly, Larry Taylor, Valerie St. John, Dennis Hawthorne, Bunty Garland.

JULIUS CAESAR (1970). *Stuart Burge*. Charlton Heston, Jason Robards, John Gielgud, Richard Chamberlain, Diana Rigg.

CRY OF THE BANSHEE (1970). *Gordon Hessler*. Vincent Price, Essy Persson, Elizabeth Bergner, Hilary Dwyer, Hugh Griffith.

A BULLET FOR PRETTY BOY (1970). *Larry Buchanan*. Fabian Forte, Jocelyn Lane, Adam Roarke, Astrid Warner, Michael Haynes.

ANGEL UNCHAINED (1970). *Lee Madden*. Don Stroud, Luke Askew, Larry Bishop, Tyne Daly, Aldo Ray, Bill McKinney.

GAS-S-S-S! (1970). *Roger Corman*. Robert Corff, Elaine Giftos, Bud Cort, Talia Coppola (Shire), Ben Vereen, Cindy Williams.

UP IN THE CELLAR (1970). *Theodore J. Flicker*. Wes Stern, Joan Collins, Larry Hagman, Judy Pace, Nira Barab.

THE VAMPIRE LOVERS (1970). *Roy Ward Baker*. Ingrid Pitt, Peter Cushing, Dawn Addams, Jon Finch, Madeline Smith.

PACIFIC VIBRATIONS (1970). *John Severson*. Surfing documentary with champion surfers.

GAMMERA VS. MONSTER X (1970). *Noriaki Yuasa*. Tsutomu Takakuwa, Kelly Varis, Katherine Murphy, Kon Omura.

TIGER BY THE TAIL (1970). *R. G. Springsteen*. Christopher George, Tippi Hedren, Dean Jagger, John Dehner, Charo.

24-HOUR LOVER (1970). *Marran Gosov*. Harold Leipnitz, Sybille Maar, Herbert Botticher, Brigitte Skay.

KAMA SUTRA (1970). *Kobi Jaeger*. Bruno Dietrich, Barbara Schones, Richard Abbott, Karen Kaehler, Persis Khambatta.

DORIAN GRAY (1970). *Massimo Dallamano*. Helmut Berger, Richard Todd, Herbert Lom, Marie Liljedahl, Maria Rohm.

WUTHERING HEIGHTS (1970). *Robert Fuest*. Timothy Dalton, Anna Calder-Marshall, Harry Andrews, Pamela Brown, Hugh Griffith.

BATTLE OF NERETVA (1971). *Veljko Bulajic*. Yul Brynner, Sergei Bondarchuk, Curt Jurgens, Orson Welles, Franco Nero.

BLOOD AND LACE (1971). *Philip Gilbert.* Gloria Grahame, Melody Patterson, Milton Selzerm, Vic Tayback, Len Lesser.

THE INCREDIBLE TWO-HEADED TRANSPLANT (1971). *Anthony M. Lanza.* Bruce Dern, Pat Priest, Casey Kasem, Albert Cole.

THE HARD RIDE (1971). *Burt Topper.* Robert Fuller, Sherry Bain, Tony Russel, William Bonner, Marshall Reed.

THE HOUSE THAT SCREAMED (1971). *Narcisco Ibanez Serrador.* Lilli Palmer, John Moulder Brown, Cristina Galbo, Tomas Blanco.

THE DIRT GANG (1971). *Jerry Jameson.* Paul Carr, Michael Pataki, Lee De Broux, Nancy Harris, Jessica Stuart.

DAGMAR'S HOT PANTS, INC. (1971). *Vernon P. Becker.* Diana Kjaer, Anne Grete, Robert Strauss, Inger Sundh, Tommy Blom.

THE YEAR OF THE CANNIBALS (1971). *Liliana Cavana.* Britt Ekland, Pierre Clementi, Delia Boccardo, Tomas Milian.

SWEDISH FLY GIRLS (aka CHRISTA) (1971). *Jack O'Connell.* Birte Tove, Susan Hurley, Inger Stender, Daniel Gelin.

CARRY ON HENRY VIII (1971). *Gerald Thomas.* Sidney James, Kenneth Williams, Joan Sims, Charles Hawtrey, Barbara Windsor.

YOG—MONSTER FROM SPACE (1971). *Inoshiro Honda.* Akira Kubo, Atsuko Takahashi, Yoshio Tsuchiya, Kenji Sahara.

THE ABOMINABLE DR. PHIBES (1971). *Robert Fuest.* Vincent Price, Joseph Cotten, Hugh Griffith, Terry-Thomas, Virginia North.

BUNNY O'HARE (1971). *Gerd Oswald.* Bette Davis, Ernest Borgnine, Jack Cassidy, Joan Delaney, Jay Robinson, John Astin.

THE RETURN OF COUNT YORGA (1971). *Bob Kelljan.* Robert Quarry, Mariette Hartley, Roger Perry, Yvonne Wilder.

MURDERS IN THE RUE MORGUE (1971). *Gordon Hessler.* Jason Robards, Christine Kaufmann, Herbert Lom, Lilli Palmer, Michael Dunn.

CHROME AND HOT LEATHER (1971). *Lee Frost.* William Smith, Tony Young, Michael Haynes, Peter Brown, Marvin Gaye, Wes Bishop.

BLOOD FROM THE MUMMY'S TOMB (1971). *Seth Holt* and *Michael Carreras.* Andrew Keir, Valerie Leon, James Villiers.

1,000 CONVICTS AND A WOMAN (1971). *Ray Austin.* Alexandra Hay, Sandor Eles, Harry Baird, Neil Hallett, Tracy Reed.

DR. JEKYLL AND SISTER HYDE (1971). *Roy Ward Baker.* Ralph Bates, Martine Beswick, Gerald Sim, Virginia Wetherell, Ivor Dean.

SOME OF MY BEST FRIENDS ARE ... (1971). *Mervyn Nelson.* Tom Blade, Carleton Carpenter, David Baker, Paul Blake, Gary Campbell.

TAM LIN (aka THE DEVIL'S WIDOW) (1971). *Roddy McDowall.* Ava Gardner, Ian McShane, Stephanie Beacham, Cyril Cusack.

KIDNAPPED (1971). *Delbert Mann.* Michael Caine, Trevor Howard, Jack Hawkins, Donald Pleasence, Vivienne Heilbron.

WHO SLEW AUNTIE ROO? (1971). *Curtis Harrington.* Shelley Winters, Mark Lester, Ralph Richardson, Hugh Griffith, Lionel Jeffries.

THE WILD PACK (aka THE SANDPIT GENERALS) (1972). *Hall Bartlett.* Kent Lane, Tisha Sterling, John Rubinstein, Butch Patrick.

SCHIZOID (1972). *Lucio Fulci.* Florinda Bolkan, Stanely Baker, Jean Sorel, Leo Genn, Alberto de Mendoza, Silvia Monti.

LOLA (aka TWINKY) (1972). *Richard Donner.* Charles Bronson, Susan George, Trevor Howard, Orson Welles, Jack Hawkins, Honor Blackman.

FROGS (1972). *George McCowan.* Ray Milland, Sam Elliott, Joan Van Ark, Adam Roarke, Judy Pace, Lynn Borden.

GODZILLA VS. THE SMOG MONSTER (1972). *Yoshimitu Banno.* Akira Yamauchi, Hiroyuki Kawase, Toshie Kimura, Keiko Mari.

BOXCAR BERTHA (1972). *Martin Scorsese.* Barbara Hershey, David Carradine, Barry Primus, John Carradine, Bernie Casey.

DR. PHIBES RISES AGAIN (1972). *Robert Fuest.* Vincent Price, Robert Quarry, Valli Kemp, Terry-Thomas, Hugh Griffith, Fiona Davis.

BLACULA (1972). *William Crain.* William Marshall, Vonetta McGee, Denise Nicholas, Thalmus Rasulala, Chrles Macauley.

THE THING WITH TWO HEADS (1972). *Lee Frost.* Ray Milland, Rosey Grier, Don Marshall, Roger Perry, Chelsea Brown, Wes Bishop.

F.T.A. (1972). *Francine Parker.* Jane Fonda, Donald Sutherland, Holly Near, Michael Alaimo, Pamela Donegan.

NIGHT OF THE BLOOD MONSTER (1972). *Jess Franco.* Christopher Lee, Maria Schell, Leo Genn, Maria Rohm, Margaret Lee.

THE DEATHMASTER (1972). *Ray Danton.* Robert Quarry, Bill Ewing, Brenda Dickson, John Fiedler, William Jordan.

CARRY ON CAMPING (1972). *Gerald Thomas.* Sidney James, Kenneth Williams, Joan Sims, Charles Hawtrey, Barbara Windsor.

PICKUP ON 101 (1972). *John Flores.* Lesley Warren, Martin Sheen, Jack Albertson, Michael Ontkean, Robert Donner.

SLAUGHTER (1972). *Jack Starrett.* Jim Brown, Stella Stevens, Rip Torn, Don Gordon, Cameron Mitchell, Marlene Clark.

CARRY ON DOCTOR (1972). *Gerald Thomas.* Sidney James, Frankie Howard, Kenneth Williams, Charles Hawtrey, Jim Dale.

RAW MEAT (aka DEATH LINE) (1972). *Gary Sherman.* Donald Pleasence, Norman Rossington, David Ladd, Christopher Lee, Sharon Gurney.

BARON BLOOD (1972). *Mario Bava.* Joseph Cotten, Elke Sommer, Massimo Girotti, Antonio Cantafora.

THE UNHOLY ROLLERS (1972). *Vernon Zimmerman.* Claudia Jennings, Louis Quinn, Betty Ann Rees, Roberta Collins, Alan Vint.

BLACK MAMA, WHITE MAMA (1973). *Eddie Romero.* Pam Grier, Margaret Markov, Sid Haig, Lynn Borden, Eddie Garcia, Laurie Burton.

BLACK CAESAR (1973). *Larry Cohen.* Fred Williamson, D'Urville Martoin, Phillip Roye, Gloria Hendry, Julius Harris, Art Lund.

SISTERS (1973). *Brian De Palma.* Margot Kidder, Jennifer Salt, Charles Durning, Barnard Hughes, Lisle Wilson.

CANNIBAL GIRLS (1973). *Ivan Reitman.* Eugene Levy, Andrea Martin, Ronald Ulrich, Randall Carpenter, Bonnie Neilson.

MANSON (1973). *Laurence Merrick.* Feature-length documentary about Charles Manson.

COFFY (1973). *Jack Hill.* Pam Grier, Booker Bradshaw, Robert DoQui, William Elliott, Allan Arbus, Sig Haig, Lee De Broux.

DEEP THRUST—THE HAND OF DEATH (1973). *Heang Feng.* Angela Mao, Chang Yi, Pai Ying, June Wu, Anne Liu.

LITTLE CIGARS (1973). *Chris Christenberry.* Angel Tompkins, Billy Curtis, Jerry Maren, Felix Silla, Frank Delfino, Jon Cedar.

DILLINGER (1973). *John Milius.* Warren Oates, Michelle Phillips, Ben Johnson, Cloris Leachman, Richard Dreyfuss, Steve Kanaly.

SCREAM, BLACULA, SCREAM (1973). *Bob Kelljan.* William Marshall, Pam Grier, Don Mitchell, Michael Conrad, Bernie Hamilton.

SAVAGE SISTERS (1973). *Eddie Romero.* Gloria Hendry, Cheri Caffaro, Rosanna Ortiz, John Ashley, Sid Haig, Eddie Garcia.

HEAVY TRAFFIC (1973). *Ralph Bakshi.* Beverly Hope Atkinson, Frank De Kova, Terri Haven, Mary Dean Lauria, Jacqueline Mills.

SLAUGHTER'S BIG RIP-OFF (1973). *Gordon Douglas.* Jim Brown, Brock Peters, Don Stroud, Ed McMahon, Gloria Hendry.

THE ITALIAN CONNECTION (1973). *Fernando Di Leo.* Henry Silva, Woody Strode, Mario Adorf, Luciana Paluzzi, Sylva Koscina.

THE SCREAMING TIGER (1973). *Chien Lung.* Wang Yu, Ma Chi, Chang Ching Ching, Lei Ming, Tzu Lan, Chin Lien.

SCHOOL FOR UNCLAIMED GIRLS (1973). *Robert Hartford-Davis.* Madeline Hinde, Renee Asherson, Dennis Waterman, Patrick Mower.

PRISON GIRLS (1973). *Thomas De Simone.* Robin Whitting, Angle Monet, Tracy Handfuss, Maria Arnold.

BATTLE OF THE AMAZONS (1973). *Al Bradley.* Lincoln Tate, Lucretia Love, Robert Widmark, Paolo Tedesco, Solvy Stubing.

BLACK JACK (1973). *William T. Naud.* Georg Stanford Brown, Brandon de Wilde, Keenan Wynn, Tim O'Connor, James Daly, Robert Lansing.

HELL UP IN HARLEM (1974). *Larry Cohen.* Fred Williamson, D'Urville Martin, Julius Harris, Gloria Hendry, Margaret Avery.

BAMBOO GODS AND IRON MEN (1974). *Cesar Gallardo.* James Inglehart, Shirley Washington, Marissa Delgado, Eddie Garcia, Chiquito.

DERANGED (1974). *Jeff Gillen* and *Alan Ormsby.* Roberts Blossom, Cosette Lee, Leslie Carlson, Marcia Diamond, Pat Orr.

SUGAR HILL (1974). *Paul Maslansky.* Marki Bey, Robert Quarry, Don Pedro Colley, Richard Lawson, Betty Anne Rees, Zara Culley.

MADHOUSE (1974). *Jim Clark.* Vincent Price, Peter Cushing, Robert Quarry, Adrienne Corri, Natasha Pyne, Barry Dennen.

HOUSE OF WHIPCORD (1974). *Pete Walker.* Barbara Markham, Patrick Barr, Ray Brooks, Anne Michelle, David McGillivray.

FOXY BROWN (1974). *Jack Hill.* Pam Grier, Antonio Fargas, Peter Brown, Terry Carter, Sid Haig, Kathryn Loder.

MACON COUNTY LINE (1974). *Richard Compton.* Alan Vint, Jessie Vint, Geoffrey Lewis, Cheryl Waters, Joan Blackman, Max Baer.

THE NINE LIVES OF FRITZ THE CAT (1974). *Robert Taylor.* Feature-length animated cartoon.

THE BAT PEOPLE (1974). *Jerry Jameson.* Stewart Moss, Marianne McAndrew, Michael Pataki, Paul Carr, Pat Delaney.

ACT OF VENGEANCE (1974). *Bob Kelljan.* Jo Ann Haris, Peter Brown, Jennifer Lee, Lisa Moore, Steve Kanaly, Connie Strickland.

TRUCK TURNER (1974). *Jonathan Kaplan.* Isaac Hayes, Yaphet Kotto, Alan Weeks, Annazette Chase, Nichelle Nichols.

DIRTY O'NEIL (1974). *Howard Freen* and *Lewis Teague.* Morgan Paull, Art Metrano, Pat Anderson, Jean Manson, Katie Saylor.

THEY CALL HER ONE EYE (1974). *Alex Fridolinski.* Christina Lindberg, Heinz Hopf, Despina Tomazini.

GOLDEN NEEDLES (1974). *Robert Clouse.* Joe Don Baker, Elizabeth Ashley, Ann Sothern, Burgess Meredith, Jim Kelly.

THE DESTRUCTORS (aka THE MARSEILLES CONTRACT) (1974). *Robert Parrish.* Michael Caine, Anthony Quinn, James Mason.

SUPER STOOGES VS. THE WONDER WOMAN (1974). *Al Bradley.* Nick Jordon, Marc Hannibal, Yueh Hua, Malisa Longo, Karen Yeh.

TRUCK STOP WOMEN (1974). *Mark L. Lester.* Claudia Jennings, Lieux Dressler, Gene Drew, Dolores Dorn, Paul Carr.

SEIZURE (1974). *Oliver Stone.* Jonathan Frid, Martine Beswick, Christina Pickles, Herve Villechaize, Troy Donahue.

WAR GODDESS (1974). *Terence Young.* Alena Johnston, Sabine Sun, Rosanna Yanni, Helga Line, Rebecca Potok, Lucy Tiller.

ABBY (1974). *William Girdler.* William Marshall, Carol Speed, Terry Carter, Austin Stoker, Juanita Moore, Nathan Cook.

MURPH THE SURF (aka LIVE A LITTLE, STEAL A LOT) (1975). *Marvin Chomsky.* Robert Conrad, Don Stroud, Donna Mills, Luther Adler.

SHEBA BABY (1975). *William Girdler.* Pam Grier, Austin Stoker, D'Urville Martin, Rudy Challenger, Dick Merrifield.

THE LAND THAT TIME FORGOT (1975). *Kevin Connor.* Doug McClure, Susan Penhaligon, John McEnery, Keith Barron.

THE REINCARNATION OF PETER PROUD (1975). *J. Lee Thompson.* Michael Sarrazin, Jennifer O'Neill, Margot Kidder, Cornelia Sharpe.

THE McCULLOCHS (1975). *Max Baer.* Forrest Tucker, Max Baer, Julie Adams, Don Grady, William Demarest, Janice Heiden.

CORNBREAD, EARL AND ME (1975). *Joe Manduke.* Moses Gunn, Rosalind Cash, Bernie Casey, Larry Fishburne III, Madge Sinclair.

THE WILD PARTY (1975). *James Ivory.* James Coco, Raquel Welch, Perry King, David Dukes, Royal Dano, Dena Dietrich.

COOLEY HIGH (1975). *Michael Schultz.* Glynn Turman, Lawrence-Hilton Jacobs, Garrett Morris, Cynthia Davis.

RETURN TO MACON COUNTY (1975). *Richard Compton.* Nick Nolte, Don Johnson, Robin Mattson, Robert Viharo, Matt Greene.

HENNESSY (1975). *Don Sharp.* Rod Steiger, Lee Remick, Richard Johnson, Trevor Howard, Peter Egan, Eric Porter.

BUCKTOWN (1975). *Arthur Marks.* Fred Williamson, Pam Grier, Tony King, Bernie Hamilton, Thalmus Rasulala, Art Lund.

PART 2, WALKING TALL (1975). *Earl Bellamy.* Bo Svenson, Luke Askew, Noah Beery, Robert DoQui, Richard Jaeckel, Angel Tompkins.

OLD DRACULA (1975). *Clive Donner.* David Niven, Teresa Graves, Peter Bayliss, Jennie Linden, Bernard Bresslaw.

KILLER FORCE (1975). *Val Guest.* Telly Savalas, Peter Fonda, O.J. Simpson, Hugh O'Brian, Maud Adams, Christopher Lee.

FRIDAY FOSTER (1975). *Arthur Marks.* Pam Grier, Yaphet Kotto, Godfrey Cambridge, Eartha Kitt, Ted Lange, Jim Backus.

SIX-PACK ANNIE (1975). *Graydon F. David.* Lindsay Bloom, Jana Bellan, Joe Higgins, Larry Mahan, Stubby Kaye, Ray Danton.

SUNDAY IN THE COUNTRY (1975. *John Trent.* Ernest Borgnine, Michael J. Pollard, Hollis McLaren, Louis Carich, Cec Linder.

DRAGONFLY (aka ONE SUMMER LOVE) (1976). *Gilbert Cates.* Beau Bridges, Susan Sarandon, Mildred Dunnock, Ann Wedgeworth.

CRIME AND PASSION (1976). *Ivan Passer.* Omar Sharif, Karen Black, Joseph Bottoms, Bernhard Wicki, Heinz Ehrenfreund.

THE DEVIL WITHIN HER (1976). *Peter Sasdy.* Joan Collins, Eileen Atkins, Donald Pleasence, Ralph Bates, Caroline Munro.

BOBBIE JO AND THE OUTLAW (1976). *Mark L. Lester.* Marjoe Gortner, Lynda Carter, Jesse Vint, Belinda Belaski, Gene Drew.

SHOUT AT THE DEVIL (1976). *Peter Hunt.* Lee Marvin, Roger Moore, Barbara Parkins, Ian Holm, Rene Kolldehoff, Jean Kent.

AT THE EARTH'S CORE (1976). *Kevin Connor.* Doug McClure, Peter Cushing, Caroline Munro, Godfrey James, Sean Lynch.

THE FOOD OF THE GODS (1976). *Bert I. Gordon.* Marjoe Gortner, Pamela Franklin, Ralph Meeker, Ida Lupino, Belinda Belaski.

A SMALL TOWN IN TEXAS (1976). *Jack Starrett.* Timothy Bottoms, Susan George, Bo Hopkins, Art Hindle, Morgan Woodward.

THE GREAT SCOUT AND CATHOUSE THURSDAY (1976). *Don Taylor.* Lee Marvin, Oliver Reed, Robert Culp, Elizabeth Ashley, Kay Lenz.

J.D.'s REVENGE (1976). *Arthur Marks.* Glynn Turman, Lou Gossett, Joan Pringle, Carl Crudup, James Louis Watkins.

FUTUREWORLD (1976). *Richard T. Heffron.* Peter Fonda, Blythe Danner, Yul Brynner, Arthur Hill, Stuart Margolin.

SPECIAL DELIVERY (1976). *Paul Wendkos.* Bo Svenson, Cybill Shepherd, Tom Atkins, Sorrell Booke, Jeff Goldblum.

SQUIRM (1976). *Jeff Lieberman.* Don Scardino, Patricia Pearcy, Jean Sullivan, Peter MacLean, R.A. Dow, Fran Higgins.

STREET PEOPLE (1976). *Maurizio Lucidi.* Roger Moore, Stacy Keach, Ivo Garrani, Ettore Manni, Fausto Tozzi, Ennio Balbo.

SCORCHY (1976). *Hikmet Avedis.* Connie Stevens, Cesare Danova, William Smith, Marlene Schmidt, Greg Evigan, Joyce Jameson.

A MATTER OF TIME (1976). *Vincente Minnelli.* Liza Minnelli, Ingrid Bergman, Charles Boyer, Tina Aumont, Spiros Andros.

THE MONKEY HUSTLE (1976). *Arthur Marks.* Yaphet Kotto, Kirk Calloway, Thomas Carter, Rosalind Cash, Rudy Ray Moore.

MADAM KITTY (1976). *Tinto Brass.* Helmut Berger, Ingrid Thulin, Teresa Ann Savoy, John Steiner, John Ireland.

THE TOWN THAT DREADED SUNDOWN (1977). *Charles B. Pierce.* Ben Johnson, Andrew Prine, Dawn Wells, Charles B. Pierce.

CHATTER BOX (1977). *Tom De Simone.* Candice Rialston, Larry Gelman, Jane Kean, Arlene Martell, Rip Taylor.

STRANGE SHADOWS IN AN EMPTY ROOM (1977). *Alberto De Martino.* Stuart Whitman, John Saxon, Martin Landow, Tisa Farrow.

THE HOUSE BY THE LAKE (1977). *William Fruet.* Brenda Vaccaro, Don Stroud, Chuck Shamata, Richard Ayres, Kyle Edwards.

THE BLACK PIRATE (1977). *Sergio Sollima* and *Alberto Silvestri.* Kabir Bedi, Carol Andre, Mel Ferrer, Angelo Infante.

THE DAY THAT SHOOK THE WORLD (1977). *Veljko Bulajic.* Christopher Plummer, Florinda Balkan, Maximilian Schell, Rado Bajic.

THE LITTLE GIRL WHO LIVES DOWN THE LANE (1977). *Nicolas Gessner.* Jodie Foster, Martin Sheen, Alexis Smith, Scott Jacoby.

BREAKER! BREAKER! (1977). *Don Hulette.* Chuck Norris, George Murdock, Terry O'Connor, Don Gentry, John Di Fusco.

RECORD CITY (1977). *Dennis Steinmetz.* Michael Callan, Jack Carter, Frank Gorshin, Ruth Buzzi, Ed Begley Jr., Rick Dees.

TENTACLES (1977). *Oliver Hellman.* John Huston, Shelley Winters, Henry Fonda, Bo Hopkins, Cesare Danova, Claude Akins.

JOYRIDE (1977). *Joseph Ruben.* Desi Arnaz, Jr., Robert Carradine, Melanie Griffith, Anne Lockhart, Tom Ligon, Cliff Lenz.

FINAL CHAPTER—WALKING TALL (1977). *Jack Starrett.* Bo Svenson, Margaret Blye, Forrest Tucker, Morgan Woodward, Leif Garrett.

THE PEOPLE THAT TIME FORGOT (1977). *Kevin Connor.* Patrick Wayne, Doug McClure, Dana Gillespie, Sarah Douglas, Tony Britton.

EMPIRE OF THE ANTS (1977). *Bert I. Gordon.* Joan Collins, Robert Lansing, Edward Power, John David Carson, Jacqueline Scott.

THE ISLAND OF DR. MOREAU (1977). *Don Taylor.* Burt Lancaster, Michael York, Barbara Carrera, Richard Basehart.

CRACKING UP (1977). *Rowby Goren* and *Chuck Staley.* Improvisational groups from Ace Trucking Company and Firesign Theatre.

ROLLING THUNDER (1977). *John Flynn.* William Devane, Tommy Lee Jones, Linda Haynes, Dabney Coleman, Cassie Yates, Luke Askew.

GRAYEAGLE (1977). *Charles B. Pierce.* Ben Johnson, Lana Wood, Jack Elam, Iron Eyes Cody, Alex Cord, Paul Fix, Jacob Daniels.

THE PRIVATE FILES OF J. EDGAR HOOVER (1977). *Larry Cohen.* Broderick Crawford, Jose Ferrer, Michael Parks, Dan Dailey.

THE INCREDIBLE MELTING MAN (1978). *William Sachs.* Alex Rebar, Burr DeBenning, Myron Healey, Ann Sweeny, Lisle Wilson.

THE CHOSEN (1978). *Alberto De Martino.* Kirk Douglas, Simon Ward, Agostina Belli, Anthony Quayle, Virginia McKenna.

MEAN DOG BLUES (1978). *Mel Stuart.* Gregg Henry, Kay Lenz, George Kennedy, Tina Louise, William Windom, Scatman Crowthers.

ISLAND OF THE DAMNED (1978). *Narciso Ibanez Serrador.* Lewis Fiander, Prunella Ransome, Maria Druille, Roberto Nauta.

HERE COME THE TIGERS (aka MANNY'S ORPHANS) (1978). *Sean S. Cunningham.* Richard Lincoln, James Svanut, Samantha Grey.

JENNIFER (1978). *Brice Mack.* Lisa Pelikan, Bert Convy, Nina Foch, John Gavin, Amy Johnston, Jeff Corey, Louise Hoven.

HIGH-BALLIN' (1978). *Peter Carter.* Peter Fonda, Jerry Reed, Helen Shaver, Chris Wiggins, David Ferry, Christopher Langevin.

OUR WINNING SEASON (1978). *Joseph Ruben.* Scott Jacoby, Deborah Benson, Dennis Quaid, Joe Penny, Jan Smithers, Joanna Cassidy.

YOUNGBLOOD (1978). *Noel Nosseck.* Lawrence-Hilton Jacobs, Tony Allen, Bryan O'Dell, Ren Woods, Vince Cannon, Art Evans.

MATILDA (1978). *Daniel Mann.* Elliott Gould, Robert Mitchum, Harry Guardino, Clive Reville, Karen Carlson, Lionel Stander.

THE LAST SURVIVOR (1978). *Ruggero Deodato.* Massimo Foschi, Ivan Rassimov, Me Me Lay, Judy Rosly, Sheik Razak Shikur.

THE NORSEMEN (1978). *Charles B. Pierce.* Lee Majors, Cornel Wilde, Mel Ferrer, Jack Elam, Chris Connelly, Kathleen Freeman.

FORCE TEN FROM NAVARONE (1978). *Guy Hamilton.* Robert Shaw, Harrison Ford, Barbara Bach, Edward Fox, Franco Nero.

CALIFORNIA DREAMING (1979). *John Hancock.* Glynnis O'Connor, Seymour Cassel, Dorothy Tristan, Dennis Christopher.

THE EVICTORS (1979). *Charles B. Pierce.* Michael Parks, Jessica Harper, Vic Morrow, Sue Ane Langdon, Dennis Fimple.

LOVE AT FIRST BITE (1979). *Stan Dragoti.* George Hamilton, Susan Saint James, Richard Benjamin, Dick Shawn, Sherman Hemsley.

SUNNYSIDE (1979). *Timothy Galfas.* Joey Travolta, John Lansing, Stacey Pickren, Andrew Rubin, Michael Tucci, Talia Balsam.

THE AMITYVILLE HORROR (1979). *Stuart Rosenberg.* James Brolin, Margot Kidder, Rod Steiger, Don Stroud, Murray Hamilton.

SOMETHING SHORT OF PARADISE (1979). *David Halpern Jr.* Susan Sarandon, David Steinberg, Jean-Pierre Aumont.

METEOR (1979). *Ronald Neame.* Sean Connery, Natalie Wood, Karl Malden, Brian Keith, Henry Fonda, Martin Landau.

SEVEN (1979). *Andy Sidaris.* William Smith, Barbara Leigh, Art Metrano, Guich Koock, Martin Kove, Susan Kiger.

JAGUAR LIVES! (1979). *Ernest Pintoff.* Joe Lewis, Christopher Lee, John Huston, Capucine, Barbara Bach, Donald Pleasence.

C.H.O.M.P.S. (1979). *Don Chaffey.* Valerie Bertinelli, Wesley Eure, Conrad Bain, Chuck McCann, Red Buttons, Larry Bishop.

DEFIANCE (1980). *John Flynn.* Jan-Michael Vincent, Theresa Saldana, Fernando Lopez, Danny Aiello, Santos Morales.

GORP (1980). *Joseph Ruben.* Michael Lembeck, Philip Casnoff, Dennis Quaid, Fran Drescher, David Huddleston, Mark Deming.

NOTHING PERSONAL (1980). *Robert Kaufman.* Donald Sutherland, Suzanne Somers, Lawrence Dane, Dabney Coleman.

MAD MAX (1980). *George Miller.* Mel Gibson, Joanne Samuel, Hugh Meays-Byrne, Steve Bisley, Tim Burns.

DRESSED TO KILL (1980). *Brian De Palma.* Michael Caine, Angie Dickinson, Nancy Allen, Keith Gordon, Dennis Franz.

Index

ABC (English), 51
Abominable Doctor Phibes, The, 194–95
Academy of Proven Hits, 25
Academy Pictures Corporation, 199
Adler, Renata, 172
Alakazam the Great, 153–54
Allen, Nancy, 235
Allen, Woody, 5, 154–55
Allied Artists, 30
Alpert, Hollis, 169
Amazing Colossal Man, The, 4, 38, 80–81
American Graffiti, 131
American International Pictures (AIP)
   advertising campaigns of, 2, 38–39, 79–80, 85, 97, 118–19, 124–25, 132–34, 153–54, 186, 195, 213–14
   approach of, 1–4
   audience and, 4, 30, 41–43, 57–58, 138–39, 247–48
   awards to, 197
   Beach Party movies, 127–37
   black action pictures, 200–6
   censorship and, 66–67, 78–79, 140–41, 165
   combinations concept and, 41, 43, 46–47, 84, 86
   cost cutting at, 1–3, 83, 151, 212, 217, 228, 231, 235–36, 244–47
   critics and, 110
   distribution and, 27–28, 30, 33–35, 58, 86–92, 161–63, 213, 239
   Dr. Goldfoot movies, 135–37
   drive-ins and, 7, 41, 58–59, 87, 90
   early financing of, 37–38
   founding of, 25–27, 29–31
   going public of, 197–98
   Hollywood-style premiers and, 184
   home screening of movies and, 81–82
   Italian movies and, 93–109
   martial arts movies, 206–8
   merger with Filmways, 6, 225, 229–36
   Museum of Modern Art retrospective, 6–7, 230–31
   Nicholson's leaving of, 198–99
   planning and, 138–39
   Poe movies and, 2, 92, 95, 109–26, 139–46
   protest movies, 5, 157–78

American International Pictures (AIP) (cont'd.)
  reviews and criticism, 62, 97, 121–22, 125, 130, 132, 146, 155, 162, 169, 172, 173, 185, 192–94, 197, 205, 211–12, 214, 218–20, 222, 236, 238–39
  screenwriters, 39
  special effects and, 2–3, 44–45, 80–81
  staff of, 85–86
  stars and, 191, 217–19
  studio of, 73–75
  teenage movies and, 4, 30, 41–43, 57–58, 127–37
  television and, 26–27, 29–30
  titles and, 212–13
  X-rated animation features, 214
  young actors and directors given breaks by, 5, 49–50, 63, 73, 77, 121, 132, 151, 177–78, 189–91, 196, 210, 211, 217–18, 239
American News (newsletter), 51
American Releasing Corporation. *See* American International Pictures (AIP)
Amityville Horror, The, 4, 6, 226–29, 235
Amsterdam, Morey, 131
Andy Hardy series, 42
Angel, Angel, Down We Go, 180–81
Anglo-Amalgamated Pictures, 37, 95, 125
Angry Red Planet, The, 152
Anson, Jay, 227
Antonelli, Laura, 136–37
Arachnophobia, 213
Arkoff, Donna, 227, 239
Arkoff, Hilda, 14, 17, 108, 178–81, 241, 253
Arkoff, Louis, 176, 217, 241, 242
Arkoff, Sam
  acting of, 82
  awards to, 109, 155
  background of, 8–14
  cerebral hemorrhage of, 22
  coin flips used to settle disputes by, 106
  home screening of movies by, 81–82
  law studies and practice of, 15–17, 19, 23, 31
  philosophy of, 1–4
  resignation of, 234, 239
  weight problem of, 108
Arkoff family, 9–10, 14, 239–42
Arkoff International Pictures, 6, 239–42
Arnaz, Desi, Jr., 218
Asher, William, 129, 132
Atomic Monster, The, 23–25
Attack of the Giant Leeches, 123
Attack of the Puppet People, 81
Avalon, Frankie, 127, 129–32, 135, 153

Baer, Max, Jr., 217
Baker, Joe Don, 207
Bakshi, Ralph, 5, 214
Bardot, Brigitte, 145
Barrymore, John Drew, 151
Barthelmess, Richard, 11
Bassett, Ronald, 143
Battle Beyond the Sun, 151
Bava, Mario, 100, 135–36
Beach Blanket Bingo, 38, 132
Beach Party, 42, 127–31, 230, 231
Beast With 1,000,000 Eyes, The, 2–3, 39–40
Begley, Ed, Jr., 5, 171
Belatramo, Mario, 107
Bergman, Ingrid, 221
Billittari, Salvatore, 102–3
Billy Jack, 173–77
Billy Jack Goes to Washington, 176–77
Bissell, Whit, 70–71
Black Caesar, 201, 202–3, 230
Black Museum, 95
Black Sunday (La Maschera del Demonio), 100–1, 135–36
Blacula, 201–2
Blaisdell, Paul, 44–45, 53
Blender, Leon, 54, 90–91, 162–63, 209
Bloch, Richard, 6, 229, 231–36
Blood of Dracula, 70, 126
Bloody Mama, 5, 38, 171, 186–89
Bogdanovich, Peter, 5, 125, 151, 158, 161
Bohrer, Jack, 160
Bonnie Parker Story, The, 78
Bono, Sonny, 178
Borgnine, Ernest, 192, 193
Born Losers, 172–76
Boxcar Bertha, 5, 189–91, 197

Boyer, Charles, 221
Brauner, Arthur, 181
Breaker! Breaker!, 207, 208
Brendel, El, 53
Brenner, Jules, 212
Brentwood, Tom, 176
Bridges, Beau, 212
British Lion, 219
Broder, Jack, 23–25, 26
Brolin, James, 226
Bronson, Charles, 5, 76–78, 93, 94
Brown, Harold, 99
Brown, Jim, 200
Brustein, Robert, 64
Buchanan, Larry, 139
Bucket of Blood, A, 79–80
Bunny O'Hare, 191–94

Cabot, Susan, 77
Cahn, Edward, 52
Caine, Michael, 235
Canby, Vincent, 162
Cannes Film Festival, 178–80, 241
Cannibal Girls, 5, 210
Cannon Films, 147
Carpenter, John, 239
Carpenter, Johnny, 19–20
Carradine, David, 189
Carradine, Keith, 218
Carreras, James, 126
Cassavetes, John, 166
Castle of the Living Dead, 100, 202
Cates, Gilbert, 212
Cat Girl, The, 95
Chakiris, George, 159
Chaney, Lon, Jr., 113
Chaney, Lon, Sr., 114
Chaplin, Charlie, 11
Chaplin studios, 73–74
Chastity, 178
Cher, 5, 178
Christa, 195
Clark, Dick, 169
Cleopatra, 93, 94
Clouse, Robert, 207
Coffy, 201, 202
Cohen, Herman, 61–63, 69, 71
Cohen, Larry, 194, 203, 240
Cohen, Nat, 37, 95, 125
Cohn, Harry, 43
Collins, Joan, 218

Columbia Pictures, 34, 43, 246
Connors, Michael, 5
Conqueror Worm, The (The Witchfinder General), 142–44
Conway, Gary, 70
Cool and the Crazy, The, 56
Cooley High, 204–6, 230
Coppola, Francis Ford, 5, 124, 146–48, 151
Corman, Roger, 2–3, 32–36
  cost cutting of, 33, 35–36, 79, 83, 139, 140, 147, 183–84, 211
  decision to quit directing, 196–97
  horror/fantasy/science fiction films of, 39–40, 43–45, 51, 71–72, 79, 83, 84, 151, 122–25, 139–42, 196–97
  Machine Gun Kelly and, 76–78
  personal characteristics of, 32–33, 83
  Poe movies and, 112, 113, 115–18
  as producer, 189, 197
  protest movies and, 158–62, 166–69
  social consciousness of, 73
  teen pictures and, 56, 72
  work habits of, 83, 122–25, 146–47, 159
Cornbread, Earl & Me, 204–5
Court, Hazel, 140–41
Crawford, Joan, 42
Crime and Passion, 62
Crist, Judith, 169
Cronenberg, David, 5, 210, 239
Crosby, Gary, 132
Crowther, Bosley, 103, 162
Cummings, Bob, 131
Curb, Mike, 167

Daley, Richard, 170–72
Davis, Bette, 191–94
Day of the Jackal, 219
Day the World Ended, 4, 43–48
Death Line, 202
Deep Thrust, 206
Degni, Lou (Mark Forest), 104
Delfont, Bernard, 221
Delon, Alain, 145
Dementia 13, 5, 146, 148
De Niro, Robert, 5, 189
Denning, Richard, 43
De Palma, Brian, 5, 217, 235
Dern, Bruce, 5, 168, 169

De Sade, 181–85
Devil's Angels, 166–67
Devil's 8, The, 85, 210
Diary of a High School Bride, 38, 79
Dickinson, Angie, 235
Dillinger, 5, 211–12
Disney, Walt, 42
   Beach Party movies and, 127–28, 131–33, 137
Disney Studios, 4, 6, 30, 229
Dr. Goldfoot and the Bikini Machine, 135
Dr. Goldfoot and the Girl Bombs, 136–37
Dr. Phibes Rises Again, 194, 195
Domino, Fats, 57
Douglas, Paul, 65
Dragonfly, 212
Dragoti, Stan, 223
Dressed to Kill, 6, 235–37, 239
Dreyfuss, Richard, 5, 211
Drive-ins, 7, 41, 58–59, 87, 90
Dudelson, Stan, 99
Dullea, Keir, 181–85

Eady Plan, 125
Eastwood, Clint, 93
Easy Rider, 177–78
Ebert, Roger, 241
Edinburgh Film Festival, 165–66
Ekberg, Anita, 96, 97
Elizabeth II, Queen of England, 219–21
EMI, 220–21
Empire of the Ants, 218
Endfield, Cy, 182
English, Marla, 39, 53–54
Enter the Dragon, 206
E.T., 250
Etkes, Raphael, 234
Evans, Linda, 5, 132

Fabian, 129
Farnum, Franklyn, 53
Fast and the Furious, The, 32–35
Feitshans, Buzz, 211
Fellini, Federico, 144, 145
Feng, Heang, 206
Fields, Freddie, 207–8
Film Finance of Italy, 104
Filmways, 6, 225, 229–36
Final Terror, The, 239

Five Guns West, 36
Flesh and the Spur, 39
Fonda, Henry, 93, 94, 218
Fonda, Jane, 145, 146
Fonda, Peter, 5, 145, 159–60, 162–65, 168, 177, 178
Foreman, Bill, 59–60
Forest, Mark (Lou Degni), 104
Foster, Jodie, 217
Fowler, Gene, Jr., 62–64
Foxy Brown, 202
Franchi, Franco, 136
Frankenstein Conquers the World, 103
Frankovich, Mike, 146–47, 156
Free, White and 21, 139
Fritz the Cat, 5, 214–15
Funicello, Annette, 127–33, 135, 137

Garland, Beverly, 83
Gas-s-s-s!, 196–97
Geisinger, Elliot, 227, 228
Gerber, Ludwig, 83
Gibson, Mel, 5, 238
Gilardi, Jack, 127–28
Girls in Prison, 2, 230
Globus, Yoram, 147
Glory Stompers, The, 167, 177
Golan, Menachem, 147
Golden Needles, 206
Golden State, 49
Goldfinger, 135
Goldstein, Milt, 223–25
Goldwyn, Samuel, 30, 50
Goliath and the Barbarians, 97–99
Goliath and the Dragon, 103, 104
Gordon, Alex, 19, 20, 23, 49–50, 53
Gordon, Bert I., 80–81, 218
Gordon, Larry, 197, 202, 210–11
Gordon, Leo, 123
Gordon, Richard, 20
Gottfried, Abe, 17
Graves, Peter, 51
Grier, Pam, 201, 203
Griffith, Chuck, 56
Griffith, Melanie, 5, 218

Hackett, Buddy, 131
Haley, Jack, Jr., 222
Hall, Monty, 156
Haller, Danny, 115, 122, 139, 166
Halloween, 239

INDEX

Hamilton, George, 223, 225
Hammer Films, 126
Hank McCune Show, 15–19, 21, 25, 29, 36–37
Hannah, Daryl, 239
Hart, Susan, 135, 198, 199
Haunted Palace, The, 125
Hayden, Sterling, 62
Hays, Will, 67
Heavy Traffic, 5, 214
Hell's Angels, 160–61, 166
Heller, Paul, 206
Hellman, Monte, 124
Hell Squad, 85
Hell Up in Harlem, 203
Hennessy, 219–21
Henshaw, Jere, 224–25
Herman, Norman, 85
Hershey, Barbara, 189
Heyward, Deke, 182
Hickman, Dwayne, 135
High School Hellcats, 38
Hill, Jack, 124
Hilton-Jacobs, Lawrence, 205
Histories Extraordinaires (Tales of Mystery and Imagination), 144–46
Holbrook, Hal, 170
Holloway, Sterling, 153
Honore, Jimmy, 85
Hoover, J. Edgar, 78
Hopkins, Anthony, 114
Hopper, Dennis, 5, 160, 167, 177–78
Hot Rod Girls, 42, 55
House of Usher, 92, 110–16, 230
How to Make a Monster, 71
Hulette, Don, 307
Huston, John, 182, 183, 218

Incredible Shrinking Man, The, 80
Ingrassia, Ciccio, 136
Ireland, John, 32
Italy, making pictures in, 93–109
It Came From Within, 5, 210
It Conquered the World, 38, 51
It Happened One Night, 34, 246
I Was a Teenage Frankenstein, 4
I Was a Teenage Werewolf, 3, 38, 61–71
  response to, 64–68

Jackson, Joe, 98
Jakob, Dennis, 124

Jeremiah Johnson, 210
Johnson, Ben, 211
Johnson, Don, 5, 217
Johnston, Eric, 67
Jones, Christopher, 170, 181
Jones, Jennifer, 180
Joyride, 218

Kael, Pauline, 237–38
Kagi No Kagi, 153, 154
Kallis, Al, 38, 39
Kandel, Aben, 62, 69
Kanter, Hal, 209
Kardish, Larry, 231
Karloff, Boris, 113, 119–24
Kasem, Casey, 167
Katzman, Sam, 180
Kaufman, Robert, 223–25
Keaton, Buster, 131
Kefauver, Estes, 66
Kellerman, Sally, 6
Kennedy, Byron, 238
Kennedy, Robert, 171
Kerr, John, 115
Kidder, Margot, 6, 217, 226
Koenig, Raymond, 201
Kramarsky, David, 2
Krantz, Steve, 205, 214, 215
Kully, Barney, 17
Kutner, Willie, 242

Ladd, Diane, 6
La Dolce Vita, 102–3
La Maschera del Demonio (Black Sunday), 100–1, 135–36
Lamour, Dorothy, 131
Landon, Michael, 5, 63–65
Lang, Fritz, 62
Langan, Glenn, 80
Langtry, Kenneth, 69
LaShelle, Joseph, 64
Laughlin, Tom, 5, 172–77
Leachman, Cloris, 211
Lear, Norman, 234
Legend of Hell House, The, 199
Leone, Sergio, 233
Letterman, David, 64, 218
Levine, Joe, 2, 3, 97
Levy, Eugene, 210
Levy, Stuart, 37

Life and Times of Judge Roy Bean, The, 210
Lippert Pictures, 30
Little Girl Who Lived Down the Lane, The, 217–18
Litto, George, 235
Loren, Sophia, 102
Lorre, Peter, 114, 118–22
Love at First Bite, 6, 126, 223–25, 235
Lucisano, Fulvio, 96–99, 101, 103–6, 108, 135–37, 149, 150
Lugosi, Bela, 23, 114
Lung, Chien, 206
Lupus, Peter (Rock Stevens), 104–5

McCarthy, Eugene, 171
McCune, Hank, 13–14, 15–19, 21, 25, 29, 36–37
McGee, Mark Thomas, 53
Machine Gun Kelly, 5, 76–78
Macon County Line, 217
MacRae, Meredith, 132
Mad Max, 5, 238
Malle, Louis, 144
Malone, Dorothy, 32
Mancia, Adrienne, 231
Mao, Angela, 206
Marlowe, Scott, 63
Marshall, William, 201
Martin, Andrea, 210
Maslansky, Paul, 5, 100, 202
Masque of the Red Death, The, 139–41
Matheson, Richard, 114–15, 119
Matter of Time, A, 221–23
Maxin Agency, 17
Mean Streets, 190, 191
Melchior, Ib, 152
Milius, John, 5, 210–12
Milland, Ray, 117, 118
Miller, George, 238–39
Milner, Jack and Dan, 45, 47
Minnelli, Liza, 221, 222
Minnelli, Vincente, 221–22
Miramax, 250
Misiano, Fortunato, 105–6
Mr. Mom, 223
Moffitt, Jack, 35
Monkees, The (TV show), 153
Monogram, 30
Monster From the Ocean Floor, The, 32

Monte, Eric, 205, 206
Moriarity, Michael, 241
Moritz, Joseph, 31, 152
Moritz, Milt, 38, 118, 172
Mulhall, Jack, 53
Murders in the Rue Morgue, 118
Murphy, Bridey, 52
Muscle Beach Party, 104
Museum of Modern Art retrospective, 6–7, 230–31

Nacirema group, 45–48
Naked Paradise, 82–84
NBC, 17–19
Near, Holly, 180
Nelson, Lori, 44–45
New Line, 249
Nicholson, Jack, 5, 63, 77, 121, 124, 125, 167–69
Nicholson, Jim, 24–27, 49, 76, 243
  advertising campaigns and, 38
  background of, 25
  Beach Party movies and, 128–29, 132, 134, 135
  death of, 199
  De Sade premier and, 184
  founding of AIP and, 25–27, 29–31
  horror movies and, 110–12, 116–21, 125
  I Was a Teenage Werewolf and, 61, 63
  leaving of AIP by, 197–99
  personal characteristics of, 91, 178
  planning and, 138–39
  as president of AIP, 156
  titles of movies and, 38, 158
Nicholson, Sylvia, 25, 31, 197
Night of the Blood Beast, 84
Nine Lives of Fritz the Cat, The, 215
Nizer, Louis, 215–16
Nolte, Nick, 5, 217
Norris, Chuck, 5, 207, 208

Oates, Warren, 211
Oblong Box, The, 146
O'Donnell, R. J., 69–70
Once Upon a Time in America, 233
Orion Pictures, 235, 241
Oswald, Gerd, 192
Outlaw Marshal, 19–21
Ox-Bow Incident, 62

Paget, Debra, 103
Palance, Jack, 150–51
Palmer, Lilli, 182
Pathe Laboratories, 37, 116–18
Perenchio, Jerry, 234
Perkins, Millie, 171
Peter Paul candy company, 17
Phantom From 10,000 Leagues, The, 43, 45, 47, 48
Phillips, Michelle, 211
Pinder, Dan, 241
Pink, Sidney, 151–53
Pirates, 233
Pirie, David, 118
Pit and the Pendulum, The, 115–16
Platters, the, 56–57
Poe, Edgar Allan, movies, 2, 92, 95, 109–26, 139–46
 reviews of, 110–11, 121–22, 125
 stars of, 111, 113–14, 118–22
Polanski, Roman, 233
Powers, James, 71
Pratt, Charles, 213
Premature Burial, 117–18
Presley, Elvis, 134
Price, Vincent
 Dr. Goldfoot movies, 135–37
 personal characteristics of, 114, 141, 187
 Phibes movies and, 194–95
 Poe movies and, 111–15, 139–45
Prisoner of the Iron Mask, 151
Producers, The, 20
Production Code, 67, 78
Protest movies, 157–78
Pryor, Richard, 5, 171
Psycho, 113
Psych-Out, 5, 169
Pula Film Festival, 149–50

Q: The Winged Serpent, 240–41

Ramos, Irene, 86
Rand, Sally, 11
Rank Organization, 221
Ransohoff, Martin, 229
Rathbone, Basil, 114, 118
Raven, The, 5, 119–22
Raw Meat, 202
Reagan, Ronald, 197

Realart, 23–25
Reed, Rex, 241
Reeves, Michael, 142–43
Reeves, Steve, 97
Reform School Girl, 38
Reitman, Ivan, 5, 210
Remick, Lee, 219
Reptilicus, 152
Republic, 30
Return to Macon County, 5, 217
Riot on Sunset Strip, 167
Rizzoli Company, 107–8
Robe, The, 29
Rock All Night, 56–57
Roeg, Nicolas, 141
Rooney, Mickey, 42, 131
Roper, Carol, 237
Roth, Joe, 239
Runaway Daughters, 50
Rush, Richard, 169
Rusoff, Lou, 39, 45, 49, 52, 103, 129, 130
Rusoff, Ted, 136, 137
Rusoff family, 14

Saland, Ronald, 227, 228
Saperstein, Henry, 154
Sarandon, Susan, 5, 212
Savona, Leopoldo, 150
Sbarigia, Giulio, 221
Schneider, Bert, 178
Schulberg, Budd, 68
Schultz, Michael, 205, 206
Scorsese, Martin, 5, 189–91, 197
Scream Blacula Scream, 202
Selznick, David O., 30, 126
sex, lies and videotape, 250
Shaft, 200, 201
Shake, Rattle and Rock, 50–51, 57
Shea, Bob, 249
She Creature, The, 52
She Gods of Shark Reef, 83, 84
Shepherd, Elizabeth, 142
Shire, Talia, 196
Show Boat, 29
Sign of the Gladiator, 96–97
Silence of the Lambs, 114
Simon, Melvin, 223
Sinatra, Nancy, 132
Singin' in the Rain, 29

Sisters, 5, 217, 235
Six, Eva, 106
Skelton, Red, 74–75
Skirball, Jack, 221
Skouras, Danny, 178–80
Skouras, Spyros, 10
Slaughter, 200
Slaughter's Big Rip-off, 200
Spielberg, Steven, 212–13
Spikings, Barry, 219
Spirits of the Dead, 145–46
Stamp, Terence, 145
Stang, Arnold, 153
Stanton, Harry Dean, 211
Stanwyck, Barbara, 62
Stark, Ray, 235, 239
Steele, Barbara, 101
Steiger, Rod, 219, 226
Stein, Jules, 178
Stein, Ronald, 84
Sten, Anna, 50
Stevens, Rock (Peter Lupus), 104–5
Stockwell, Dean, 169
Story of Louis Pasteur, The, 28n
Strasberg, Susan, 168, 169
Strock, Herbert, 70, 71
Stroud, Don, 188
Stulberg, Gordon, 199
Sugar Hill, 5, 202
Surf Party, 134
Swedish Fly Girls, 195–96

Tales of Mystery and Imagination (Histoires Extraordinaires), 144–46
Tales of Terror, 118
Tank Commandos, 85
Taxi Driver, 188
Taylor, Robert, 215
Teenage Caveman, 72–73
Teenage Mutant Ninja Turtles, 228
Tentacles, 171, 218–19
Terror, The, 124–25, 147
Thom, Robert, 171, 180
Thornton, Ralph, 62
3 in the Attic, 158, 181
Thunder Over Hawaii, 82–84
Tiffin, Pamela, 132
Time of Indifference, 171
Titra Sound Corporation, 102, 238
Tomb of Ligeia, 139–42
Topper, Burt, 85, 210

Torn, Rip, 200
Torres, Joan, 201
Towne, Robert, 141
Transamerican, 215–16
Travelian, John, 51–52, 165
Trial of Billy Jack, The, 174–76
Trip, The, 158, 167, 178, 231
Truck Turner, 201, 202
Turman, Glynn, 205, 206
Twentieth Century Fox, 28n, 199, 239

United Artists, 20, 75, 215
Up the Creek, 241

Vadim, Roger, 144, 146
Van Cleef, Lee, 93
Variety Clubs children's charities, 156
Variety magazine, 8, 11–12
Varsi, Diane, 170
Vaughn, Robert, 5, 72–73
Venice International Film Festival, 106, 164
Vereen, Ben, 6, 196
Viglietta, Rocco, 178
Viking Women and the Sea Serpent, 71–72
Voyage to the Planet of Prehistoric Women, 151

Wald, Jerry, 68–69
Walking Tall, 213–14
Ward, Rachel, 239
Warner Brothers, 28n
War of the Zombies, The, 151
Warriors 5, 150
Weary River, 11
Weintraub, Fred, 206
Welch, Raquel, 132
Wellman, William, 62
Wexler, Bess, 122
What's New, Pussycat?, 154
What's Up, Tiger Lily?, 5, 154–55
Whitney, Jock, 30
Who Slew Auntie Roo?, 171
Why Must I Die?, 139
Wicked Stepmother, 194
Wild Angels, The, 158–66, 231
Wild in the Streets, 158, 170–72, 230
Wilkes, Keith, 204
Williams, Cindy, 196
Williamson, Fred, 201, 202

Wilson, 28n
Winters, Jonathan, 153
Winters, Shelley, 94, 171, 186–89, 218
Witchfinder General, The (The Conqueror Worm), 142–44
Women in Film, 236–37
Wood, Edward, Jr., 23

Yi, Chang, 206
Young Racers, The, 147–49
Yu, Wang, 206
Yugoslavia, 149–50

Zeckendorf, William, 117
Zimbert, Richard, 204